LANGUAGE AND LITERACY SERIES

Dorothy S. Strickland, Celia Genishi, and Donna Alvermann SERIES EDITORS

ADVISORY BOARD: RICHARD ALLINGTON, KATHRYN AU,
BERNICE CULLINAN, COLETTE DAIUTE, ANNE HAAS DYSON, CAROLE EDELSKY,
JANET EMIG, SHIRLEY BRICE HEATH, CONNIE JUEL, SUSAN LYTLE, TIMOTHY SHANAHAN

Once Upon a Fact: Helping Children Write Nonfiction
CAROL BRENNAN JENKINS & ALICE EARLE

Research on Composition: Multiple Perspectives on Two Decades of Change
PETER SMAGORINSKY, ED.

Critical Literacy/Critical Teaching: Tools for Preparing Responsive Literacy Teachers
CHERYL DOZIER, PETER JOHNSTON, & REBECCA ROGERS

The Vocabulary Book: Learning and Instruction
MICHAEL F. GRAVES

Building on Strength: Language and Literacy in Latino Families and Communities
ANA CELIA ZENTELLA, ED.

Powerful Magic: Learning from Children's Responses to Fantasy Literature
NINA MIKKELSEN

On the Case: Approaches to Language and Literacy Research (An NCRLL Volume)*
ANNE HAAS DYSON & CELIA GENISHI

New Literacies in Action: Teaching and Learning in Multiple Media
WILLIAM KIST

On Qualitative Inquiry: Approaches to Language and Literacy Research (An NCRLL Volume)*
GEORGE KAMBERELIS & GREG DIMITRIADIS

Teaching English Today: Advocating Change in the Secondary Curriculum
BARRIE R.C. BARRELL, ROBERTA F. HAMMETT, JOHN S. MAYHER, & GORDON M. PRADL, EDS.

Bridging the Literacy Achievement Gap, 4–12
DOROTHY S. STRICKLAND & DONNA ALVERMANN, EDS.

Crossing the Digital Divide: Race, Writing, and Technology in the Classroom
BARBARA MONROE

Out of this World: Why Literature Matters to Girls
HOLLY VIRGINIA BLACKFORD

Critical Passages: Teaching the Transition to College Composition
KRISTIN DOMBEK & SCOTT HERNDON

Making Race Visible: Literary Research for Cultural Understanding
STUART GREENE & DAWN ABT-PERKINS, EDS.

The Child as Critic: Developing Literacy through Literature, K–8, Fourth Edition
GLENNA SLOAN

Room for Talk: Teaching and Learning in a Multilingual Kindergarten
REBEKAH FASSLER

Give Them Poetry! A Guide for Sharing Poetry with Children K–8
GLENNA SLOAN

The Brothers and Sisters Learn to Write: Popular Literacies in Childhood and School Cultures
ANNE HAAS DYSON

"Just Playing the Part": Engaging Adolescents in Drama and Literacy
CHRISTOPHER WORTHMAN

The Testing Trap: How State Writing Assessments Control Learning
GEORGE HILLOCKS, JR.

The Administration and Supervision of Reading Programs, Third Edition
SHELLEY B. WEPNER, DOROTHY S. STRICKLAND, & JOAN T. FEELEY, EDS.

School's Out! Bridging Out-of-School Literacies with Classroom Practice
GLYNDA HULL & KATHERINE SCHULTZ, EDS.

Reading Lives: Working-Class Children and Literacy Learning
DEBORAH HICKS

Inquiry Into Meaning: An Investigation of Learning to Read, Revised Edition
EDWARD CHITTENDEN & TERRY SALINGER, WITH ANNE M. BUSSIS

"Why Don't They Learn English?" Separating Fact from Fallacy in the U.S. Language Debate
LUCY TSE

Conversational Borderlands: Language and Identity in an Alternative Urban High School
BETSY RYMES

Inquiry-Based English Instruction
RICHARD BEACH & JAMIE MYERS

The Best for Our Children: Critical Perspectives on Literacy for Latino Students
MARÍA DE LA LUZ REYES & JOHN J. HALCÓN, EDS.

Language Crossings
KAREN L. OGULNICK, ED.

What Counts as Literacy?
MARGARET GALLEGO & SANDRA HOLLINGSWORTH, EDS.

Critical Encounters in High School English: Teaching Literary Theory to Adolescents
DEBORAH APPLEMAN

Beginning Reading and Writing
DOROTHY S. STRICKLAND & LESLEY M. MORROW, EDS.

Reading for Meaning
BARBARA M. TAYLOR, MICHAEL F. GRAVES, & PAUL VAN DEN BROEK, EDS.

* Volumes with an asterisk following the title are a part of the NCRLL set: Approaches to Language and Literacy Research, edited by JoBeth Allen and Donna Alvermann.

(Continued)

Once Upon a Fact

HELPING CHILDREN
WRITE NONFICTION

Carol Brennan Jenkins and Alice Altfillisch Earle

Foreword by George Kamberelis

Teachers College, Columbia University
New York and London

To our dads, in loving memory:

Patrick Brennan and Michael D. Altfillisch

———————————

Published by Teachers College Press, 1234 Amsterdam Avenue, New York, NY 10027

Library of Congress Cataloging-in-Publication Data

Jenkins, Carol Brennan.
　　Once upon a fact : helping children write nonfiction / Carol Brennan Jenkins and Alice Altfillisch Earle ; foreword by George Kamberelis.
　　　p.　cm.—(Language and literacy series)
　　Includes bibliographical references and index.
　　Contents: Contents: Writing workshop: are children choosing to write nonfiction?—Patterns of intertextuality in nonfiction reports—Strategic nonfiction writers: Caitlyn and Colin—Experience-only nonfiction writers: Vanessa and Kristin—Text-bound writers: Kyle and Patrick—Nonfiction report writing: lessons learned.
　　ISBN 0-8077-4682-7 (cloth : alk. paper)—ISBN 0-8077-4681-9 (pbk. : alk. paper)
　　1. English language—Study and teaching (Elementary) 2. Report writing—Study and teaching (Elementary). I. Earle, Alice Altfillisch. II. Title. III. Series.

LB1576.J39 2006
372.6—dc22

2005046738

ISBN-13
978-0-8077-4681-3 (paper)
978-0-8077-4682-0 (cloth)

ISBN-10
0-8077-4681-9 (paper)
0-8077-4682-7 (cloth)

Printed on acid-free paper
Manufactured in the United States of America

13　12　11　10　09　08　07　06　　8　7　6　5　4　3　2　1

Contents

Foreword

FOR OVER THREE DECADES NOW, literacy researchers have studied children's writing development and how to facilitate it most effectively. This work has been informed variously by the American writing process movement, Australian systemic functional linguistics, and Vygotskian-inspired cultural historical activity theories. Some of this work has been primarily theoretical. Some of it has been mostly empirical. Some of it has been largely pragmatic. Whether theoretical, empirical, or pragmatic, Australian, American, or Soviet, scholarship on children's writing has been relatively insular and nonsystematic (as compared to research on reading comprehension, for example). Only a few scholars have engaged in sustained programs of research, and even fewer have worked to integrate ideas from various theoretical perspectives to understand and explain children's writing in ways commensurate with its complexity, dynamism, and richness. Jenkins and Earle are among those few. Based on over a decade of sustained engagement with composition theory and careful empirical research on classroom writing practices, *Once Upon a Fact* is a rich book: a gift for writing theorists, literacy researchers, and classroom teachers alike. It is comprehensive in its scope, smart in its execution, critical in its stance, and unusually self-reflexive.

Reminiscent of such books as Martin and Rothery's *Writing Project Report 1981*, Langer's (1986) *Children's Reading and Writing*, and Newkirk's (1989) *More Than Stories*, this book embodies a unique synthesis of diverse theoretical constructs; it offers new insights based on rigorous and innovative qualitative research strategies; and it has considerable pragmatic value both for pedagogy and future research. The book also showcases a remarkable range of children's informational writing, from almost pure examples of what Bereiter and Scardamalia (1987) called "knowledge telling" to compelling examples of what they called "knowledge transformation."

Once Upon a Fact is written in a style that is as refreshing as it is engaging—a hybrid genre somewhere between a research report and a story. In the tradition of exceptionally talented "kid watchers" such as Yetta Goodman and Anne Haas Dyson, Jenkins and Earle describe "being with children" with a kind of verisimilitude that is enviable. Weaving narrative webs from interview snippets and field notes, for example, they show with remarkable ease and clarity how the effects of instruction and the effects of children's out-of-school learning coalesce in a sea of genres, voices, styles, ideologies, tactics, functions, uses, and audience concerns as children write informational texts on topics they know and care about.

These narrative webs embody a delightful balance of voices. Findings are neither too raw nor too cooked. Jenkins and Earle narrate the story. Their child participants sing the chorus. And both the narration and the chorus interact with the voices of published authors. The overall effect is harmonic and richly portrays authorship itself as complex, contingent, emergent activity.

Gathering theory. Jenkins and Earle offer a succinct yet eloquent synthesis of key theoretical constructs relevant to understanding and explaining how children reason their way through novel, complex, and difficult text-making activities—the ebb and flow of cognitive load, the multiple negotiations with resources and audiences, the impasses, the breakthroughs. Key constructs are gathered together from a broad range of theoretical domains, including situated learning, genre studies, intertextuality studies, and stylistics. Particularly useful are the authors' arguments about how genre, intertextuality, style, and voice constitute interanimating streams of activity within children's situated writing practices and how rich understandings of each activity require understanding the others as well.

Documenting children's writing. Perhaps the greatest strength of this book is how Jenkins and Earle document children's writing practices with precision and richness. They offer multiple penetrating insights into how the children think and what they do as they become interested in particular subject matter, gather together multiple intertextual resources, experiment with assembling, disassembling, and reassembling these resources, and generate texts they are proud of. More important, the authors show how these various sociocognitive processes intersect, transverse, and transform one another as children move from nascent levels of competence to more mature ones.

Creating typologies. But the authors do not stop at displaying complex trajectories of text-making activity. They also create several analytically powerful typologies. One is a typology of child writers that allows them to locate their participants on a continuum from extremely proficient to much less proficient. This typology will be useful to classroom researchers and teachers alike for "seeing" and "understanding" children differently. Another is a typology of intertextual activity that includes thematic intertextuality (similarities between borrowed and redeployed ideas, themes, and actual language), organizational intertextuality (structural similarities with respect to genre conventions), and orientational intertextuality (relations between voices and ideology in source texts and emerging texts). They go on to use this typology to show how different forms and degrees of intertextual poaching exert different effects on the emerging genres children produce (and vice versa). Both the content and the form of their arguments here will be valuable to other researchers who want to study similar articulations of relevant constructs.

Imagining pedagogy. Once Upon a Fact contributes in important ways to the decade-plus long debate about the relative effectiveness if teaching children how to write in/with different genres. By carefully staging different kinds of instructional interventions, the authors show that immersion is necessary but not sufficient for genre learning. They go on to argue that the most effective learning occurs when immersion is coupled with clear rhetorical tasks and purposes, demonstrations, and responsive teaching, underscoring the importance of "showing" and not just "telling" as a central activity of writing pedagogy. And without being prescriptive, the authors provide compelling sketches of how to imagine and enact instruction motivated by this advice.

Troubling assumptions. This book embodies a level of self-reflexivity uncommon in academic work. Making the familiar strange, Jenkins and Earle detect both absences and presences in what they observe and what children tell them about their writing processes and written products. From this self-reflexive activity emerge a host of key questions about both children's writing and the authors' pedagogical and research practices: "Why did so few children take notes while conducting research on topics they would write about?" "Why did so many children appropriate so much material verbatim and have such difficulty understanding how to 'write it in your own words'?" "How could we [the authors] have been more effective helping children think and write as scientists?"

To conclude, *Once Upon a Fact* is an interesting and useful book. It deploys and integrates relevant theoretical constructs in novel ways. It embodies rigorous empirical research on children's situated writing practices. And it indexes key ideas for effective classroom writing pedagogies. Like genres and intertexts themselves, the book constitutes a metaphorical starting point for future research on children's writing and classroom writing pedagogies, a finite account with infinite suggestive potential. Jenkins and Earle challenge our taken-for-granted ways of understanding these topics and impel us toward imagining them in new ways.

George Kamberelis
State University of New York at Albany

REFERENCES

Bereiter, C., & Scardamalia, M. (1987). *The psychology of written composition.* Hillsdale, NJ: Erlbaum.

Langer, J. A. (1986). *Children reading and writing: Structures and strategies.* Norwod, NJ: Ablex.

Martin, J., & Rothery, J. (1981). *Writing project report 1981* (Working Papers in Linguistics No. 2). Sidney, Australia: University of Sidney, Department of Linguistics.

Newkirk, T. (1989). *More than stories: The range of children's writing.* Portsmouth, NH: Heinemann.

Acknowledgments

OUR FIRST DEBT OF GRATITUDE goes to the eighteen 3rd graders, who shared their unbridled enthusiasm for life, learning, and literacy, and who reminded us, on a daily basis, not to underestimate their powers of intellect. We thank each and every child, as well as the school community, which supported this endeavor.

We are also grateful to Mary Catherine O'Connor, professor of linguistics at Boston University, who suggested that we apply for a Spencer Grant to pursue our investigation of intertextuality and who guided our early efforts with sage counsel and good humor. To Maggie Mode, our thanks for helping us prepare the grant proposals and for offering words of encouragement. And to the Spencer Foundation, and particularly, Marti Rutherford, we express our gratitude for supporting our research with a Spencer Foundation Small Grant as well as a Communication and Mentoring Grant.

We extend special gratitude to Carol Chambers Collins, acquisitions editor at Teachers College Press, for believing in this book and for shepherding it through the revision process with perspicacity and patient understanding. Carol's high standards and probing questions enhanced the manuscript immeasurably. We thank Wendy Schwartz for her critical review of the manuscript, especially her insights about gender and literacy.

To George Kamberelis, whose work in the area of genre development and intertextuality significantly advanced our understanding and served as an anchor for this book, we extend our deep appreciation. And in the spirit of Sir Isaac Newton's intertextual insight, "If I have seen further, it is by standing on the shoulders of giants," we gratefully acknowledge other giants who have influenced our thinking about children's nonfiction writing: Mikhail Bakhtin, Roland Barthes, Jay Lemke, Ann Dyson, Judith Langer, Tom Newkirk, Donald Graves, Nancie Atwell, Lucy Calkins, and many others.

And to our families, we profess heartfelt gratitude for their support and encouragement—to our mothers, Louie Altfillisch and Mary Brennan; to our husbands, Charlie Earle and Ted Jenkins; to Alice's children, Caroline, Daniel, David, Michael, and Norman; and to Carol's brother, Tom, and sisters, Patricia and Kathy. We thank you for giving us the gift of time to pursue this adventure, for extending unconditional love and support, and for cheering us on through thick and thin. We could not have done this without you.

Writers, Genres, and the Web of Intertextuality

As writing workshop opens, Sarah begins her story "The Good Haunted house." Later that morning, she reads her piece to Connor and Judy, who sit at her table. The following week, Judy writes the story "The hauted house." In asking about the origin of her story idea, Judy replies, "Sarah did a story about a good haunted house, so I did 'The hauted house.' Mine's sort of bad, though, because the girls live right in the haunted house and don't know it. But at the end of the story, the ghost comes out with his children and they come to life and they are good." Two days later, Connor writes "The Haunted House," explaining that he wrote it because it was Halloween time. When asked where he got the idea to write this story, he comments, "Everyone at my table was doing stories about haunted houses and I thought it was a good idea. And I like *Casper the [Friendly] Ghost* [TV cartoon]."

The following week, the ripple effect continues. This time, Connor leads with a story called "The Mysteryous Teacher." One week later, Sarah begins "The Mysteryis Kid" and Judy, "The Mistiris Kid." Interviews again underscore the power of peer influence. For instance, Sarah explains, "Connor did a story about a mysterious something so I got the idea from him, but mine is different."

Indeed, this is the classroom context that Donald Graves (1983) envisioned in his classic book *Writing: Teachers and Children at Work*, a context in which children choose their own writing topics and genres, write at their own pace, and share their work with peers and teachers. Graves noted that through sharing, "children pick up a heavy percentage of topic ideas from each other" (p. 28).

What happens, though, if children choose to write only personal narratives, stories, and an occasional poem during writing workshop across the schoolyear? Such has been our observation over the last few years in examining the writer's notebooks of 3rd graders. As a classroom teacher (Alice) and a teacher educator (Carol) who have collaborated on various literacy projects over the last 15 years, we have informally tracked 3rd graders' genre

---

With the exceptions of Vanessa and Jeffrey, all of the children's names in this book are pseudonyms.

1

preferences and noted that, when given control over their genres and topics, children often begin the schoolyear with personal narratives—accounts of soccer games, family trips, and birthday parties. Soon, probably because of the allure of Halloween as well as immersion in quality picture books and chapter books during reading workshop, story writing begins and continues to sustain their writing efforts throughout the year. Missing from their notebooks, however, is nonfiction writing—writing that, in the words of award-winning nonfiction writer Russell Freedman (1992), has as its "basic purpose . . . to inform, to instruct, and hopefully to enlighten" (p. 3). Missing from their notebooks, then, are informational reports on sharks or dinosaurs; biographies of sports icons or historical figures; procedural texts such as directions, how-to sequences, or recipes; news articles; and persuasive pieces (e.g., essays, letters, and editorials), just to name a few.

While children's literature experts caution that it is becoming increasingly difficult to define the literature of fact (Cullinan & Galda, 1994; Hepler, 1998), they explain that nonfiction typically includes subgenres such as biography, autobiography, how-to texts, photographic essays, alphabet books, and, the largest subgenre, informational texts. Informational texts explore the sciences (e.g., biological, physical, earth), the social sciences (e.g., history, geography, economics, cultures), and the humanities (e.g., art, music, dance) (Tomlinson & Lynch-Brown, 1996). In addition, journal and diaries are often included under the nonfiction umbrella (Harvey, 1998; Huck, Hepler, & Hickman, 1987); therefore, the personal narratives that our 3rd graders wrote about family trips and baseball games can technically be classified as nonfiction. However, for the purposes of this book, we are establishing personal narratives as a genre separate from nonfiction because of its life-story recounting focus (Stotsky, 1995), much in the same way that Britton, Burgess, Martin, McLeod, and Rosen (1975) assigned personal narratives to expressive writing, not to the transactional mode of writing that includes the report, the business letter, or the persuasive essay (see Chapter 1 for discussion). Therefore, when we use the term *nonfiction* (or *informational* and *expository*) writing throughout this book, we are referring to informational writing that excludes personal narratives.

Does it matter that nonfiction writing has not been pursued by our young writers? The case for the importance of nonfiction was first argued in the 1980s (Chall & Jacobs, 1983; Chall, Jacobs, & Baldwin, 1990; Christie, 1987; Langer, 1986). These experts demonstrated that success in school is tied to proficiency with nonfiction, "the type of prose that accounts for approximately 80% of the reading and writing experiences students in the United States encounter during their school careers" (Langer, 1992, p. 33). Competence with exposition, of course, extends beyond school to the work place. In *The Disciplined Mind*, Howard Gardner (1999), writes:

With economic growth comes the shift to the information society, the knowledge society, the learning society. More and more people work in the sectors of human services and human resources, and, especially, in the creation, transformation, and communication of knowledge. Workers may well be hired and fired on the basis of what they know, how well they learn, and what they have contributed recently to relevant knowledge bases. No one will be able to rest on past school or educational laurels. Only those who can demonstrate their continued utility in a knowledge-suffused society can expect to reap the rewards of that society indefinitely. (pp. 48–49)

Descriptions such as Gardner's of the challenges facing the nation, and consequently its schools, abound. Concerns that the present generation will not be prepared to face the demands of a technologically advanced society or to assume the responsibilities of a democracy are heightened by reports about the poor performance of students on the National Assessment of Educational Progress (NAEP) as well as on international assessments in subjects such as literacy, history, and science (Anderson, Hiebert, Scott, & Wilkinson, 1985; Finn & Ravitch, 1988).

Beyond the exigency of school and workplace success is the research that documents children's intrigue with nonfiction literature (Anderson, Higgins, & Wurster, 1985; Caswell & Duke, 1998; Kletzien & Dreher, 2004; Monson & Sebesta, 1991; Pappas, 1991). Teachers who have launched literature-based animal studies of any kind know the levels of exhilaration and wonderment that children bring to such study (Duthie, 1996; Jenkins, 1999; Roop, 1992; Spink, 1996). Nonfiction literature not only engages the intellect but also evokes aesthetic sensibilities (Rosenblatt, 1978; Spink, 1996; Tower, 2002).

Thus, convinced of the centrality of nonfiction literacy to success in life's multiple spheres, educators have ratcheted up the call for nonfiction reading over the last 10 years (Caswell & Duke, 1998; Duke, 2000; Duke & Bennett-Armistead, 2003; Fountas & Pinnell, 1999, 2001; Harvey, 1998; Kamberelis & Bovino, 1999; Pappas, 1991, 1993; Stead, 2002). However, a review of the literature about children's affinity for nonfiction writing in the context of writing workshop has yielded contradictory findings. Some researchers have concluded that when the principles of choice/ownership, time, and response are honored, non-narrative writing prospers (Graves, 1973; Newkirk, 1987; Sowers, 1985). Others have found that children do not choose to write nonfiction in classrooms where the same principles anchor writing workshops (Chapman, 1995; Duke, 2000; Kucera, 1995). For example, Cheryl Kucera (1995) offered the following reflection on her efforts to implement writing workshop as described by Atwell (1987) with her middle school students:

At the end of the school year, I sat at a desk that was covered by a welter of papers, folders, and stick-on notes. I knew true despair. Not only had I not seen examples of persuasive and expository writing, but I had also observed a decline in my students' development of sentence variation, complexity and spelling. The students loved writing creative or personal narratives and poetry. They never voluntarily wrote an expository or persuasive piece. Never! (Kucera, 1995, p. 181)

Firm in the conviction that exposition is essential to the writing lives of young children, we set out to investigate this conundrum with the support of two Spencer Foundation grants. Our project involved the participation of 18 3rd graders who lived in Alice's literature-rich, literacy-intensive classroom. During writing workshop (Atwell, 1987; Calkins, 1991), these 3rd graders chose their own topics, genres, and writing timelines. Mini-lessons, conferences with peers and with teachers, as well as group and partner share time were also integral parts of the writing workshop.

The focus of our research was twofold. First, we set out to determine whether varying degrees of exposure to nonfiction literature would prompt nonfiction writing and, if not, to ascertain whether immersion in nonfiction in conjunction with instruction would result in expository writing. Experts concur that immersion in nonfiction literature is a necessary condition for the production of nonfiction writing (e.g., letters, reports, directions, essays, biography, autobiography, news articles, editorials) (Fountas & Pinnell, 2001; Kamberelis & Bovino, 1999; Pappas, 1991, 1993). Unclear, though, is whether immersion, along with other writing workshop principles of choice, time, and response, rounds out the necessary conditions for nonfiction writing. Is explicit instruction in nonfiction also needed? Key questions included the following:

- If children are free to choose their own writing topics and genres, are invited to share their pieces, and are immersed in nonfiction literature, will nonfiction writing flourish?
- If this literacy context, in and of itself, does not prompt nonfiction writing, will the addition of direct instruction in nonfiction writing result in expository engagement?

Second, confident that at some point during the study some 3rd graders would choose to write nonfiction, we also set out to investigate the range of intertextual links forged during each act of composing. Literally defined, *intertextuality* means "between or among texts." Roland Barthes (1977), a literary theorist, noted that the Latin derivation of the word *text* is "a tissue, a woven fabric" (p. 159), an apt metaphor for acknowledging the interconnectedness of every author's work to those of others. As J. R. R. Tolkien (1965) put it, "Speaking of the history of stories . . . we may say that the Pot of Soup, the Cauldron of Story, has always been boiling, and to it have continually been added new bits, dainty and undainty" (pp. 26–27).

J. K. Rowling, for example, surely dipped into the "Cauldron of Story" to concoct her phenomenally successful *Harry Potter* books. Rowling stood on the shoulders of many literary giants to craft not "original" works but rather offshoots in the rich tradition of high fantasy. Saltman's (2002) analysis of the intertextual links between *Harry Potter* and other masterful works is a testimony to Rowling's command of literary classics and mythology. To Charles Dickens, Rowling owes her orphaned protagonist who must defend himself in an unjust world, as well as the use of invented language (e.g., Muggles, Quidditch) and word play (e.g., "Diagon Alley for the diagonal, crooked alley that house the wizard shops. . . .") (Saltman, 2002, p. 1). To Roald Dahl, she owes the Victorian characterization of the abusive family, not to mention the devilish humor. To J. R. R. Tolkien and C. S. Lewis, she owes the construct of a parallel universe in which good battles and conquers evil, standard fare of high epic fantasy. Of course, all of these writers foraged ancient mythology and folklore to craft their tales (Saltman, 2002).

Like J. K. Rowling, our 3rd graders also "danced in the footsteps" (*Publishers Weekly*, 1998) of literary mentors. Recall the various versions of the haunted house stories, mentioned in the opening of this introduction. During interviews, we asked our young authors about the origins of their stories. Sarah, the first to write a Halloween story, explained that she got the idea to write "The Good Haunted house" because "Halloween is coming and I like scary stories." When asked where she got the idea to write about a haunted house, Sarah replied as follows:

> SARAH: Well, I've read all the *Goosebumps* books 'cuz I love them. And one was called *Welcome to the Dead House*. And it was about, see these kids move into a new house and it's haunted, but their parents don't believe it.
> CAROL: And is your story like this R. L. Stine story?
> SARAH: I changed mine so that the ghosts are friendly and help the kids.

Thus, *Goosebumps* served as Sarah's primary intertext—the text that influenced her choice of genre and topic and that infiltrated the plot development of her story. While the "text" in Sarah's case was a book, *text* is defined as "any chunk of meaning that has unity and can be shared with others. A song, dance, poem, oral story, mathematical equation, or sculpture are all texts from which learners can draw connections as they construct their understandings about a current evolving text" (Short, 1992, p. 315). While secondary intertextual links were not probed, it is likely that other "texts" permeated her story making. Perhaps, like Connor, who cited Sarah's story and the television cartoon *Casper the Friendly Ghost* as his intertexts, Sarah also activated, consciously or unconsciously, this cartoon, or horror movies she had seen, or stories she had heard.

Thus, Sarah's and J. K. Rowling's acts of writing should not be viewed as the acts of soul-searching solitary writers, creating "original" works. Rather, the act of composing plunged both authors into the web of all previous "textual" experiences. In collaboration with these previous sources, Sarah and Rowling strove to "assimilate, rework, and reaccentuate" (Bakhtin, 1986, p. 89), shaping stories that in the end bore their imprints. This web, of course, included not only published sources (book, film, TV) but also peer authors. Figure Int.1 presents an intertextual map of the various versions of the Halloween story that our 3rd graders, who sat at tables (not desks), wrote. For example, at table 1, Patrick's "The Dead Football Player on Halloween," written on September 30th, triggered Maureen's "Return of the dead Football player" and Patrick's subsequent "Return of the Pumpkin People." In the midst of this Halloween story spree were three children (table 3) who wrote personal narratives about Halloween, but no stories. (Note: As will be explained in Chapter 1, four children were unable to participate in the study; three special-needs students (SPED in Figure Int.1) were out of the classroom during writing workshop, and one student didn't return the consent form.)

While research on intertextuality and story writing has begun to take hold (Bearse, 1992; Cairney, 1990, 1992; Lancia, 1997; Sipe, 2001), research on the intertextual links that young writers make while composing nonfiction is in its infancy (Kamberelis & Bovino, 1999; Kamberelis & Scott, 1992; Many, 1996; Oyler & Barry, 1996). We set out to investigate such links.

PURPOSE OF THE BOOK

Because our findings add to the growing body of research that affirms the remarkable sociocognitive activity of the young mind, this book will be of interest to classroom and preservice teachers, teacher educators, and literacy researchers. Although researchers have examined the intertextual links children make during story writing, little comparable research has been undertaken for the nonfiction genre. Our 3rd graders demonstrated multifaceted intertextual knowledge about report writing, much of it appropriated from their exposure to nonfiction literature and to life experiences. This knowledge enabled them to pursue report writing with confidence; none of the children expressed a reluctance or inability to pursue their topics. Without formal instruction during 3rd grade, a number of 3rd graders (1) consulted multiple nonfiction sources (books, people, and media), (2) paraphrased the ideas of others, (3) inserted what Bakhtin (1984) called "stylizations," for example, statements of dramatic effect or opinion to engage readers, (4) included their own experiences, (5) crafted titles for reports, and (6) divided information into chapters and included chapter headings. Not surprisingly, though, their understandings across many of these facets were incomplete,

TABLE 1

Maureen	Patrick
"Return of the dead Football Player"	"The Dead Football Player on Halloween"
"Lola bunny makes the basketball team on Halloween"	"Daffy Duck on Halloween"
	"Return of the Pumpkin People"

Colin	(SPED)
"Bugs Bunny on Halloween Night"	
"Mo Vaughn on Halloween Night"	

TABLE 6

Jake	Caitlyn
"Monsster on the Loose"	"Halloween Story"
	"Frankin Turkey"

Jessica	Jason
"Gosty"	"Halloween Party Story"
"The Skullaten Who got Loose"	
"The Halloween Mistery"	

TABLE 3

Josie

Kyle

Kristin

TABLE 5

Judy
"The Halloween Kidnapper"
"The hauted house"
"The bad wich"

Connor
"The Haunted House"
"The Goblin"

Sarah
"The Good Haunted house"
"Bats in the Belfree"

TABLE 2

Vanessa	Phil
"The Three whithis"	"The Magic Halloween"
"The Haunted Mainchon"	
"Towere of Trore [terror]"	

Ted	(SPED)
"Halloween Gosts"	

TABLE 4

Andrea	Nonparticipant
"The curse of Wherewolf hill"	

(SPED)	Danielle
	"Gost Shoe's"

Figure Int.1. Intertextual web of Halloween stories written by the 3rd graders during September and October. Table 3 penned personal narratives about Halloween, but no stories.

suggesting the need for responsive instruction that scaffolds what they know with developmentally appropriate insights and strategies.

It is also the intent of this book to examine why a literature-rich environment that espoused the principles of choice, time, response, and immersion was sufficient to ensure story writing, but not nonfiction writing. We found that after 2 months of varying degrees of exposure to nonfiction literature, only 2 of our 18 3rd graders chose to experiment with the nonfiction genre in response to a dinosaur unit in their science textbook. The fact that other researchers (Chapman, 1995; Duke, 2000) also have noted that neither immersion in nonfiction literature nor free choice prompts exposition suggests a more proactive stance on the part of the teacher. If children do not choose to write nonfiction, there can be no social ripple effect. As the third phase of our study revealed, nonfiction writing soared as soon as the reports of our first two nonfiction writers were showcased and ongoing instructional demonstrations were implemented, reaffirming the vital place of instruction.

And finally, this book discusses instructional implications, lessons learned in the trenches, working side by side with our 3rd graders. Because only two 3rd graders chose to write nonfiction reports toward the end of the second phase of the study, we designed the instruction implemented during the final phase without knowing the breadth and depth of the intertextual understandings that these youngsters possessed. The result was instruction that we are quick to admit was off the mark. Having had the subsequent opportunity to analyze and appreciate the vitality of intertextuality in their reports, we have generated a set of instructional suggestions to guide our future work with nonfiction writers. At their core, these guidelines advocate for public acknowledgment and inspection of the ways in which all writers lean on the "texts" of others in order to craft their own. From the first inkling of an idea (thematic intertextuality), to the ways in which we organize these ideas (organizational intertextuality), to the voices we appropriate (orientational intertextuality) in order to express these ideas, we absorb the words and structures of others, and then work to make them our own (Bakhtin, 1986; Lemke, 1992). Our mission, then, is to help children understand that every writer enters this intertextual zone where he or she summons the words, ideas, and forms of others with grateful acknowledgment, and then corroborates, extends, challenges, parodies, and/or resists in order to make his or her contribution to the topic at hand (Bakhtin, 1986).

ORGANIZATION OF THE BOOK

In Chapter 1, we survey the research on children's nonfiction writing and explore the debate about how best to induct children into the nonfiction genre. With this research as a backdrop, we detail the three phases of the study, highlighting the curricular activities during each phase as well as the data collection and analysis procedures. Frequency data revealed that neither exposure to nor immersion in nonfiction literature, in and of itself, served as a catalyst for nonfiction writing; only two children chose to write exposition after 2½ months. On the other hand, instructional interaction and peer influence prompted a significant rate of nonfiction writing during the final phase; all but one child wrote a minimum of one report.

Chapter 2 then introduces the construct of intertextuality and reviews the small body of research investigating intertextuality and children's literacy. It then presents our findings with respect to the range of the intertextual patterns, which revealed that what children know about the genre of the nonfiction report is intricately tied to their conscious and unconscious appropriations of others' nonfiction works (literature, film, television).

In Chapters 3–5, we shift the lens from our cross-sectional findings to individual writers and their intertextual understandings about the nonfiction reports. Inductive analyses of the interviews and written products revealed that the 3rd graders adopted four differing stances to the task of report writing (Many, Fyfe, Lewis, & Mitchell, 1996): strategic, experience-only, memory-only, and text-bound. In Chapter 3, the reports and interviews of Caitlyn and Colin are used to illuminate the advanced understandings of the strategic writer. These young writers chose topics anchored in personal experiences but extended by consultation of multiple sources; rather than allow these intertextual sources to drive the organization and voice of their reports, each strove to carve out his or her own point of view. Chapter 4 showcases the reports of two 3rd graders that were anchored exclusively in their personal experiences and tied intertextually to information learned from others (e.g., instructors, parents, peers, media). Chapter 5 rounds out our case studies. Here, we present the reports of two text-bound writers, Kyle and Patrick, who viewed texts as the sole source of authority. Each leaned heavily on his intertexts while constructing his reports. Efforts to address their verbatim copying revealed the complexity of this construct for youngsters.

And finally, in Chapter 6, we consider the pedagogical implications of our findings, first in terms of children's reluctance to adopt nonfiction during writing workshop, and then with respect to the wealth of their intertextual understandings. We share the lessons we learned and offer a preliminary set of instructional guidelines to guide our future endeavors. Believing that "children grow into the intellectual life of those around them" (Vygotsky, 1978, p. 88), we will strive to create a learning environment that acknowledges their remarkable cognitive abilities, the profound influence of social interaction and textual sources on these abilities, and the central role that teachers play in nurturing, clarifying, and extending expository understandings.

Writing Workshop: Are Children Choosing to Write Nonfiction?

VANESSA, A 1ST GRADER, arrived at the dinner table and announced to her family that she had "some news" to report. Vanessa then read her news broadcast presented in Figure 1.1, which she had written independently and of her own volition that afternoon.

To the astonishment of her parents, Vanessa had been soaking up the live media coverage of the Gulf War that afternoon while sitting at the kitchen table, talking to her mother about her day at school and eating her snack. This piece stood in contrast with the writing samples in her 1st-grade writing folder, which contained both teacher-prompted journal entries ("If I had three wishes, . . ."; "My favorite month is . . .") and self-selected entries, as well as a few stories about talking bears, a haunted house, and a pumpkin that weighed 100 pounds.

According to the early theories of children's writing development, however, Vanessa should not have been cognitively capable of writing this expository piece on the Gulf War. The pioneering work of James Britton and his colleagues (1975) and James Moffett (1968) posited that children are not ready to handle the complexities of informational reading and writing. Vanessa's ability not only to "read the world" (Freire, 1985, p. 18) but also to craft her message in a culturally appropriate genre and deliver it in a social setting is representative of the current research which has debunked Britton and colleagues' (1975) and Moffett's findings (1968).

We begin this chapter, then, with a brief overview of this early research on children's writing development (Britton et al., 1975; Moffett, 1968) and its influence on Donald Graves (1983), who revolutionized the teaching of writing at the elementary level. We then survey the current research on young children's nonfiction genre development and discuss the debate about genre instruction. Having established the vitality of the nonfiction genre in young children's writing, we then set the stage for the first part of our study, which sought to explore why our 3rd graders chose not to write nonfiction during writing workshop. We present our research questions, a description of our classroom context, and the curricular events of the three phases of the study. The data collection and analysis procedures are also described, as well as our findings with respect to children choosing to write nonfiction writing.

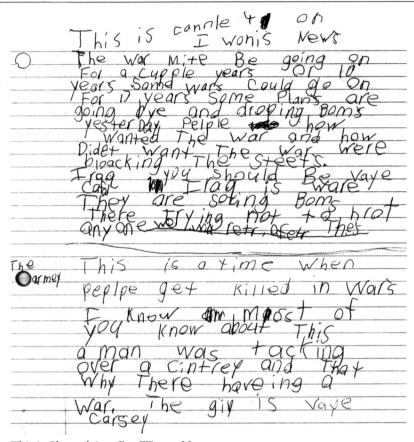

This is Channel 4 on Eye Witness News.
The war might be going on for a couple of years or 10 years. Some wars go on for 17 years. Some planes are going by and dropping bombs. Yesterday, people who wanted the war and who didn't want the war were blocking the streets. Iraq, you should be very careful. Iraq is where they are sending bombs. They're trying not to hurt anyone. We will be return after this.

This is a time when people get killed in wars. I know most of you know about this. A man was taking over a country and that's why they're having a war. The guy is very crazy.

Figure 1.1. Vanessa, a 1st grader, wrote this broadcast on the Gulf War and read it to her family during dinner. Reprinted from *Inside the Writing Portfolio: What We Need to Know to Assess Children's Writing,* by Carol Brennan Jenkins. Copyright © 1996 by Carol Brennan Jenkins. Published by Heinemann, a division of Reed Elsevier, Inc. Portsmouth, NH. Reprinted with permission.

NONFICTION WRITING DEVELOPMENT AND THE YOUNG CHILD

In their classic study *The Development of Writing Abilities*, Britton and his colleagues (1975) surveyed the types of writing that students were asked to do in British schools. Using this database, they identified three major functions of writing—expressive, poetic, and transactional—and proposed that these functions occur in a fixed developmental sequence. Expressive writing (often called personal narrative or journal writing) constitutes the child's earliest form of writing—highly fluid, informal, egocentric in viewpoint, and occurring in a shared, familiar context. It is "the language close to the self" (p. 90). While acknowledging that "it is certainly not the case that every child's first attempts at writing are expressive . . ." (p. 82), they argued that expressive writing stands at "the matrix from which differentiated forms of mature writing are developed" (p. 83). It is only in later years, when children develop an awareness of audience—an audience they would like to entertain or to inform—that they transition to the more advanced forms of poetic and transactional writing. Poetic writers operate within certain literary boundaries as they arrange "sounds, words, images, ideas, events, and feelings" (Britton, 1993, p. 177) in deliberate ways to compose a story or a poem. Transactional writers, on the other hand, take on the challenge of describing, explaining, instructing, and/or persuading in order "to *get something done* in the world" (Britton, 1993, p. 169; emphasis in original).

Moffett (1968), dismayed by the quality of student writing, used Piaget's construct of egocentrism to propose a writing curriculum that also placed personal narratives at the center of the writing experience across the elementary years. He argued that "as one struggles to put personal experience into language, the experience itself becomes perceived, clarified, distanced, symbolized, ordered, understood, and even mastered in a new way" (Moffett & Wagner, 1976, p. 320). Thus, by instituting a sequence of writing assignments that entailed "writing about self"—such as sensory writing and memory writing—teachers could ensure that students would advance to increasingly higher levels of abstraction and generalization.

Britton's and Moffett's call for the primacy of expressive writing was clinched with Donald Graves's (1983) *Writing: Teachers and Children at Work*, in which he stated:

> When children attempt to recall information in a personal narrative, they have a much stronger sense of chronology, as well as of the missing information. The next easiest is fantasy or fiction, where children must recall imagined information and locate in their own contrived stories the proper place for the data. Many children can do this, but it is usually more difficult than in personal narratives. In the content area where the order is determined by the logical relationships of information, the task is even more difficult. (p. 155)

Interestingly, however, Graves's privileging of the personal narrative over nonfiction writing ran counter to the findings of his own doctoral research (1973) on children's writing processes. When the 2nd graders in his study were given an opportunity to self-select topics, both girls and boys chose to write about "animals and living things," by a wide margin (30%). The next most popular category (17%) was what Graves called "primary territory"; the 2nd graders wrote about themselves, their family, and their classrooms, with almost twice as many girls doing so. Graves also noted high percentages of boys writing about "secondary territory" topics such as airplanes, police and war, and sports, and about "extended territory" topics such as presidents, space flights, history, and war. That said, Graves in his later works (1989, 1994) does advise teachers to integrate nonfiction writing into the curriculum by anchoring exposition primarily in direct experiences, observations, and interviews.

The earliest challenges to Britton and colleagues' and Moffett's notions about young children's inability to handle exposition were sounded by case study researchers and classroom teachers. Bissex (1980) found that the earliest writings of her son Paul, age 5, spanned the genres. He created cards, typed five-page stories, designed a gameboard, wrote a newspaper, and penned signs (DO NAT DSTRB GYNS AT WRK) that he hung on his door and in his block area. Likewise, Schickedanz (1990) documented a range of genres with which her son experimented from age 4 to age 6. Sowers (1985) found that 1st graders' earliest form of writing was expository, characterized by "all-about" books in which they penned everything they knew about a particular topic, such as dinosaurs.

In her landmark study, Langer (1986) established that

> even at age 8, the children differentiate clearly between the uses of exposition and of story telling. They describe story and report differently, attribute different uses to them, select different topics for use with each, and organize them differently. This differentiation is based on a primary distinction between truthful presentation of facts and imaginative creation of fiction. (p. 52)

Subsequent research has demonstrated that the ability to produce distinct genres, including a range of non-narrative genres, begins as early as kindergarten and becomes increasingly more sophisticated (Chapman, 1994, 1995; Donovan, 2001; Kamberelis & Bovino, 1999; Newkirk, 1987; Zecker, 1996). For example, curious as to whether young children are cognizant of the differing linguistic patterns in fiction and nonfiction, Pappas (1993) asked kindergartners to pretend-read two unfamiliar stories and two unfamiliar nonfiction books. Pappas documented increasing sensitivity to the distinctive features of these two genres at two major levels: patterns of global organization and patterns of language texture. With respect to nonfiction global organization, the children organized their reenactments by (1) introducing the topic, (2) describing the attributes of the topic, (3) giving the characteristic events associated with the topic, and (4) providing a final summary. The kindergartners also demonstrated sensitivity to the three patterns of texture that are particular to informational texts: choice of pronouns (e.g., use of *it*, not *you* or *she*), verb tense (present, not past), and degree of description. Extending Pappas's work, Casbergue (1996) found the same degree of linguistic knowledge with respect to global organization and texture patterns in the nonfiction writing samples of kindergartners and 1st and 2nd graders.

Newkirk (1987), one of the first researchers to challenge Britton's and Moffett's theories, analyzed the structural features in the non-narrative writing samples that children in grades 1 to 3 produced during writing workshop without any specific instruction in expository writing. He found a general progression of eight structures that included basic lists in the early grades to ordered paragraphs by 3rd grade. For example, while 1st and 2nd graders constructed a high percentage of attribute lists (an unordered list of statements about a topic that may contain affective and informational statements), only a small percentage of 3rd graders did so. Third graders, on the other hand, were the only ones to write ordered basic paragraphs.

In a year-long naturalistic investigation of 1st graders' genre experimentation, Chapman (1995) validated and extended Newkirk's work. She examined the written genres of six 1st graders who participated in a literature-based reading program and daily writing workshop. Using Newkirk's analytic scheme to diagram the relationships among clauses as well as the hierarchical structure of each child's piece, Chapman found 15 genres, which ranged from various types of action-based chronologies, such as recounts based on personal experiences and imaginary narratives, to various types of object-oriented genres, such as labels, lists, and attribute series. Labeling (59%) constituted children's most frequent genre in September; expanded records (personal narrative of two or more clauses) (31%) and attribute series (24%) were most prevalent at the end of grade 1. However, even though the 1st graders lived in a literature-rich classroom and participated in weekly teacher-led nonfiction writing, they chose not to write nonfiction during writing workshop; personal narratives and stories prevailed. "In the case of this study, recall that despite the Wednesday 'project day' and the children's exposure to 'scientific writing,' the focus pupils did not chose to engage in this kind of writing during Writing Workshop" (p. 189). In discussing this predicament, Chapman speculated that because the teacher did not read nonfiction literature and did not tell children they could chose to write nonfiction, the children may not have been primed for or may not have understood this option.

Chapman's distinction between non-narrative writing (essentially labels, lists, and personal narratives) and nonfiction writing (scientific writing) with respect to developmental trends is noteworthy. In fact, researchers (Hicks, 1990; Kamberelis & Bovino, 1999) who have probed specific nonfiction genres suggest less clear-cut support for genre understandings. For example, Hicks (1990) asked kindergartners, 1st graders, and 2nd graders to watch a 14-minute version of the silent film, *The Red Balloon*, and to execute three narrative tasks. One task asked each child to give an online narration (in the role of a sportscaster) while rewatching a 3-minute segment of the film. To ready the child for this simulated live broadcast, the examiner read a scripted lead-in prompt. Directly following this task, a second genre-specific prompt was read, which asked the child to relate the contents of the 14-minute film as a news reporter. One hour later, each was asked to retell the film as a story. Hicks found that although the children were able to retell the film's content, they evinced an incipient but unstable understanding of these genres. For example, while they appropriately used more past tense verbs and more sequential connectors (*and, and then*) in their storytelling and news reporting than in their online narration, none adopted the global strategies often used to mark these genres (e.g., "Stay tuned" during online narration). Marked similarity among the three narrations was found, suggesting that these youngsters had difficulty adopting the varying narrator roles. In addition, the order of the tasks significantly affected their performance. For example, kindergartners and first graders who gave the news reports first continued to use the past tense in their "sportscasts." Hicks (1990) concluded that genre understandings of primary children are nascent and that "children from grades K-2 may be unable to produce clearly defined discourse genres, since their repertoire of genre knowledge may be somewhat collapsed in comparison to that of mature speaker[s]" (p. 100). It is interesting that Vanessa's broadcast (Figure 1.1) included two of the global strategies that characterize news broadcasts ("This is Channel 4 Eye witness News"; "We will be right back after this"), as well as use of past tense and temporal connectives (e.g., *yesterday, when, after*), which were rarely employed by Hicks's sample population. Vanessa's decision to generate her Gulf War broadcast for genuine communicative purposes, rather than to fulfill a research agenda, reminds us that context and intention are critical variables in assessment of genre performance (Freedman, 1993). While Hicks's findings demonstrate that young children have difficulty shifting among genres on demand, further research is needed to pinpoint what children know specifically about genres, such as the news report and the broadcast, not only in terms of linguistic markers, but also in terms of criterial attributes and organizational structure.

In an intriguing study that specifically investigated what young children understand about the genres of story and the nonfiction report, Kamberelis and Bovino (1999) asked kindergartners, 1st graders, and 2nd graders to write two stories and two science reports under two conditions—scaffolded and nonscaffolded. Under the scaffolded condition, each child was asked to recall a familiar/favorite story and to reproduce it; on another day, each was asked to recall information "about animals that you remembered from a book you know" (p. 169) and to write a report about an animal. Under the nonscaffolded condition, each child was asked to pretend that he or she was an author and to write an original story and an original science report about an animal. Thus over four separate days, four pieces were generated by each child, working one-on-one with a researcher. All children participated in grade-appropriate thematic units on animals (habitats, life cycles), which included fiction and nonfiction trade books, during the 6-week period prior to the study. No formal instruction on genre characteristics was provided, but informal discussions about text characteristics occurred in all classrooms.

Analyses of the writing samples revealed that the kindergartners, 1st graders, and 2nd graders possessed a strong command of the narrative genre under both the scaffolded and nonscaffolded conditions. Their stories contained the obligatory features of story (e.g., initiating event, sequence event, final event), as well as appropriate linguistic markers, such as past tense verbs, temporal connectives (e.g., "and then," "next," "finally"), and co-referential devices (such as pronoun referents).

With respect to the expository genre, though, Kamberelis and Bovino (1999) noted, "Although most children composed prototypic stories in response to the request to write stories, fewer children produced prototypic science reports and quite a few had difficulty instantiating this genre" (p. 153). They noted that many samples, especially those of the younger children, were not prototypical of informational reports. Moreover, many youngsters produced hybrid reports that combined features of both fiction and nonfiction. Although many of their reports were not as well-developed as their stories, a number of nascent understandings about the expository genre were noted. Using Pappas's scheme of obligatory features of exposition, Kamberelis and Bovino (1999) found that across grade levels, children used significantly more of these obligatory features in their reports than in their stories. Not surprisingly, the reports of 1st and 2nd graders were better developed than those of the kindergartners. The linguistic device of co-classification, necessary for creating cohesion in a nonfiction text, permeated their reports, with significantly more co-classification markers in the reports of the 1st and 2nd graders. With the exception of kindergartners under the nonscaffolded condition, the children consistently used present tense verbs to mark the stable nature of factual information in their reports. Another linguistic feature, logical connectives (markers such as "because," "although," "therefore"), characteristic of nonfiction, was coded very infrequently, appearing only in the reports of the older children.

In addition to demonstrating that young children do possess increasingly sophisticated levels of genre knowledge, Kamberelis and Bovino (1999) also noted another intriguing finding: "Almost without exception, children tended to produce more well-formed texts in [the] scaffolded condition. . . . As non-social apprenticeship contexts, these artifacts seemed to speak through the children, allowing them to engage in text-making activities beyond their ability to do so independently" (p. 163). The fact that the children were more successful at generating stories and reports in particular genres when they were calling up and reenacting familiar texts than when they were attempting to author original pieces brings to the forefront the powerful scaffold that literature provides. Citing Vygotsky's attention to the role of imitation in learning, Kamberlis and Bovino urge educators to acknowledge the mediational power of cultural artifacts.

Taken together, these studies suggest that primary school children are capable of not only writing in a variety of genres but also abstracting features of particular genres in increasingly sophisticated ways. Certain genres appear to be absorbed more readily than others, with lists, letters, and personal narratives well within the repertoire of 1st and 2nd graders (Chapman, 1995; Newkirk, 1987; Zecker, 1996) and with story writing emerging at the end of first grade (Chapman, 1995) and solidifying in second grade (Kamberelis & Bovino, 1999). Nonfiction genres such as science reports, news reports, and online broadcasts, however, appear to be less stable for primary children (Hicks, 1990; Kamberelis & Bovino, 1999), although their report writing was significantly stronger when scaffolded by trade books (Kamberelis & Bovino, 1999).

Taking our cue from these researchers, we speculated that the invitation to write nonfiction during writing workshop coupled with immersion in high-quality nonfiction literature would spur nonfiction writing. In the event, though, that a rich literacy context would not induce exposition, we also considered the place of instruction. We turn now to the debate about genre instruction.

THE DEBATE ABOUT GENRE INSTRUCTION

How best to induct children into the dynamic nature of genre has been the subject of much debate. A number of genre theorists (Freedman, 1993; Gee, 1989; Genishi, 1992) have endorsed the model of incidental learning (also called the natural learning model). Freedman (1993) argues that, because genres are not static text structures but rather social actions of writers attempting to influence readers in particular ways, they need to be learned tacitly through immersion and authentic engagement. Thus, a teacher implementing the incidental model with the intention of introducing children to editorial writing would create a "facilitative environment" (Freedman, 1993, p. 237). The teacher would immerse students in a wide range of exemplary editorials, explore how and why the authors of these editorials came to take a stand on particular issue, invite students to brainstorm issues about which they felt passionately, and set the stage for students to craft editorials that would be published. While Freedman (1993) contends that this model "leaves room for some explicit teaching"(p. 237), she believes that a heavy dose of direct instruction in genres is not only unnecessary but potentially harmful. She contends that the rules of genres are too complex and numerous to be taught explicitly—so complex, in fact, that many teachers haven't mastered the intricacies of certain genres and often teach students erroneous genre features and rules. Gee (1989) concurs that "discourses are not mastered by overt instruction . . . but by enculturation (apprenticeship) into social practices through scaffolded and supported interaction with people who have already mastered the Discourse" (p. 7).

Researchers have begun to document the power of authentic endeavor. As already noted, Chapman (1995) found that 1st graders do experiment with a variety of genres (although the nonfiction report was not evident) in increasingly advanced ways. She concluded that her study "provides strong support for the notion that young children learn much about genre without explicit instruction in generic features through immersion in a literacy-rich environment" (p. 188).

Other researchers have corroborated Chapman's (1995) findings. Zecker (1996) asked kindergartners and 1st graders to produce three genres (grocery list, letter, and story) across the year. She found that the grocery list was the easiest genre for both groups, followed by the personal letter, with 85% of the kindergartners' letters (and 100% of the 1st graders') meeting the primary content and structural criteria by the end of the year. Subsequent studies have substantiated the increase in genre knowledge across the primary grades (Donovan, 2001; Kamberelis & Bovino, 1999).

The incidental learning model, however, has been contested by Delpit (1988), who has charged that while children who live in middle-class, literacy-rich homes may abstract the forms and functions of literate activity, there is little evidence that this process-oriented approach works for children of color or poverty. According to Delpit, these children need explicit instruction within the context of authentic reading and writing endeavors. To deny children this instruction is to deny them access to the dominant culture, to successful participation in society. Delpit has been joined in her call for explicit instruction by a group of Australian genre theorists (Christie, 1993; Cope & Kalantzis, 1993; Kress, 1993, 1999). Alarmed by the poor writing performance of children who had participated in writing-process classrooms that treated writing as a single generic experience (essentially personal narratives), Australian genre theorists (Eggins, Wignell, & Martin, 1993; Martin, 1985) surveyed the school curriculum for genres that students must master to succeed in school. Noting the importance of nonfiction genres, they argued against a genre-neutral writing-process curriculum and advocated explicit instruction in genres to ensure that all children, especially those from diverse backgrounds, have equal access to the genres of power. As Kress (1999) writes, genre theory and practice make

> writing . . . no longer an individual expressive act, but a social, conventional act *performed* by an individual, *any* individual. . . . The impulse for writing has shifted: from desire to power, from the individual to the social, from expression to communication, from creativity to conventionality, from authenticity (a question of fit with personal truth) to appropriateness (a question of fit with social truth). No wonder there was a debate, and a fierce debate. Genre theory threatened to unmake everything that proponents of the English language arts thought they had stood for over the preceding 20 years. (pp. 463–464)

The work of many genre theorists is anchored in Vygotsky (1978), who posited that while oral language is acquired naturally through social interaction, literacy is not as easily acquired. Such acquisition hinges not only on the social milieu but also on the active intervention of more knowledgeable others. As Vygotsky (1962) argued, "Instruction is one of the principal sources of the school child's concepts and is also a powerful force in directing their evolution; it determines the fate of his total mental development" (p. 85). Although many genre theorists agree that children must participate in meaningful literacy events, they argue that such immersion is not enough. Rather, both process and product must enter the educational equation if children are to experience the full power of literacy.

This perspective has been borne out by recent research. Wollman-Bonilla (2000) investigated the effect of teacher-led collaborative science writing on the writing of four 1st graders. The children wrote daily entries about various curricular activities, including science inquiry, which were sent home for reply from family members. At the beginning of the school year, the teachers explicitly modeled various genre-specific forms (e.g., experiment, report) to guide the construction of their science journals; they implicitly modeled the lexicogrammatical features (verb tense, technological vocabulary) during joint collaborations. Over time, the modeling decreased in that the collaborative messages were begun together but finished independently by the children. Analysis of the children's science writing revealed four major genre categories: the report, experiment recount, experiment procedure, and explanation. The predominant genre (60%) was the report. The children's messages included introductory statements and descriptions of attributes or characteristic events, as well as the use of present tense and of scientific language. The report was followed in popularity by the experiment, with the 1st graders including features such as aim of investigation, methods used, and results found; only a third included conclusions. The children were successful to a limited degree in adopting the lexicogrammatical features of experiments.

Wollman-Bonilla (2000) concluded that young children can be successfully inducted into scientific writing via teacher-led collaborative writing followed by independent practice.

Tackling the explicit–implicit instruction debate head-on, Yeh (1998) examined the effects of two literacy contexts on the ability of culturally diverse 7th graders to construct persuasive essays. In one set of classrooms, students participated only in the immersion activities. Once or twice a week, these students "read pro and con arguments on a given topic, participated in a classroom debate, received pre-writing instruction, then planned, wrote, and revised argumentative essays" (Yeh, 1998, p. 61). These immersion students wrote eight essays over 6 weeks but received no explicit instruction on the generic principles of argumentation. In the other classrooms, students received explicit instruction in argumentation as well as immersion in the debate and peer-response activities described above. Yeh (1998) found that students who received instruction and who participated in the immersion activities wrote significantly better essays and revealed greater understanding of argument strategies. Burkhalter (1995) compared the performance two classes of 4th and 6th graders who received instruction in persuasive writing and two classes at each level who received no instruction. She found that all students who received instruction wrote significantly better pieces than children without instruction. While 6th graders scored higher on their essays than 4th graders, 4th graders wrote essays that met the criteria for effective persuasive essays.

Culling the expanse of this research data, we designed our study with the conviction that our 3rd graders were capable of writing nonfiction across a range of subgenres. Concurring with Kamberelis and Bovino (1999) and others about the interdependency of the reading and writing processes, and with the New London Group (1996) on the necessity of both "situated practice"—defined as "immersion in a community of learners engaged in authentic versions of such practice" (p. 84)—and overt instruction, we framed the phases of our study as follows.

THE STUDY

As reported in the introduction of this book, the focus of our research was twofold. First, we investigated whether a literature-rich, literacy-intensive classroom that exposed 3rd graders to varying degrees of nonfiction literature would prompt nonfiction writing. And, if not, would immersion in nonfiction in conjunction with direct instruction result in expository writing? Second, we examined the range of intertextual links that children forged when they chose to write nonfiction. The study was organized into three phases; the research questions guiding each phase included the following:

Phase 1. When given free choice of topics and genres, and exposure to one piece of nonfiction literature per week, with what frequency do 3rd graders choose to write nonfiction during writing workshop? What intertextual patterns (thematic, orientational, and organizational) are evident in their nonfiction writing?

Phase 2. Given the same classroom context, will increased exposure to nonfiction (three times a week) affect frequency rates? What intertextual patterns (thematic, orientational, and organizational) are evident in their nonfiction writing?

Phase 3. Will continued immersion in nonfiction in conjunction with explicit instruction in nonfiction report writing affect the frequency rate? What intertextual patterns (thematic, orientational, and organizational) are evident in their nonfiction writing?

This chapter addresses only the questions with respect to frequency with which the 3rd graders adopted nonfiction writing during each phase; the next chapter focuses on the patterns of intertextuality adopted. We begin with a description of the classroom context. We then describe the curricular events of each phase of the study, the data collection and analysis procedures, and our findings with respect to children choosing to write nonfiction writing.

Participants

COME BACK *SOON* (AND THATS AN *ORDER*!!)
DEAR MRS. EARLE,
WE REALLY MISS YOU. I DON'T THINK WE'RE PAYING ATTENTION TO THE SUBSTITUTE TEACHER. I KNOW WHAT YOU FEEL LIKE. I LOST MY DAD TOO. I KNOW YOU WILL ALWAYS REMEMBER HIM. HAVE YOU GUESSED WHO I AM YET. I'M . . . !!
LOVE,
Caitlyn

With tears in her eyes, laughing and crying at the same time, Alice read this and other cards written by her 3rd graders the week she returned to school following her father's death. Caitlyn, a new student in the school, who had lost her father several years earlier, was forthright in sharing her life with the class. A real horse nut, she took riding lessons and competed in equestrian events. Not surprisingly, horses dominated much of her writing and reading. Slender, with light blond hair and blue-green eyes, she became quite a social butterfly in the classroom.

Caitlyn was just one of the twenty-two 3rd graders in Alice's classroom, 18 of whom participated in our study. (*Note:* Three special-needs children were unable to participate because of scheduling conflicts. In addition, one boy's writing was not included in our database because his parent did not return the consent form after a number of requests.) Caitlyn and her peers attended a public elementary school in a suburban, middle-class New England town. Per capita income in 1999 was $33,510, with 45% of the adult population being college graduates and 10% of families living below the poverty level. Although the number of non-White residents moving into the community was increasing as of the 1999 census, non-Whites made up 7.5% of the total population at the time (U.S. Census Bureau, 2000).

Our school, one of three elementary schools in the public school district, had approximately 500 students in grades K–5, with four 3rd-grade classrooms. Of the 10 females and 8 males who participated in our study, 1 was African American, 1 was bilingual, and the remainder were European American. Three students qualified for the federally subsidized lunch program. Six students lived in a single-parent household, 2 lived in a family where one of the parents was a stepparent, and the remaining 10 lived with both biological parents. Parental occupations spanned a wide range: administrative assistants, a professional body builder, business executives, a computer technician, educators, health club instructors, laborers, lawyers, a medical technician, managers, a physician, and salespeople. Seven of the 18 general education students received counseling services from the school adjustment counselor.

Alice's classroom was the inclusion 3rd grade for the building. The school's inclusion model included both in-class and pull-out dimensions because the special-needs teacher also worked in an inclusion 2nd grade. As noted above, because three children were with the special-needs teacher in the learning center during reading and writing workshop, they were unable to participate in our study.

Table 1.1 summarizes the sex, ethnicity, and literacy standing of our 18 3rd graders. Literacy standing was determined by assessing the 3rd graders' reading and writing portfolios. Those who were reading chapter books with a reading level of 4th grade (or higher) on a regular basis and writing effective pieces (as judged by teacher-assessment rating scales) are designated as "advanced" in Table 1.1. Third graders reading chapter books on grade level and writing grade-appropriate pieces are designated as "on grade level." The six receiving support services from the literacy specialist were working toward grade-level proficiency. One student, Caitlyn, participated in a gifted and talented pull-out program once a week for 2 hours. Eligibility for this program began with a teacher recommendation and was ultimately based on three sources of data: parent and teacher checklists, school performance, and the Torrence Test of Creativity.

Table 1.1. Sex, Ethnicity, and Literacy Standing of 3rd-Grade Participants, as Determined by Portfolio Assessment and Support Services

	Sex	Ethnicity	Literacy Standing
Andrea	F	European American	On grade level
Caitlyn	F	European American	Gifted and talented
Colin	M	European American	Advanced
Connor	M	European American	On grade level
Danielle	F	European American	On grade level
Jake	M	European American	On grade level
Jason	M	European American	On grade level
Jessica	F	European American	Literacy support services
Josie	F	European American (bilingual)	Literacy support services
Judy	F	European American	On grade level
Kristin	F	European American	Advanced
Kyle	M	European American	Literacy support services
Maureen	F	European American	Literacy support services
Patrick	M	European American	On grade level
Phil	M	African American	Literacy support services
Sarah	F	European American	On grade level
Ted	M	European American	Literacy support services
Vanessa	F	European American	On grade level

In 1st and 2nd grade, most of these children had learned to read in a literature-based reading series. They also received whole-class phonics instruction through a published program called *Won Way Phonics* (Bradley, 1996). During 1st grade, many participated in shared reading of predictable books at the start of the year and later wrote their own predictable books. They were allowed and encouraged to use invented spelling when writing. In 2nd grade, writing activities varied by classroom. In one classroom, children were part of a pen pal program. Three of the four 2nd-grade teachers had children choose a New England state and write a one-paragraph report; the fourth teacher had children choose and write an animal report. This was the extent of the 2nd graders' nonfiction writing. When they arrived in Alice's classroom, they had no experience with reading and writing workshops.

Finally, as participants in this study, we interacted with our 18 3rd graders in a variety of ways across the phases of this study: conferring during writing workshop, interviewing, recording observations, implementing read-alouds, teaching formally and informally, and so forth. (Our specific roles during each phase are highlighted in the Phases of the Study section of this chapter.) As a classroom teacher (Alice) and a teacher educator (Carol), we have collaborated extensively on various literacy projects since 1990. For example, in addition to two Spencer Grants, which funded this research on nonfiction writing, we have worked together on a portfolio assessment project, a pen pal project between 3rd graders and college students, and an author study. Certified as an elementary teacher and a teacher of reading, Alice taught 1st grade for 2 years, Chapter I students for 5 years, and 3rd grade for 18 years. Carol, who has worked in the field of literacy education for more than 30 years as a classroom teacher, reading specialist, and teacher educator, teaches courses in literacy and conducts in-service workshops.

We turn now to a description of the classroom context: what Alice did to prepare for the first week of school, to induct children into daily routines, and to launch reading and writing workshops.

Classroom Context

Literacy-bound: August and the first 2 weeks of school. During August, Alice sent a letter welcoming each student to her classroom and asking, among other things, that they bring a writer's notebook and books to read during reading workshop and free time. Parents also received a letter of introduction that included Alice's beliefs about learning and an invitation to write a letter about their child, responding to questions such as: What are your child's interests and talents? What is important for me know about your child? How does your child feel about school? Several parents shared insightful observations and voiced the hope that their child would develop more interest in reading during the coming school year.

As children entered on the first day, they sat at tables instead of desks in order to foster the social interaction that is the key to learning and literacy (Vygotsky, 1978). Because social responsibility was also central to this classroom community, the 3rd graders discussed what makes a caring and responsive learning environment and designed signs and posters displaying rules of conduct (Charney, 1991). They also shared in classroom responsibilities by selecting and executing a weekly job: emptying pencil sharpeners, distributing notices, feeding pets, watering plants, patrolling cubby and coat areas, and straightening the game and library areas.

The daily routine, laced with literacy activities, was also introduced. After students put away their belongings, they met at the rug area. A student manager read the menu and took the lunch count, which was given to the messenger to deliver to the office. Then the leader of the day chose a patriotic song for the class to sing and led the Pledge of Allegiance. The leader then read an excerpt that had been rehearsed from a favorite part of a book or from his or her own writing. Questions and supportive comments or requests for clarification from the audience followed. At the conclusion of opening activities, children transitioned to reading and writing workshops (see the next sections). Math instruction, also based on a workshop model that included mini-lessons, cooperative group work, partner, and individual activities, rounded out the morning.

After lunch and specialist activities, students gathered on the rug for a daily oral-language session. Two students served as class secretaries in charge of recording incorrect sentences from the teacher's edition of the language textbook on chart paper. The secretaries, with teacher guidance, then asked the class to offer editorial changes along with justifications. Based on their responses, ideas for future mini-lessons were recorded. Students then worked on individual activities until afternoon recess and executed classroom jobs (described earlier). Daily whole-class instruction for science or social studies then ensued. At the end of the day, the class gathered on the rug to contribute to the "News of the Day," an activity which asked the children to review the highlights of the day. Contributions were recorded on chart paper. Later in the week, two student reporters summarized these notes, which were published in the weekly news and sent home to each family.

During the first week, the 3rd graders also set up the classroom library. They were asked to unpack well over a thousand trade books and magazines from boxes onto the rug, and then, tapping what they knew about genres, organize them according to genre on bookshelves and in labeled plastic buckets. When completed, they had shelved approximately 550 picture books and chapter books, 650 informational books, 100 magazines such as *Ranger Rick*, *National Geographic for Kids*, *Sports for Kids*, and 20 poetry and joke books. Thus, general talk about the range of genres constituted one of the earliest mini-lessons.

Other mini-lessons specific to the procedures for writing and reading workshop (Atwell, 1987) were also implemented during the first few weeks, such as (1) generating rules for workshop time, (2) demonstrating the status of class procedure used at the beginning of every workshop, (3) brainstorming/recording writing topics and genres and completing idea lists, (4) discussing and distributing guidelines for writing notebooks, (5) demonstrating how to keep reading and writing record sheets, and (6) responding to reading and writing surveys.

Writing workshop. In mid-September, Alice recorded the following memory of a recent personal event on a chart as children listened with the goal of demonstrating that "writing comes from the events of our daily lives, from what appears at first glance to be trivial" (Graves, 1994, p. 36). Alice then transformed these seed ideas into a first draft as children attended and interacted.

SEED IDEAS	FIRST DRAFT
right at dirt road with soccer field sign	Turning my car off the paved street onto a dirt road at the sign,
"I'll get there before the half"	"Soccer Fields," I bump up and
worry if I should put car in second gear	down, leaving a cloud of dust behind me. Crawling past pas-
bump up and down, leave dust clouds behind me	tures of yellow grass that remind me of South Dakota summers, I
tall yellow grass reminds me of South Dakota pastures	make it to the top of a hill and see the green school shirts far to the
reach soccer field and see ——, not varsity	right. I pull closer and roll to a stop. Hoping I've made it before
Wrong field	the half, I scan the faces of the kids and get a sinking feeling. "Wrong field!"

Students then tried their hand at exploring this approach during the silent writing time and later shared their work with partners.

Such is an example of one of the mini-lessons that Alice frequently taught at the opening of writing workshop. Mini-lessons usually sprang from the children's writing needs and interests, as well as from curricular mandates, and focused on a wide array of topics, including strategies and skills experienced writers use, the writing process, and the assessment process. As already noted, informal instruction on the range of genres occurred as the 3rd graders set up the classroom library. In addition, as the 3rd graders brainstormed the range of genres in which people write as well as possible topics, their ideas were posted. The 3rd graders were told that they could choose to write in genres and on topics of their choice during writing workshop. With respect to genre-specific instruction, only mini-lessons on personal narratives, as just illustrated, were taught prior to phase 1. No mini-lessons on story writing were taught during any phase, and no nonfiction lessons were taught until phase 3 of the study in December.

Sustained silent writing for 30–40 minutes constituted the mainstay of writing workshop. The 3rd graders chose their own topics, genres, and timelines. As soon as the children began writing, Alice took the status of the class, visiting each child individually to talk about his or her piece and then recording the writing topic and phase of the writing process (draft, revision, etc.) next to the child's name on a record sheet attached to a clipboard (Atwell, 1987). Conferences with individual children followed. These consisted of listening to excerpts, providing feedback, discussing revisions and editing, or teaching skills and strategies when appropriate. The workshop often concluded with peer conferences or sharing. In addition, whole-group sharing of writing conducted by a student leader, with students reading pieces and receiving feedback from the class and teacher, was also scheduled on a regular basis. Writing workshop was scheduled three times a week.

In October, students were introduced to portfolio assessment across a series of mini-lessons. They selected a favorite/best entry from their writer's notebooks and, during a conference, explained why it was their favorite and what made it a good piece of writing. In the spirit of the collaborative portfolio, Alice also chose what *she* considered to be their best work and shared her insights with the writer. Both choices were added to the student's portfolio. In addition, students were introduced to reading and writing self-assessment scales at the end of the first term (and each subsequent term). After students rated themselves and Alice rated them, they met to compare results (writing samples and rating scales) and to set goals for the next term.

Reading workshop. Alice's 3rd graders enjoyed the same freedom to select their own books from the well-stocked classroom library to read and respond to at their own pace. Paralleling the writing workshop, reading workshop (Atwell, 1987) included mini-lessons on topics that ranged from the reading process to the skills and strategies fluent readers use, including word analysis. Sustained silent reading for 30–40 minutes then ensued. During silent reading, Alice conferred with individual students and met with students in small reading-response groups, where they took turns reading favorite passages from their books and responding to questions and comments from the group. Each child also wrote a dialogue journal (Atwell, 1987)—a letter sharing his or her personal response to a book—every other week. Alice returned a letter to each child, acknowledging his or her content and sharing her response. Portfolio assessment also ensued.

In sum, Alice strove to ensure her 3rd graders' literacy success by fostering the appropriate conditions for learning—immersion, demonstration, expectation, responsibility, use, approximation, and response (Cambourne, 1988). We turn now to a description of the three phases that exposed children to nonfiction literature in varying degrees and included direct instruction during the final phase.

Phases of the Study

Each phase was 4 weeks in duration, beginning at the end of September and ending the second week in January (but not including Thanksgiving week, winter break, and the first week in December due to teacher illness). In addition to the nonfiction literature read aloud during each phase, the 3rd graders also read their science and social studies textbooks, as well as current events articles in the weekly news magazine *Time For Kids*. These phases are summarized in Figure 1.2.

Phase 1: Will limited exposure to nonfiction prompt nonfiction writing? The first phase investigated whether minimal exposure to nonfiction literature would result in nonfiction writing. One informational book along with three fictional pieces (storybooks or chapters from a children's novel) were read aloud each week. Cognizant of children's well-documented interest in animals (G. Anderson et al., 1985; Kirsch, 1975) and committed to keeping some degree of curricular continuity, we chose four informational books to support the 3rd graders' year-long study of the vernal pool (transitory wetland). Two weeks prior to the first visit to the town's vernal pool, two books were read and discussed: *Box Turtle at Long Pond* (George, 1989) and *Frogs* (Gibbons, 1993). Two weeks after the visit, two other books were shared: *Salamanders* (Billings, 1981) and *Dragonfly* (Bernhard & Bernhard, 1993). The book selection process involved perusal of many books on vernal pool animals; the four chosen met the criteria of high-quality nonfiction (Huck et al., 1987). These read-alouds, which evoked both aesthetic and efferent responses, were highly interactive (Doiron, 1994; Moss, 1995; Oyler & Barry, 1996; Tower, 2002; Vardell & Copeland, 1992); the 3rd graders interjected many comments and asked questions. Strategies such as anticipation guides and KWL charts were implemented to tap prior knowledge and to enhance comprehension. No suggestion to write nonfiction during writing workshop was given.

    With respect to our teaching roles, Alice assumed full responsibility for organizing and implementing the reading and writing workshops. Minilessons taught during this phase focused on additional procedural aspects of writing workshop (e.g., the purpose and procedures of conferences with teachers and peers as well as peer or whole-class share) and on the writing process (e.g., rehearsal, drafting, revising, editing, and publishing). Alice used her personal narrative on the soccer game to model the writing process for the class. She read the fiction books during read-aloud time three days a week. During the first week, she read four chapters of Judy Blume's (1972) *Tales of a Fourth Grade Nothing*. Over the next two weeks, she read the remaining chapters. During the final week, she read the picture book *My Great Aunt Arizona* (Lamb, 1992) and began the chapter book *Morning Girl* (Dorris,

PHASE 1

This 4-week phase, beginning the last week in September, investigated whether minimum exposure to nonfiction literature (one book per week) would prompt nonfiction writing during writing workshop. The nonfiction read-alouds are listed on the left; the science/social studies curricular topics are listed on the right. Because no nonfiction was written during this phase, no intertextual patterns were analyzed.

Box Turtle at Long Pond	Rosh Hashanah
Frogs	Living things/nonliving things
Salamanders	Rocks (observations/experiments)
Dragonfly	Vernal pool (field trip/observations)
	Columbus
	Current events

PHASE 2

This 4-week phase (last week of October and first three of November) investigated whether increased exposure to nonfiction literature (three read-alouds per week) would prompt nonfiction writing during writing workshop. The read-alouds are listed on the left; curricular topics are listed on the right. Two reports were written in response to a textbook unit on dinosaurs/fossils. Writers were interviewed about intertextual links; analysis of intertextual patterns began.

The Wright Brothers (3 chapters read per week)	Fossils
Tapenum's Day	Dinosaurs
People of the Breaking Day	Flight
	Veteran's Day
	Native Americans
	Current events

PHASE 3

This 4-week phase (the second and third week of December and first two of January) investigated whether three nonfiction read-alouds per week and instruction on nonfiction reports would prompt nonfiction writing during writing workshop. The read-alouds are listed on the left; curricular topics are listed on the right. A total of 26 reports were written by all but one participant. Writers were interviewed about intertextual patterns; reports were coded and analyzed.

Hungry, Hungry Sharks	Pearl Harbor
Magic School Bus Inside a Beehive	Geography
Magic School Bus Inside a Hurricane	Maps
Magic School Bus Inside the Human Body	Environments
Magic School Bus Lost In Space	Drugs
Magic School Bus In the Time of the Dinosaurs	Christmas/Hannukah
On the Bus with Joanna Cole	Martin Luther King; civil rights
Faithful Elephants	Current events
I Have a Dream	
Martin Luther King Jr. and the March Toward Freedom	

Figure 1.2. Overview of the three phases of the study, including nonfiction read-alouds and curricular topics.

1992). In order to increase her profile in the classroom, Carol spent one day a week during phase 1 reading the aforementioned nonfiction books to the class.

Writing workshop (30–40 minutes' duration) was convened three times during each week of this first phase. We interviewed each 3rd grader during writing workshop at least once a week about entries in their writer's notebooks, completing interview protocols. Alice interviewed the 3rd graders whom we didn't have time to interview during the writing workshop during the week. (Because none of the children chose to write nonfiction during this phase, it was easy to keep on top of their output.)

Phase 2: Will increased exposure to nonfiction trigger nonfiction writing? Hypothesizing that greater immersion would influence experimentation with nonfiction, we had the 3rd graders listen to and talk about nonfiction literature three times a week during phase 2. During the first 3 weeks of this phase, three chapters of the Newbery Honor book *The Wright Brothers* (Freedman, 1991) were read each week to support the 3rd graders' curricular study of flight. Because no nonfiction writing had occurred during phase 1, we speculated that perhaps ongoing immersion in one nonfiction topic (combined with activities such as designing their own planes) might prompt experimentation with exposition. During the last week, *Tapenum's Day* (Waters, 1996) and *People of the Breaking Day* (Sewall, 1990) were read as part of curricular study on the Wompanoag nation. These social studies trade books were selected to balance the science focus during the first phase as well as to vary genre exposure (biography during this phase). Again, no suggestion to write nonfiction was made.

To counterbalance Carol as the nonfiction reader during phase 1, Alice read the aforementioned nonfiction literature each week during this second phase. The chapter book during this phase (and the next) was Patricia MacLachlan's (1991) *Journey*; Alice read three chapters a week. Carol spent 1 day a week in the classroom during this phase, primarily conducting interviews. Carol also took responsibility for making copies of the nonfiction entries written by the children and for tracking and copying the sources that students reported they used to construct these texts (e.g., if the source was a nonfiction book, each page was copied).

Mini-lessons during this phase focused on two areas. First, Alice revisited the writing process with the goal of having 3rd graders select a favorite piece and move it through the writing process. Because Alice had modeled the process with her personal narrative on the soccer game and because the personal narratives were more manageable in terms of length (half to a full page in general), the 3rd graders were encouraged to revise and edit personal narratives. In addition, Alice introduced the "show, not tell" rule that good writers employ—the importance of vivid verbs and sentence variety. Second, a number of mini-lessons were also implemented to introduce the 3rd graders to the purpose and procedures of portfolios and the process of self-assessment. As the first school term came to a close, the 3rd graders completed rating scales on their writing as well as reflections on their progress as writers.

As in phase 1, the 3rd graders participated in writing workshop (30–40 minute duration) three times a week.

Phase 3: Will increased exposure to nonfiction and instruction prompt nonfiction writing? The final phase included completion of MacLachlan's (1991) *Journey*, (fiction read-loud) begun during phase 2, and continued immersion in a variety of the nonfiction works three times a week as well as instruction in the nonfiction report (the genre that the first two nonfiction writers chose to write during phase 2). The works of Joanna Cole, particularly *The Magic School Bus* books (Cole, 1986c, 1987, 1989, 1990, 1992, 1994, 1995a), constituted much of the nonfiction literature during this final phase, along with the following books: *Faithful Elephants* (Tsuchiya, 1997), *Martin Luther King, Jr. and the March Toward Freedom* (Hakim, 1991), and *I Have a Dream* (King, 1997). The decision to use *The Magic School Bus* series was anchored in a survey that the 3rd graders had completed about favorite nonfiction authors, with Cole taking the lead by a wide margin. *The Magic School Bus* books are typically classified as informational storybooks—books that weave fact into a fictional storyline. Preliminary research has revealed that 3rd graders retained significantly more scientific information from an informational storybook than from an information book on the same topic (Leal, 1993; 1995). Leal concluded that informational storybooks, such as *The Magic School Bus* series, engage student interest and permit a deeper level of processing of factual information. With this endorsement, we moved ahead. The first two *Magic School Bus* books were read aloud in their entirety. Because of the multigenre nature of these books, each was read across two sessions. For the remaining *Magic School Bus* books, however, the story lines and selected "reports" of Ms. Frizzle's kids were read to accommodate time constraints. To keep the readings alive, these "reports" were read chorally by the class (using the overhead projector), assigned to particular children to read, or read by us.

Because of the volume of nonfiction writing, Carol spent 2 full days and a morning in the classroom during the first 2 weeks of this phase and every day of her winter break (January 5–16)—teaching, interviewing, and so forth. We interviewed the children daily, with Carol doing most of the interviewing while Alice taught other curriculum areas. Carol continued to collect copies of children's work and the intertextual sources.

Alice and Carol co-planned the instructional lessons; Carol taught the three weekly lessons. A synopsis of these 12 lessons follows:

Day 1. Discussion about nonfiction report writing was launched by placing Jessica's "A report on Fossils," the first nonfiction report written during phase 2, on the overhead. After Jessica read the first few pages of her 15-page report, the class was asked to guess where she had gotten the idea to write about fossils. Jessica confirmed or rejected their intertextual links. Kyle then read his report on fossils/dinosaurs (also written during phase 2) and shared intertextual links. The call for other "experts" was sounded. The lesson concluded with a request that children, during free time, think about the question "What Makes a Good Report?" and record their ideas on the poster.

Day 2. Because the 3rd graders' ideas about what made a good report centered on what writers do ("research," "experiment") rather than on the criteria of a good report, we backtracked and brainstormed what we might include if we were writing a report on sharks. Details were recorded on a semantic map, and the children then generated headings. We then read Joanna Cole's (1986b) *Hungry, Hungry Sharks* and compared content coverage, adding new ideas to our map and deleting misconceptions. After posting another blank "What Makes a Good Report?" chart, the 3rd graders brainstormed the following criteria of a good report: (1) "Don't make stuff up; give true facts," (2) "Keep related facts together," (3) "Don't copy; say it in your own words," and (4) "Add some humor." We explained that these criteria would be revisited and revised after we studied more about nonfiction. The 3rd graders then completed a survey on favorite nonfiction authors.

Day 3. Danielle's piece on tropical fish was placed on the overhead to illustrate the place of personal experience in report writing. Then, to reinforce the concept of headings, each table was handed an overhead that contained a section from *Hungry, Hungry Sharks* (Cole, 1986b) (which contains no headings) and was asked to read the content and to write a heading that Cole might have included. Groups shared and explained their headings. Later in the day, two 4th graders, invited as guest speakers, arrived to read a kangaroo report they had written in 3rd grade and to explain their research process. After the speakers left, the 3rd graders listened again as we reread the kangaroo report and discussed which criteria of a good report were met.

Day 4. Results of the nonfiction author study survey were shared; Joanna Cole won almost half of the votes. As Cole's books were presented, one of the 3rd graders suggested that we categorize the books. For example, they suggested *A Dog's Body* (Cole, 1986a) be placed beside *A Bird's Body* (Cole, 1983) because "they are about animals' bodies," and that *A Chick Hatches* (Cole, 1976) be placed beside *My New Kitten* (Cole, 1995b) because "it's a new chick that has just hatched like a new kitten that's born." A general introduction to text structures (sequence, compare/contrast, and description) ensued. The difference between Cole's *Magic School Bus* books (informational storybooks) and her other books (informational books) was also discussed.

Day 5. The class performed a Readers' Theatre of *The Magic School Bus Inside a Beehive* (Cole, 1996). Third graders wrote and shared personal responses about their encounters with bees. At their suggestion, we drafted a letter inviting the vice principal to class to talk about his experiences as a beekeeper.

Day 6. Students recorded as many bee facts as they could recall from *The Magic School Bus Inside a Beehive* (Cole, 1996) on "combs," which, when later edited, were pasted on a "honeycomb." We discussed the relationship between the nonfiction information in the storyline of *The Magic School Bus Inside a Beehive* (Cole, 1996) and the nonfiction information in Ms. Frizzle's "kids'" reports. We examined the text structure of sequence in the "kids'" bee dance reports, emphasizing signal words such as *first, then, next,* and *finally.* Alice acted out the sequence of one of the bee dances and asked the 3rd graders to guess the dance.

Day 7. Other reports of Ms. Frizzle's "kids" were used to introduce the text structures of description and compare/contrast. Signal words in each text structure were highlighted. We then explained that, when reading their writer's notebooks, we noticed that some of them had written description, comparison, and sequence passages in their reports, just like Joanna Cole—*before they even knew about these kinds of special reports.* We promised to showcase these nonfiction reports (with permission) in the next session.

Day 8. The nonfiction reports of the 3rd graders who had included sequence, comparison, and description structures were placed on the overhead and discussed. Writers were encouraged to use these patterns during report writing. We then played a game in which students identified the text structures of the *Magic School Bus* "kids'" reports to reinforce these structures. In response to the question about how we might let Joanna Cole know that we enjoyed reading her books, the children eventually suggested that we write our own *Magic School Bus* book to send to her.

Day 9. The vice principal arrived with his beehive, his beekeeper suit, and his honey-excavating equipment. When asked what they knew about bees, the 3rd graders directed him to their "honeycomb" and shared their knowledge. He then donned his beekeeping suit and demonstrated how to remove honey from the combs. We again talked about the role of experience in writing nonfiction.

Day 10. After discussing the science focus of the *Magic School Bus* books, we brainstormed ideas for our *Magic School Bus* book. Because the 3rd graders had made three field trips to a vernal pool, they decided to make this the focus of their book. After listing the vernal pool animals, the

3rd graders signed up for research teams (turtles, salamanders, etc.) and discussed how to find resources. (This collaborative project extended beyond the study.)

Day 11. Using excerpts from the *Magic School Bus* books, we revisited the concept of headings by examining headings that Ms. Frizzle's kids used in their reports. We also introduced other text arrangements, such as bulleted summaries and experiments, found in the *Magic School Bus* books.

Day 12. The poster that the 3rd graders completed at the end of the first session was reintroduced to discuss their ideas about what writers do to write a good report. To heighten awareness about the research process central to nonfiction writing, the children listened to excerpts of Joanna Cole's (1996) autobiography, *On the Bus with Joanna Cole*, in which she talks about reading many books on her topic and about her note-taking strategy (e.g., recording interesting facts on sticky notes). Our original criteria for a good nonfiction report were reassessed and revised.

Data Collection and Analysis

Data were collected in order to (1) determine the frequency with which children chose to write nonfiction pieces during each phase and (2) identify the patterns of intertextuality that emerged in their nonfiction texts. (*Note:* In this chapter, we report our findings with respect to the frequency data. In the next chapter, we define intertextuality and report our findings about the patterns of intertextuality.) Sources of data included the 3rd graders' writer's notebooks, interview transcripts, trade books/materials used by the students to write reports, science and social studies textbooks, and informal classroom observations. Records were kept of all books (fiction and nonfiction) read to the children across the three phases, the science and social studies topics/ units taught during each phase along with chapters read in textbooks, any movies watched, and any major projects/experiments they completed.

Frequency data were collected each week during each phase. Each 3rd grader was asked to bring his or her writer's notebook to the interview and to read and talk about the piece(s) written that week. If the piece was fictional, the 3rd grader was asked only to share the origin of the story idea, primarily to acclimate him or her to this question about thematic intertextuality. Responses were recorded on an interview protocol. Because the focus of this study was nonfiction, no analysis of intertextual links in fictional pieces was undertaken. If the piece was nonfiction, the 3rd grader was asked to explain its thematic and organizational origins, and then to read each line of the piece and explain its source (orientational intertextuality). If the child mentioned source materials, he or she was asked to retrieve these materials and locate information noted during the interview. All interviews were audiotaped; only interviews about the nonfiction pieces were transcribed and analyzed. These interviews usually occurred as soon as a nonfiction piece was started, with multiple interviews following depending on the length of the report.

Lemke's (1992) patterns of intertextuality and Kamberelis and Scott's (1992) topology of voice provided the theoretical framework for analyzing the intertextual links in the 3rd graders' nonfiction writing. Data collection and analysis procedures for this dimension of the study are presented in Chapter 2.

FINDINGS

First we report the findings with respect to the frequency rate of adoption of nonfiction writing under the varying conditions of each phase; and then we discuss these findings.

Phase 1: Third Graders Choose Not to Write Nonfiction

Four trade books that tied to the vernal pool science curriculum were read during this 4-week phase; one nonfiction book each week. Two books were read prior to the first field trip to a local vernal pool; two books were read after the trip. However, exposure to books on turtles, frogs, salamanders, and dragonflies yielded no nonfiction writing. (*Note*: To clarify, we were not expecting reports on vernal pool creatures per se. Rather, we speculated that talk about animals in general might result in animal reports of any kind.) The 3rd graders chose only to write personal narratives and fiction during writing workshop.

Table 1.2 presents the number of the specific genres in which each 3rd grader wrote across each phase of the study; the 3rd graders are organized in their table groups. At first glance, the wide variability in terms of the numbers of pieces produced is curious. How is it that Colin at table 1 wrote only 3 pieces across the 4 weeks of this phase, while Kyle managed to write 11 pieces? Inspection of their notebooks reveals differences in their choice of genres and in the length and duration of these pieces. Colin wrote two personal narratives at the beginning of this phase, both about football practice. The first personal narrative was started and finished on the same day; the second took 2 days to complete. During the second week of this phase, Colin began a story called "Bugs Bunny on Halloween Night." This four-page story took eight sessions to write. Colin wrote about half a page (skipping no lines) per writing workshop. Kyle (table 3), on the other hand, wrote 11 personal narratives that included entries about after-school activities, school events, and soccer practice. All except one were started and completed the same day. Entries varied in length from a half to a full page (skipping lines).

Table 1.2. Number of Specific Genres Written by Each 3rd Grader Across Each Phase of the Study

	Phase One			Phase Two			Phase Three			
	PN	F	NF	PN	F	NF	PN	F	NF	P
Table 1										
Colin	2	1	0	0	4	0	0	1	2	0
Patrick	3	5	0	2	2	0	0	0	2	0
Maureen	6	3	0	1	1	0	0	2	1	0
Table 2										
Vanessa	3	3	0	0	4	0	0	4	2	0
Phil	2	3	0	0	4	0	0	5	2	0
Ted	3	5	0	0	4	0	2	2	1	0
Table 3										
Kyle	11	0	0	8	1	1	0	1	1	0
Kristin	9	0	0	4	2	0	0	2	1	0
Josie	8	0	0	8	0	0	0	1	0	0
Table 4										
Andrea	4	4	0	3	2	0	0	2	1	0
Danielle	6	2	0	1	2	0	0	0	3	0
Table 5										
Connor	2	3	0	0	3	0	0	1	1	0
Sarah	2	1	0	0	3	0	0	0	2	3
Judy	2	3	0	0	6	0	0	0	1	3
Table 6										
Jason	2	2	0	0	4	0	0	5	2	0
Jessica	2	6	0	2	5	1	0	0	2	0
Caitlyn	3	2	0	0	2	0	0	0	1	0
Jake	3	2	0	0	2	0	0	3	1	0
Totals	73	45	0	29	51	2	2	29	26	6

Note: The 3rd graders are organized by the tables at which they sat. PN = personal narrative; F = fiction; NF = nonfiction report; P = poem.

In sum, 73 personal narratives were penned during this first phase with topics such as soccer games, birthday parties, family outings, and Halloween costumes predominating. Most of these personal narratives (length: half to a full page) were "one-shot" pieces, completed the day they were started. In contrast, of the 45 stories produced, many were written over the course of two or three workshops and some across five or more workshops. Extending the writing of one piece over time, a process that necessitates rereading previous text in order to advance the storyline, marks an important step in the evolution of a young writer (Calkins, 1983; Simmons, 1990, 1992).

Phase 2: Two 3rd Graders Write Nonfiction Reports in Response to a Textbook Unit on Dinosaurs

During the second 4-week phase, the nonfiction read-alouds were increased to three times a week. Immersion in this literature did not prompt nonfiction writing. However, a unit on fossils and dinosaurs anchored in the science textbook caught the fancy of two 3rd graders. During the week following a fossil/dinosaur unit, Jessica began "A report on Fossils," relying solely on her recall of what she had learned about fossils. The following week, Kyle, unaware that Jessica was writing a report on fossils, also began a piece titled "fossils and Dinosaur Bones." Kyle also wrote his report from memory, accessing no nonfiction resources. This dinosaur unit had triggered the eagerly awaited emergence of nonfiction. We drew no attention to these two nonfiction reports during phase 2; we silently celebrated and wondered if a ripple effect would take hold.

These dinosaur reports arrived at a time when story writing was strongly ensconced. As Table 1.2 shows, 51 stories were penned during this phase. All but one 3rd grader wrote at least one story, with Halloween tales predominating. Notable was the increased length and duration of these stories as compared to those written in phase 1. The length of these stories ranged from 1 page to 7, with an average of 3½ pages. The number of writing workshops to complete these stories spanned 2 to 6 days, with the majority written across 2 or 3 days (78%). A significant drop in personal narratives was noted between the first two phases (see Table 1.2). Of the 29 personal narratives, 20 were written by the same threesome at table 3 who also had written only personal narratives during phase 1.

Phase 3: Twenty-Six Nonfiction Reports Written During This Immersion/Instructional Phase

During this final phase, the 3rd graders continued to listen to nonfiction books three times a week. In addition, they participated in 12 lessons that explored the genre of nonfiction report writing. During the opening lesson, the nonfiction reports of Jessica and Kyle (phase 2 writers) were showcased on the overhead. Conversation about where they had gotten their ideas to write about dinosaurs/fossils was pursued. During the second lesson, the class brainstormed ideas about what they might include in a report about sharks and then compared these ideas with Joanna Cole's (1986b) *Hungry, Hungry Sharks*. By the end of this first week, six 3rd graders had begun writing nonfiction reports of their own volition; by the end of the second week, an additional five chose to write nonfiction. By the end of the third week, all but one child had chosen to write a nonfiction report. A total of 26 reports (including Jason's report, which was begun during the interim week) were written during this final phase.

With the momentum for nonfiction taking hold by the second week, a decline in both personal narratives and stories was noted (see Table 1.2). Only two personal narratives were written during this final phase; 29 stories were drafted, with two 3rd graders writing five each. Six one-verse poems also were written by Judy and Sarah, who sat at table 3.

In sum, then, with respect to nonfiction writing across phases 2 and 3, a total of 28 reports were composed. As Figure 1.3 reveals, two children wrote 3 reports, seven children wrote 2 reports, and eight children wrote 1 report. Twenty (or 22 if the dinosaurs in Jessica's fossil report and the Florida panther in Ted's Everglades report are included) of the 28 reports were on animals. These reports ranged in length from three sentences to 15 pages. Fifteen 3rd graders wrote at least one report of two or more full pages in length.

Culling the total of number of writing samples for each phase yields some interesting observations. As Table 1.2 reveals, a total of 118 pieces were written during the first phase. The majority of these pieces were personal narratives started and completed the same day. While fewer pieces were generated during phase 2 (n = 82), the length and duration of many pieces increased dramatically. For example, many 3rd graders wrote multichapter stories over an extended period of time. The final phase yielded the least amount of writing. Fifty-seven pieces (excluding the 6 poems) were written. This drop in productivity may have been due, in part, to the timing of this phase; the first 2 weeks were before the December break and the final 2 after the New Year. The excitement before the holidays and the slow recharge after may have compromised productivity. Also significant, though, was the time spent reading nonfiction books during writing workshop as report writing commenced. In the next section, we discuss this integration of nonfiction books into writing workshop, as well as our conclusions about the conditions under which nonfiction flourishes.

DISCUSSION

At the beginning of the schoolyear, our 3rd graders brainstormed possible writing topics and genres and were told that they had control over topic and genre choice during writing workshop. Examination of their writer's notebooks, however, revealed that none had chosen to write nonfiction during the first few weeks of school. Interested in the suggested link between nonfiction literature and nonfiction writing (Daniels, 1990; Kamberelis & Bovino,

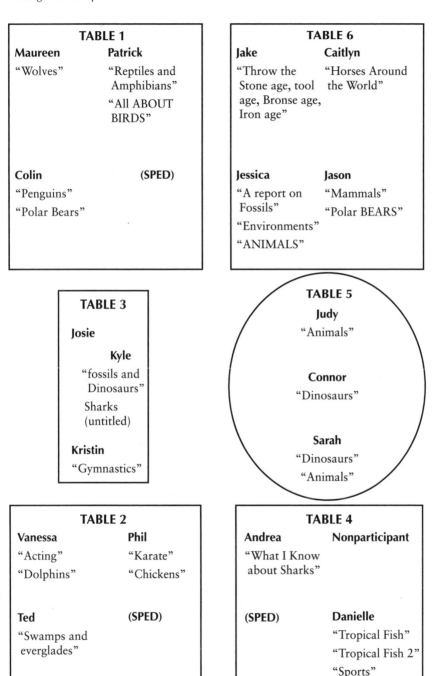

Figure 1.3. Titles of the 28 reports written by the 3rd graders; 26 were written during the final 4-week phase.

1999; Pappas, 1991), we read nonfiction trade books to the 3rd graders (once a week during phase 1; three times a week during phase 2) over a 2-month period.

We found that the invitation to choose their own topics/genres and exposure to a variety of nonfiction trade books did not prompt exposition during the first two phases. However, participation in a fossil/dinosaur unit anchored in the science textbook resulted in two nonfiction reports during phase 2. This finding prompted us to reexamine decisions we made about book choice, book immersion, and the invitation to write in genres of their own choice.

Because preliminary research suggests that book choice may be an important variable with respect to scaffolding children's writing (Donovan & Smolkin, 2002), we wonder if we would have achieved different results if we had selected books that tapped children's intrigue with dinosaurs or sharks during the first phase, rather than books that supported the science curriculum on the vernal pool. Our efforts to scaffold the knowledge learned during the read-alouds with an inquiry-based curriculum that included field trips may not have been enough to match the prior knowledge and visceral excitement that talk about sharks generated during our initial lessons in phase 3. Likewise, our speculation that sustained engagement over time with one topic (Wright brothers/flight) was not realized. In hindsight, we should have involved the 3rd graders in the selection of the nonfiction read-alouds. Perhaps, too, the issue of who read these books may have factored in. We made the decision that Carol would read the nonfiction books during phase 1 to facilitate her integration into the classroom. While the 3rd graders responded enthusiastically to these read-alouds, they may have viewed these sessions as "outside" of the daily routine.

In addition to the issue of book choice, we now wonder what constitutes book "immersion." During phase 1, the 3rd graders listened to three fictional pieces and one nonfiction book each week. During phase 2, this ratio was flipped, with three nonfiction read-alouds and one fiction per week. While Graves (1994) notes that "children need to hear good nonfiction read aloud to them" (p. 323), he doesn't specify how much exposure is needed. Likewise, Calkins (2001) remarks that "it's terribly important for children to listen to nonfiction texts read aloud" (p. 54) but doesn't recommend how often these read-alouds should be integrated, either. Other than the call to give children "equal access" to fiction and nonfiction (Duke, 2000; Kamberelis & Bovino, 1999; Pappas, 1993), we haven't been able to locate any research that addresses the specifics of nonfiction immersion. Perhaps if our 3rd graders had listened to nonfiction literature every day of the week during phase 2, right before the onset of writing workshop, they might have pursued nonfiction writing.

It is our hunch, though, that the search for the "right" kinds of book and for the magical immersion number may not resolve the issue of why children aren't choosing to write nonfiction during writing workshop. As Freedman (1993) notes, "we must remember that exposure to written discourse is a necessary but not a sufficient condition" (p. 238) for literacy acquisition. Central also are the roles of affect (i.e., the attitude and motivation of the learner) and of intention (i.e., the need to respond to/act on what is learned) (Freedman, 1993). For example, we know that toddlers' language acquisition is significantly accelerated when mothers are trained to provide information about language through expansions, modeling, elicitation of responses, and praise during book reading as compared to mothers who just read books aloud. This study exemplifies immersion and intention working hand in hand. Thus, it may be the merger of book choice and immersion with intention to write nonfiction that makes the difference. Such were the conditions that underscored our instructional phase. The pivotal acts of showcasing the reports of our first two trailblazers and of calling for other nonfiction "experts" to voluntarily write reports launched report writing. Peer influence and talk about how authors (peer and published) craft nonfiction reports, along with inspection of their works, sustained this momentum. Twenty-six reports were written during the instructional phase.

While we are quick to acknowledge that we prioritized the "report" subgenre with our choice of books on turtles, frogs, and so forth during the first phase and the "biography" subgenre (Wright brothers) during the second phase, peer influence essentially established the "report" as the genre of choice. Perhaps because the first two reports focused on dinosaurs or perhaps because of children's timeless fascination with animals, animal reports, in particular, reigned. During phase 3, three dinosaur reports, two shark reports, three reports titled "Animals" (which addressed multiple animals in one report), and a range of other animal reports (penguins, polar bears, wolves) were penned (see Figure 1.3). In all likelihood, the unspoken allegiance to animal reports evolved because of the social dynamic among the 3rd graders. Note the comments of students at table 5 when asked about the origins of their reports (see the Thematic Intertextuality section in Chapter 2):

CONNOR: I figured everybody was writing something different, like Jessica was writing fossils. Jason was writing mammals, and Patrick was writing reptiles. So I picked dinosaurs.
SARAH: Well, Connor, he started to write about dinosaurs, so I kind of copied him because I liked the idea, but he had different topics on dinosaurs than I did. I started with small dinosaurs and he didn't.
JUDY: Sarah and Connor were doing dinosaurs and I wanted to do something different. But I wanted to do nonfiction 'cuz they're doing nonfiction.

As Dyson (1989, 1993, 1997, 2000) has so powerfully documented, young children use written language to negotiate the intersecting social worlds of the classroom—official and unofficial—and the home. Children, including those from diverse cultures, use the rich language resources of popular culture, cultural traditions, and the curriculum to participate and to position themselves in social relationships. They independently access a range of genres such as stories, jokes, pop songs, raps, and cartoons in order to make sense of their experiences and to carve out their social niche. Because the act of writing is accompanied by much talk, drawing, and dramatic play, children are coaxed by peers and friends to explain, elaborate, justify, and defend their ways of knowing. "Through the genres they use, the discourse traditions they draw upon, and the social stances they adopt, composers enact their roles as social players, anticipating the responses of their listeners and readers" (Dyson, 1993, p. 133).

To trace the history of the social players in our classroom is to shed light on one of the pivotal reasons for the nonexistence of nonfiction writing during the first 2 months of school. Namely, when given free choice children write what their peers write. Peer solidarity began with their affinity for personal narratives, prompted by Alice's aforementioned "seed" mini-lesson. Sharing these entries, informally and formally, clinched their early proclivity for expressive writing, reminding us that "literacy events do not take place in isolation, but in relation to a discourse community of which the reader or writer is, or wishes to become, a member" (Haneda & Wells, 2000, p. 432). Desire to maintain membership in the social club was evidenced in their shift away from personal narratives to Halloween stories (and subsequently our aforementioned story writing in general). The camaraderie—social and literary—among the earlier dinosaur writers (Connor, Sarah, Judy) had manifested itself at the beginning of the schoolyear with their haunted house stories (see Figure Int.1). Intertextual influences were evident at other tables. For example Patrick and his table peers penned "Daffy Duck on Halloween," "Bugs Bunny on Halloween Night," and "Lola bunny makes a basketball team on Halloween." As October progressed, every 3rd grader wrote a Halloween story, with the exception of two children and one table, whose members wrote only personal narratives about Halloween, perhaps just enough to keep their memberships alive.

Such social and literary camaraderie, though, was not true of all tables. Phil and Vanessa were best friends who argued frequently because Phil resented it when Vanessa "copied" him. According to Phil, if he brought in a certain magazine, Vanessa would bring in the same magazine the next day. To keep the peace, Vanessa made an effort not to copy Phil's work during writing workshop. Thus, while Vanessa was writing "Haunted Mainchon," Phil was writing "Bond and the Spice Girls." Vanessa wrote her first nonfiction piece on acting in mid-December (see Chapter 4); Phil waited 3 weeks to write his first report. Asked about this delay, he replied, "After *The Magic School Bus* [a nonfiction read-aloud], I'm going to come in with lots of non-fiction . . . about karate. . . . So after a lot of fiction, I think I'm going to catch up with everyone else." When asked if he felt behind, Phil commented, "No, not really. But I just want to see how it feels to get out and write lots of nonfiction and I hope Vanessa doesn't try to copy me." The underlying tension between Vanessa and Phil suggests that peer influence is a complex phenomenon—one not to be viewed through a romantic lens. It calls to mind Lensmire's (1994) findings about the ways in which children use writing to create and sustain social hierarchies in the classroom for the purpose of including and excluding peers. It may matter greatly which child writes the first piece of nonfiction; the social status of this child may determine whether peer influence is activated.

Peer solidarity may have manifested itself in yet another way during the final phase, contributing to the decision not to write nonfiction earlier on. Recall that Jessica and Kyle, our nonfiction pioneers, wrote their fossil reports from memory, prompting the question: Why didn't they access any books? We suspect that the answer ties to the context of writing workshop, to the implicit rules that the 3rd graders established before and after the nonfiction momentum began. As noted earlier, the two genres that dominated writing workshop prior to the onset of nonfiction were personal narrative and fiction. Because there was no need to consult print material of any kind in order to recount what they did over the weekend or to weave a tale, the notebook was the only material on their desks during writing workshop. Given this unspoken rule, Jessica and Kyle crafted reports from memory without consulting any resources. However, during their presentation of their individual reports, answers to questions about where they acquired their knowledge about dinosaurs and fossils illuminated not only the science textbook and curricular events, but also the trade books (e.g., Jessica had read all four of Aliki's books on dinosaurs/fossils) that each had independently read in school and at home. Hence, the day after the endorsement of their report writing, nonfiction books began to clutter our 3rd graders' desks. Without any direction from us, the 3rd graders established a new norm during writing workshop that sanctioned the use of nonfiction books. With the exception of one video game report, memory-based reports ceased to be written during phase 3.

FINAL THOUGHTS

We began this book with the unsettling observation that our 3rd graders, who had brainstormed a range of genres and topics available to writers and who had been granted the freedom to choose their genres and topics during writing workshop, were choosing not to write nonfiction. Recall that the only genre that received instructional attention during the first 3 months of the school year was the personal narrative. Because our 3rd graders had no experience with writing workshop in previous grades, Alice followed Graves's (1983, 1994) advice about the power of personal narrative to ease children into writing. Not surprisingly, personal narrative became the genre of choice at the beginning of the school year. During the last week of September, however, Sarah struck out on her own and wrote a Halloween story, which triggered a flood of such stories (see Figure Int.1). No mini-lessons were implemented on story, no teacher prompting to write story was made, and yet story writing emerged. Even with the shift to three nonfiction and one fiction read-alouds per week during phase 2, story predominated (see Table 1.2). Why did story writing infiltrate this classroom, but not nonfiction, with the exception of two writers, during the first two phases? Beyond the pull of Halloween, the simple fact is that story is the privileged genre in school (Applebee, Langer, Mullis, & Jenkins, 1990; Duke, 2000; Langer, 1986; Putnam, 1991) and at home (Sulzby & Teale, 1987). Immersed in a lifetime of story, our 3rd graders spun their tales with confidence and peer endorsement. Story writing edged out the personal narrative by a wide margin in phase 2 of our study. Thus while the catalyst for genre choice can be either a peer or the teacher, it is the social dynamic among writers that propels and sustains a particular genre across time.

Recall also that the potential for nonfiction report writing occurred with the arrival of two reports on fossils/dinosaurs, prompted by the fossil unit in the science textbook. Jessica wrote her report on November 12; one week later Kyle began his report without knowledge of Jessica's report. The 3-day week of Thanksgiving followed, with no other 3rd grader choosing to write nonfiction. During the first week of December (an interim week due to teacher sickness), Jason, who sat at Jessica's table, began his three-page report on mammals. Whether this trickle of nonfiction would have spurred others to write nonfiction over time, we don't know, as our instructional phase, which put nonfiction front and center, commenced the second week of December. Our speculation, based on informal analyses of writer's notebooks from past years and on the literature (Chapman, 1995; Duke, 2000; Kucera, 1995), is that nonfiction would not have swept through this classroom. Why not? The reasons appear multifaceted:

• Engagement with story writing energized writing workshop. The penning of stories about haunted houses and dead football players not only held great appeal but also played to the children's strength in terms of their ability to tap their well-developed schema for story. Two months of varying degrees of immersion in nonfiction literature couldn't stack up against years of story immersion. And perhaps more important, story writing satisfied their social need to belong; Halloween stories granted them membership in the writing club (see Dyson, 1993, 2000; Lensmire, 1994; Smith, 1988). Why consider writing any other genre?

- Even though we explained to the children that they could write nonfiction during writing workshop and generated possible topics at the beginning of the school year, we failed to abide by our own "show, don't just tell" dictum with respect to genre choice. Rather than just telling the 3rd graders that they could choose to write nonfiction, we should have shown them reports (as well as other subgenres) penned by peers (from previous years or from other sources). Nonfiction writing soared as soon as the reports of our first two nonfiction writers were showcased, along with the call for other "experts" to write reports if they chose to do so, and with continued immersion in nonfiction literature.
- Hindering the adoption of nonfiction, too, may have been the unspoken norm established by the 3rd graders, namely, that the only material permitted on desks during writing workshop was their writer's notebook. This norm forced our trailblazing nonfiction writers to write their fossil reports from memory. Both Jessica and Kyle retrieved knowledge learned during a fossil/dinosaur unit that had included such activities as discussing the fossil chapter in their science textbook, examining real fossils, watching a *National Geographic* video, and making clay models of trilobites. In addition, as we learned during interviews, their affinity for this topic extended beyond the school curriculum. For example, Kyle had participated in six "dinosaur digs" with his family at the Roger Williams Zoo Park in Rhode Island, had seen the movie *Jurassic Park*, and had read books about dinosaurs. Each had "lived" this topic in the "presence" of experts, affording them the confidence and knowledge to write their reports without consulting any resources. This lends credence to Donald Graves's (1994) observation that in order to write nonfiction, "children need to know something about the content of their first report subjects before they even begin" (p. 316). However, on learning that Jessica and Kyle had read books before writing their reports, the 3rd graders, without guidance or permission from us, established a new implicit norm: It's okay to consult books during writing workshop. Nonfiction books littered their desks during writing workshop. As will be explored in subsequent chapters, however, once the floodgate opened and the 3rd graders established the precedent of consulting trade books, a number pursued topics about which they seemed to have little knowledge, resulting, in some cases, in verbatim copying. Thus, while not knowing about a topic was not a deterrent as long as text consultation was permitted, the quality of the report writing varied greatly. Interestingly, for the most part neither set of writers (memory-based or text-based) achieved the level of success that the strategic writers did. As will be discussed in Chapter 3, the most advanced

writers were those who not only entered report writing with considerable previous knowledge but also accessed print material in order to supplement their knowledge and find appropriate organizational and orientational ideas.

On a final note, while we have acknowledged the powerful force of peer influence, it is important to clarify that it may not guarantee the expository engagement of every child. In our study, one child was not swept into the nonfiction writing momentum. As a reluctant writer, Josie spent the first 3 months writing only personal narratives. Just as her peers shifted from story writing to exposition, she transitioned from personal narratives to story writing—crafting a seven-page, six-chapter piece. Because this story took over a month to write, Josie did not write any nonfiction during our study. To ensure that all children are inducted into the world of exposition, it makes sense to periodically suspend the principle of choice during writing workshop and to devote a 2- or 3-week block of time to genre study (Calkins, 1994; Duthie, 1996). The finding that most children did not experiment with nonfiction during phases 1 and 2 suggests that it is not judicious to stand by and hope that nonfiction will take root in elementary classrooms. In Chapter 6, we offer suggestions about effective instructional practices based on our findings and on current thinking/research about nonfiction literacy.

Patterns of Intertextuality in Nonfiction Reports

AFTER READING A BIOGRAPHY about Abraham Lincoln, Maureen asked her 1st graders to respond in their journals. During a writing conference the next day, Jeffrey, an accomplished artist, read his piece, presented in Figure 2.1, "Read my lips. No more slavery." Taken with Jeffrey's sensibilities, Maureen asked where he got the idea for this entry. Jeffrey explained that he had heard President Bush say, "Read my lips. No new taxes," on television (the campaign pledge that would come back to haunt George H. W. Bush in the 1991 election). No mention of President Bush had occurred during the class discussion. Jeffrey, like Vanessa (see Figure 1.1), poignantly reminds us that children can and do "read the world" (Freire, 1985, p. 15).

Jeffrey constructed Lincoln's pledge with the tacit understanding that "stories lean on stories, art on art. And we who are the tellers and the artists do what has been done for all the centuries of tellings: We thieve (or more politely) borrow and then we make it our own" (Yolen, 1991, p. 147). This phenomenon of literary "thieving" is known as intertextuality. Intertextuality focuses on the connections that readers and writers forge as they move from one text to another, with *text* defined as any sign (literature, television, film, dance, art, a road sign, a smile) used in social interactions (Short, 1992). The construct of intertextuality has its origins in the work of Russian literary critic Mikhail Bakhtin. In his analysis of Dostoevsky's novels, Bakhtin (1986) traced the diverse social viewpoints of fictional characters and proposed his theory of heteroglossia, a construct that Kristeva (1986) would later coin as intertextuality:

> The unique speech experience of each individual is shaped and developed in continuous and constant interaction with others' individual utterances. . . . Our speech, that is all our utterances (including creative works), is filled with others' words, varying degrees of otherness and varying degrees of "our-own-ness," varying degrees of awareness and detachment. These words of others carry with them their own expression, their own evaluative tone, which we assimilate, rework, and reaccentuate. (p. 89)

Essentially, Bakhtin disputes the notion of text as the autonomous work of a solitary writer. Rather, he posits that every text has the fingerprint of

Figure 2.1. Jeffrey's (grade 1) appropriation of President George H. W. Bush's campaign pledge. Reprinted from *Inside the Writing Portfolio: What We Need to Know to Assess Children's Writing,* by Carol Brennan Jenkins. Copyright © 1996 by Carol Brennan Jenkins. Published by Heinemann, a division of Reed Elsevier, Inc. Portsmouth, NH. Reprinted with permission.

every other text. Writers absorb a world of ideas—historical, social, and political—from their social milieus and then reiterate, modify, oppose, and/or reenvision these ideas in order to craft their own texts. Every text, therefore, reverberates with the voices of others. Moreover, these echoing voices materialize in the form of speech genres that Bakhtin (1986) describes as "relatively stable typical forms of construction of the whole" (p. 87). Speech genres are the blueprints of discourse—language maps that give form to and are embedded in our social interactions. Knowledge of speech genres enables us to exchange greetings, resist advertisements, write scientific reports, and, in Jeffrey's case, create political pledges. While the construct of intertextuality has been the subject of extensive scrutiny in the literary world (Allen, 2000; Fairclough, 1992), it is a relative newcomer to education (Bloome & Egan-Robertson, 1993). In this chapter, we begin by reviewing the small body of literature on intertextuality and children's writing. We then present our findings on the range of intertextual links—thematic, organizational, and orientational—that our 3rd graders forged when they chose to write nonfiction during writing workshop.

INTERTEXTUALITY AND CHILDREN'S WRITING

In 1966, Bill Martin Jr., children's author and educator, gave teachers and children the gift of *Sounds of Language*, a literacy program developed to challenge the basic tenets of Dick-and-Jane basals that had dominated reading instruction for decades. *Sounds of Language*, which would become the prototype for new basal reading programs in the 1990s, offered young readers delectable stories, poems, chants, and songs—all written by acclaimed authors. As part of this program, Martin (1972) offered 10 teaching strategies, one of which involved children in "innovating on literary structure" (p. 19). Children were taught "to utilize the author's pattern for expressing their own thoughts. By borrowing the underlying structure of a poem or story they have come to know, they are . . . building a bridge between the linguistic facts of their worlds and the linguistic facts of the printed page" (p. 19). These "innovations," popularized by Don Holdaway (1979), became standard fare in literature-based classrooms during the 1980s and 1990s. Teachers immersed children in predictable stories such as *Brown Bear, Brown Bear, What Do You See?* (Martin, 1967) and then invited them to author their own versions (e.g., "Huge Bear, Huge Bear, What Do You Hear?" [Holdaway, 1979, p. 78]). Bill Martin went on to publish his own innovations, *Polar Bear, Polar Bear, What Do You Hear?* in 1991 and *Panda Bear, Panda Bear, What Do You See?* in 2003, a trend followed by other authors such as Laura Numeroff, who appropriated her first book, *If You Give a Mouse a Cookie* (1985) to pen *If You Give a Moose a Muffin* (1991) and *If You Give a Pig a Pancake* (1998).

It's not surprising, then, that young writers like Jeffrey "borrowed" from literary mentors during writing workshop and that their teachers began to write about the power of literature to influence children's writing. Early attention to intertextuality was spearheaded by the keen observations of classroom teachers, such as Nancy Atwell (1987), Mary Ellen Giacobbe (1988), Ellen Blackburn (1985), and Susan Sowers (1985).

Recent studies have corroborated their insights by tracing the vitality of intertextuality in children's writing. Cairney (1990) asked 6th graders: "Do you ever think of stories you've read when you are writing a story" (p. 480)? Ninety percent acknowledged borrowing ideas from story plots without directly copying the plots (although some did borrow plots directly). Interestingly, 31% noted that they used content from nonfiction books in their stories. Bearse (1992) found that while only 61% of 3rd graders were able to verbalize intertextual links, all had appropriated, to varying degrees, fairy tale leads, characters, and/or plot details in their stories. Four children transferred elements of several fairy tales into their pieces. Lancia (1997) examined 2nd graders' stories written during writing workshop across a schoolyear and corroborated the high rate of literary theft of plot and character as well as the transfer of factual information from nonfiction material into stories. In another intriguing investigation to prompt intertextual connections by reading a text set of Rapunzel fairy tale variations, Sipe (2001) found that 1st and 2nd graders made seven types of intertextual links. Notable was the extent of personal connections (18%) made to the first Rapunzel story as compared to the text-to-text connections (3%) and then the dramatic decrease in personal connections (3%) and increase in text-to-text connections when the second version was read. This text-to-text intertextuality remained high across the remaining versions. Sipe (2001) concluded that the wealth of intertextual connections prompted by use of a text set ultimately strengthened the children's schema for story.

Undoubtedly driving the intertextuality noted in these studies is the power of the social context. Cairney (1992) was one of the first to discuss the centrality of the social dynamic in the intertextual process. He traced the ripple effect of one 1st grader's published retelling of a read-aloud that resulted in spin-offs on the original story by 10 peers. Integral to the creation process were high levels of dramatic play, note writing, letter writing, and endless conversation. Social interaction among students and between teacher and students abounded, bolstering authorship efforts. As Cairney (1992) and others (Bloome & Egan-Robertson, 1993; Dyson, 1997; Harris, Trezise, & Winser, 2002; Hicks, 1997) have demonstrated, intertextuality is a process of "social construction, located in the social interactions that people have . . ." (Bloome & Egan-Robertson, 1993, p. 308). As noted in Chapter 1, the seminal work of Dyson (1989, 1993, 1997, 2000) in particular illuminates how children use written texts not only to participate in social relationships but also to attain social status in the classroom. Such use of written language to construct a classroom hierarchy has also been documented among 3rd graders (Lensmire, 1994).

While the thrust of the intertextual research has been on children's fictional writing, the few studies that have investigated intertextuality and nonfiction literacy offer promising findings. For example, Oyler and Barry

(1996) found that 1st graders made multiple and varied intertextual connections during interactive read-alouds of informational books. Connections to personal experiences constituted the most frequent type of intertextuality; other intextextual links included poems, television shows, songs, and other texts. The increase in the number of links made as the year progressed was tied to the teacher's acknowledgment of the children's intertextual contributions and to the practice of having the 1st graders retrieve the texts mentioned during discussion, and then showing the connection to the class. With respect to nonfiction writing, Kamberelis and Scott (1992) found that when children had the opportunity to explore their cultural heritage, their personal narratives and essays resonated with the polyphonic voices in their lives—family, friends, church, community, and historical mentors. And in the process these children began to forge personal, social, and political identities. In addition, while Kamberelis and Bovino (1999) didn't investigate intertextual ties per se, their finding that young children generated more generically successful reports when reenacting familiar nonfiction texts than when attempting to author original pieces supports the power of literature to scaffold writing.

Only one study could be located that included the examination of intertextual links that children made when writing reports. In investigating the connections that 11- and 12-year-olds made while writing a report on World War II and a piece of historical fiction set in the same time period, Many (1996) found major differences between the genres. To craft their stories, students integrated information from a rich WWII database (trade books, plays, newspapers, films, photographs, artifacts, audio- and videotapes, etc.). Although encouraged to access the same resources while writing their reports, students relied almost exclusively on nonfiction texts. During interviews about their reports, the students talked about information learned from the wide array of resources but weren't able to infuse these details into their reports. Many (1996) speculates that students just didn't know how to integrate information from the wide range of genres into their report writing.

It is to this nascent body of research that we add our study. What children know about the genre of nonfiction is intricately tied to their conscious and unconscious appropriations of others' works (literature, film, television, etc.). With knowledge about the genre understandings that children bring to their nonfiction writing gleaned from intertextual juxtapositions, we will be able to support and to extend their efforts.

INVESTIGATING INTERTEXTUAL LINKS: DATA COLLECTION AND ANALYSIS

Recall that in Chapter 1 we described the two-pronged focus of our study. First, we set out to determine whether varying degrees of exposure to nonfiction literature would prompt our 3rd graders to write nonfiction during writing workshop, and, if not, whether the addition of explicit instruction would influence their rate of expository adoption. These findings were discussed in Chapter 1. Second, we investigated the intertextual patterns that our 3rd graders forged when choosing to write nonfiction. It is in this chapter that we present these findings.

Lemke's (1992) patterns of intertextuality and Kamberelis and Scott's (1992) topology of voice provided the theoretical framework for analyzing the intertextual links. Using Halliday's semantic grammar, Lemke (1992) identified three patterns of intertextuality—thematic, orientational, and organizational—that describe the influence one or more texts (e.g., any sign— literature, television, film, people used in social interactions) may have on the construction of a new text:

- *Thematic intertextuality* refers to the semantic congruity between two or more texts (written or oral). To illustrate, let's say that Haley writes a report on the extinction of dinosaurs based on a *National Geographic* documentary. Haley's report would be considered co-thematic because it "is seen as being 'on the same topic' or 'about the same thing'" (Lemke, 1992, p. 258).

- *Organizational intertextuality* examines the structural compatibility between or among texts. If Haley appropriates the cause-and-effect structure of the *National Geographic* documentary in her piece, the texts would be considered genre-compatible. If, however, Haley uses the information from the documentary to write a humorous limerick, her piece would remain co-thematic but not co-generic (no genre compatibility) (Lemke, 1992).

- *Orientational intertextuality* addresses the degree to which one text adopts the point of view, or voice, of one or more other texts. As noted earlier, Bakhtin (1986) posited that the words we utter are the words of others— voices that we absorb and act on in order to find our own voice. We appropriate these polyphonic voices in a variety of ways: (1) by directly quoting the words of others, or by imitating or paraphrasing what we have heard or read, (2) by stylizing what we have heard or read in order to "create the same effect as the other might have" (Kamberelis & Scott, 1992, p. 371), (3) by parodying the words of others to poke fun or to ridicule, and (4) by polemicizing the utterances of others for the purpose of undermining and resisting (Kamberelis & Scott, 1992). By asking Haley to explain the origin of each sentence in her dinosaur report, we discover the voices (e.g., the direct quotes, the paraphrases, the stylizations) she appropriated from the documentary and, in all likelihood, from other sources.

If Haley's report reveals a close juxtaposition with the *National Geographic* documentary across all three dimensions—same topic, same voice, same organizational structure—it would be considered an intertext of the documentary (Lemke, 1992). The greater the degree of uniformity across these patterns, the greater the intertextuality.

As reported in Chapter 1, each 3rd grader in our study read and talked about his or her piece(s) during taped interviews. If the piece was nonfiction, the child was asked to discuss the (1) thematic origin ("Where did you get the idea to write about . . . ?"), (2) organizational origin ("Where did you get the idea to organize your report this way?"), and (3) orientational intertextuality (for each sentence in the report, the child was asked "Where did you learn that information?"). Writers who mentioned source material(s) in response to these questions were asked to retrieve these materials and locate information noted during the interview.

Using the constant-comparison method (Glaser & Strauss, 1967), we read the 28 reports written by the 3rd graders, their interview transcripts, and the corroborating sources repeatedly to identify recurrent patterns of response within each of the three dimensions of intertextuality. The search for common patterns began with the first two nonfiction reports that were written during phase 2, and a preliminary coding system was devised for each dimension of intertextuality. As other reports were written and analyzed during the final phase, the coding system was tested and revised. Not surprisingly, a number of new codes were added and some original codes were deleted or revised. The revised coding system was then applied to all the nonfiction reports. The reports were divided between the authors, coded independently, then exchanged to verify accurate coding. Discrepant codings were discussed and recoded.

FINDINGS: PATTERNS OF INTERTEXTUALITY

Thematic Intertextuality

To investigate the primary intertextual origins of the 28 nonfiction reports, we asked each 3rd grader, "Where did you get the idea to write about . . . ?" Four sources of fairly equal distribution were reported: personal experience, trade books, people, and the curriculum. Eight writers noted the influence of the school curriculum:

Because we're learning about fossils.

Because I studied penguins last year.

Seven writers identified personal experiences as the source for their reports:

I know all about acting.

I take Karate and I'm a blue belt and this is what I had to go through to get it.

Six others identified trade books:

I decided to start with kittens because I saw that book.

I got this book on chickens.

Six noted the influence of others, primarily peers, in their choice of topic:

Everyone was writing something different. Caitlyn was writing fossils and Kyle was doing mammals so I did dinosaurs.

My dad—he's an expert.

One 3rd grader mentioned two of these sources in her initial statement: "I found a sports book . . . and I flipped through the pages and I saw a pool table. And it looked cool and you know Andrea . . . she's my neighbor and I went to her house and we played pool 'cause she has a little pool table."

Thus, every 3rd grader was able to identify an intertextual source that fed his or her nonfiction writing, although, as discussed in Chapter 1, the intertextual source that triggered all reports was the presentation of Jessica's and Kyle's fossil/dinosaur reports during our first day of instruction.

Organizational Intertextuality

The influence of the organizational structure of the original source(s) on each nonfiction report was analyzed at two levels: top-level text organization and paragraph organization. Top-level text organization refers to the framework that an author chooses to use to organize his or her content. For example, decisions are made about (1) access features such as table of contents, index, and glossary and (2) organizational features concerning the division of content (e.g., chapters, headings, subheadings). In order to analyze top-level organization, we juxtaposed the organizational structure of the original source(s) and the organizational structure of the 3rd grader's report. So, for example, if the organizational setup of the original source included a table of contents followed by chapters whose content was subdivided under headings, would the third grader appropriate, in part or in full, this setup for his or her report? At the paragraph level, the analysis focused on the degree to which the young writer aligned the flow of his or her sentences with those of the published author(s). Findings with respect to these two levels are summarized in Table 2.1.

Top-level text organization. During interviews, the 3rd graders were asked about the organization of their reports as well as that of their primary source(s). The intertext's top-level organization was compared to the child's report to determine the degree of alignment. Five patterns of intertextual alignment, presented in Table 2.1, were found.

Title only. The most prominent pattern was the simplest in organization. Seven 3rd graders wrote nine reports that contained only a title followed by continuous text—no division of content. Four crafted reports based solely on their personal experiences (see Chapter 4). The remaining three writers who wrote title-only reports accessed only one trade book, all of which were classified as photo essays.

Table 2.1. Tally of Intertextual Organizational Patterns at the Top Level and Paragraph Level

Organizational Intertextuality	Number of Occurrences
Top-level text organization	
Title only	9
Multiple alignment	8
Self-alignment	7
Selected alignment	3
Perfect alignment	1
Total	28
Paragraph organization	
Selected alignment	19
Self-alignment	19
Perfect alignment	11
Multiple alignment	9
Total	58

Note: "Organizational intertextuality" refers to the influence of the organizational structures of original sources on the reports of the 3rd graders. "Top-level text organization" refers to the overall structure of a text with respect to both the division of content (chapter, heading, subheading) and access features (table of contents, index, and the like). Each 3rd grader's report ($n = 28$) was coded for its degree of organizational alignment with the original source's (or sources') top-level organization. "Paragraph organization" refers to the degree of alignment found between the sentences in each paragraph in each 3rd grader's report and those in the original source(s) that influenced the creation of that paragraph.

Multiple alignment. This complex top-level organization of multiple align-ment ranked second in frequency. This code was applied to any top-level organization in which the child appropriated chapter headings from two or more intertextual sources, thereby creating a new sequence for his or her own report. Eight 3rd graders' reports were coded as such. Examples of multiple alignment include Sarah's dinosaur report (discussed below) and Colin's penguin report (see Chapter 3).

Self-alignment. This code was applied to seven reports that contained head-ings created by the 3rd-grade authors. Essentially these writers struck out on their own to devise headings for their content. Obvious examples of self-alignment ($n = 2$) were found in the reports of the memory-only writers. Ja-son, who didn't access any print material while writing his mammal report, created five headings; each heading identified a specific ocean mammal ("Killer Whales," "Narwak," etc.). Other interesting examples included the reports of two writers who consulted one or more trade books that contained no organizational scheme (other than a book title). For example, Andrea crafted her own sequence of chapter headings for her shark report (see the "Discussion" section). Finally, three other writers chose to ignore their trade book's organizational framework, designing their own headings.

Selected alignment. Three writers selectively aligned their headings with those of their intertexts. Each accessed only one resource, surveying the headings in the original source and appropriating particular headings. For example, Maureen chose to adopt verbatim only two headings from a book on wolves. By selectively aligning her headings, she created a report that was sequenced differently from the original.

Perfect alignment. Of the 28 reports, only one was penned by a writer who appropriated the exact same sequence of headings found in his original source.

Paragraph organization. At the paragraph level, the organizational flow of the child's sentences was compared to the flow of sentences in the intertext(s) (unless none was used). Because the focus was on organizational intertextuality, it did not matter whether the child's sentences were direct quotes, partial di-rect quotes, paraphrases, or a combination thereof. It did matter, however, that the child's text meet the following criteria for a paragraph: "the state-ments in the paragraph be related to the topic of the paragraph (the criterion of unity) and that the clause-length statements—a minimum of three—be logi-cally connected (the criterion of coherence)" (Newkirk, 1987, p. 134). (In-dentation was not required.) Fifty-eight paragraphs across 19 reports were analyzed for ways in which the 3rd graders organized their information. Nine reports were eliminated because they did not meet the paragraph criteria. For example, Jessica's 15-page fossil report, which contained 12 "chapters," was eliminated because each "chapter" was classified as an attribute series— a random amalgam of affective ("I love fossils!") and descriptive statements (Newkirk, 1987). Jake's report based on his recall of a video game was excluded because the criterion of coherence was not met. Our findings at the paragraph level, summarized in Table 2.1, included the following.

Selected alignment. Tying for first place was the popular strategy called selected alignment. Half of the 3rd graders crafted paragraphs (*n* = 19) by selecting only some sentences/ideas from paragraphs in their original sources. For example, Phil selected what he perceived to be the prominent details across 11 pages in Joanna Cole's (1976) *A Chick Hatches* for his "Chicken" report:

ORIGINAL TEXT	PHIL'S TEXT
At nine days the fetus is starting to look like a chick. The beak is formed. The wings are shaped like a chicken's wings. Even the little stump of a tail is there. . . . On the chick's beak, you can see the egg tooth. This tooth is a sharp little bump that will help the chick break the shell. A few days after hatching, the egg tooth will drop off. (Cole, 1976, pp. 23–33)	Do you no that it takes 9 days for a chicken to form and that when it brakes out of its egg you can see a egg tooth . . .

Many children explained that they chose particular sentences because they were interesting or contained information readers wouldn't know; some admitted that it would be too much to copy the whole paragraph.

Self-alignment. The equally popular strategy of self-alignment was also adopted. Nineteen paragraphs were constructed independently (without reference to print material) by 3rd graders who relied on their personal knowledge and/or personal experience. For example, Caitlyn drew on her knowledge about jumping classes, learned from direct experience and her riding instructor, to craft the self-aligned paragraph found on the second page of her horse report (see Chapter 3). The text she consulted while writing her report did not address these jumping classes. The highest percentage of these self-aligned paragraphs were penned by children who either wrote exclusively from memory or exclusively from personal experiences (see Chapter 4).

Perfect alignment. Four 3rd graders wrote 11 paragraphs that matched the flow of the original source. Three of these writers essentially copied a paragraph from a text using either direct quotes or partial direct quotes. Kyle, for example, copied verbatim eight paragraphs from his intertexts while writing his shark report (see Chapter 5). The fourth writer crafted one of her paragraphs by taking the dictation of a peer who was very knowledgeable about sharks.

Multiple alignment. When a writer constructed a paragraph by fusing information acquired from more than one original source (e.g., books, people, media), it was coded multiple alignment. Three 3rd graders wrote nine paragraphs that merged information from more than one source. Eight of these paragraphs were crafted by our two most advanced writers, Caitlyn and Colin, whose reports are profiled in Chapter 3.

Orientational Intertextuality

The 3rd graders were interviewed to ascertain the voices that they adopted while writing their reports. For each sentence in each report, the writer was asked, "Where did you learn that information?" The children's responses revealed seven intertextual voice patterns (see Table 2.2).

Personal-knowledge paraphrase. The most prominent voice pattern used by the 3rd graders was the personal-knowledge paraphrase (28%)—the appropriation of others' ideas but not their exact words. This code was created to distinguish content paraphrased from memory as opposed to content paraphrased while consulting a published text (which was coded as a textual paraphrase). For example, when a writer attributed information in a particular sentence to a television program, a movie, a person, a book read or listened to in the past, his or her sentence was coded as a personal-knowledge paraphrase (with the source identified). Because these paraphrases were retrieved from memory, most could not be checked. (*Note:* If the child stipulated a memory source but used print material while writing some part of his or her report, it was checked to ensure that the information wasn't paraphrased from this source. Few instances were noted.) It is important to qualify that the bulk of these personal-knowledge paraphrases (71%) were attributed to the four children who wrote their nonfiction reports exclusively from memory. Three of these four children were the first to write reports before the nonfiction momentum took hold in the classroom. Because these memory-only reports tied to curriculum units that involved instruction, textbooks, trade books, and media, most of their sentences in these three reports were coded as paraphrase—multiple. The fourth memory-based report, written during phase 3, contained 12 sentences based on a video game.

Table 2.2. Frequency of Voice Appropriations at the Sentence Level

Orientational Intertextuality	Number of Occurrences	Percent of All Sentences
Personal-knowledge paraphrase		28
Multiple sources	76	
Trade book	31	
Media	28	
People	27	
Unknown	18	
Total	180	
Direct quote		18
Text	81	
Caption	32	
Total	113	
Stylization		14
Personal opinion	32	
Dramatic effect	32	
Diagram	20	
Asks question	2	
Total	86	
Textual paraphrase		13
Text	76	
Caption	4	
Total	80	
Partial direct quote		12
Text	68	
Caption	6	
Total	74	
Personal-experience paraphrase	76	12
Picture observations	17	2
Double-coded voices	7	1
Total number of sentences:	633	

Note: "Orientational intertextuality" refers to the voices that the 3rd graders adopted while writing their reports. Building on the work of Kamberelis and Scott (1992) and Bakhtin (1986), we noted seven voice patterns. Each sentence in each writer's report was coded in relation to the original source(s) when possible.

The remaining 29% of the personal-knowledge paraphrases were sprinkled throughout 10 other reports. As Table 2.2 shows, our 3rd graders integrated information recalled from trade books, the media, and people into their reports. When a writer was unable to attribute a particular sentence to a source (usually because of the generic nature of the information [e.g., "Birds fly."]), it was coded paraphrase—unknown.

Direct quote. While the appropriation of unmarked direct quotes ranked second (18%), three writers accounted for 67% of the total ($n = 113$). Kyle included 20 direct quotes from various texts as well as 25 verbatim captions in his report on sharks; Patrick incorporated 26 direct quotes into his reptile/amphibian report. (These two writers are profiled in Chapter 5.) Judy's seven-sentence report contained a string of five direct quotes taken solely from captions and two personal-knowledge statements. These three writers relied heavily on direct quotes; 60% or more of their reports contained direct quotes. Six other children were responsible for the remaining 37% of unmarked direct quotes, ranging from 1 to 11, with an average of 4.3. Interestingly, two of these six writers also correctly enclosed some sentences in quotation marks.

Stylization. Kamberelis and Scott (1992) describe stylization as the appropriation of another's words to "create the same effect as the other might have" (p. 371). The 3rd graders' reports were analyzed for ways in which they reached out to their audience. Four stylization patterns were noted. Statements of dramatic effect (e.g., "Can you believe it!") and personal opinions had the highest frequencies ($n = 32$ for each pattern). Also notable were diagrams/pictures ($n = 20$) that three children included in their reports to engage readers. In addition, two writers captured their readers' attention by posing a question (e.g., Phil's chicken report). All five writers who based their reports on personal experiences (see Chapter 4) included an average of two and a half stylized statements. Five others who relied on textual resources included at least one stylized statement in their reports. They absorbed the ways in which television/movie writers and book authors appeal to audiences and used this tacit knowledge to create the same effect in their own pieces.

Textual paraphrase. Textual paraphrases tied directly to the print material used by the 3rd graders during writing workshop. If a writer used print material (a book, magazine, or peer's report, for example), he or she was required to bring the material to conferences and locate sentences that were consulted. When it was evident that the writer had read a sentence in a text, absorbed its meaning, and restated its contents in his or her own words, it was coded as a textual paraphrase, and the source and page number were noted. Half of the children successfully paraphrased information. A total of

80 sentences were paraphrased across 15 reports. As the following examples show, many writers used the read-a-line-and-restate strategy:

ORIGINAL TEXT	THIRD GRADER'S PARAPHRASE
But they [whales] keep in touch through the sounds they make. (Patent, 1993, p. 27 [caption])	To communicate they make noises.
I picked up this kitten. He was the first to open his eyes. I named him Dusty. (Coles, 1995, n.p.)	When kittens are born, their eyes are closed.

Partial direct quote. Seventy-four sentences were coded as partial direct quotes (12%). This code was applied to any sentence that contained both paraphrased and verbatim text. In general, students wrote part of the sentence in their own words, and copied the remainder from the original source. As the two following examples show, however, the verbatim appropriations ranged from a phrase to a significant chunk of the original sentence. As Patrick's excerpt below reveals, he scooped the segment ("finding a good place to nest"), adjusted it syntactically, and then went off on his own tangent. Connor, on the other hand, thought he had avoided plagiarism by splitting Seymour Simon's original sentences into simple sentences, and then copying major chunks.

ORIGINAL TEXT	EXCERPT FROM PATRICK'S REPORT
Each species of bird has evolved to make the most of a particular habitat . . . by feeding on the plants or animals there and finding a good place to nest. You may have to look hard, because many birds blend into their surroundings to hide from their enemies. (Gill, 1990, p. 6)	Birds find good places to put nest because if its in a tree and it was'nt stirdy enough and it fell and the baby birds didn't know how to fly they'll get hert.

ORIGINAL TEXT	EXCERPT FROM CONNOR'S REPORT
Tyrannosaurus, the "tyrant lizard," was the biggest meat-eating dinosaur. This huge and terrifying hunter measured forty feet in length, stood nineteen feet high, and weighed seven tons. (Simon, 1991a, p. 26)	Tyrannosaurus means "tyrant lizard." It was the biggest meat eating dinosaur. It was fourty feet in length. It weighed 7 tons.

With the exception of Judy (whose aforementioned report contained five unmarked direct quotes and two personal-knowledge paraphrases), all 3rd graders who consulted text resources included at least one partial direct quote. Some included many in one report: Connor included 14 partial direct quotes, and Sarah included 9.

Personal-experience paraphrase. This paraphrase was reserved for sentences that tied directly to the writer's personal experience—knowledge learned directly by doing. Four 3rd graders wrote reports based exclusively on their hobbies (see Chapter 4); Caitlyn merged her personal experience with book and television information (see Chapter 3). These five writers accounted for 72% of the personal-experience paraphrases. The remaining 28% of the personal-experience paraphrases were integrated into text-based reports by four other writers.

Picture observation. Five writers generated 17 sentences by studying the illustrations or photographs in their trade books. For example, Danielle crafted the following three sentences by examining photographs of guppies: "They have beautiful dizzins [designs] on them. They are black and orange. And some of them are black and white." None of these observations was included in the intertext that she consulted. (*Note:* Intertexts were checked across all writers to ensure that the content in their sentences didn't originate in the body of the text or in the captions.)

Double-coded voices. Three 3rd graders independently identified two sources of voice for a single sentence in their reports. For example, in a paragraph about the difference between a horse and a pony, Caitlyn wrote: "If she [the mother] was a pony then the foal wold be a pony." When asked about its source, she replied, "Well, I sorta just read it [in Jackie Budd's (1995) *Horses*] and I watch TV a lot—the Pony Channel on the Disney Channel." This sentence was coded for paraphrasing a book as well as for paraphrasing media; three other sentences of Caitlyn's were double-coded.

DISCUSSION

Ideational Origins

One of the most frequent questions asked of acclaimed authors is, "Where do you get your ideas?" Their usual reply: "Everywhere." As Newbery winner Avi (1991) notes:

The answer is everywhere. Ideas don't come whole cloth. They are amalgams of random thoughts, observations, moods, squeezed into shape by the way I look upon the world. (p. 2)

As our thematic findings reveal, children also cast a wide net for their ideas. During interviews, the 3rd graders readily acknowledged the influence of sources such as personal experiences, trade books, people, and curricular units. Undergirding this array of thematic sources was the primacy of peer influence (Chapter 1). Although attribution was distributed fairly evenly across the sources noted above, unspoken allegiance to the animal report was pivotal, prompted by the showcasing of Jessica's and Kyle's fossil/dinosaur reports (see Chapter 1). With the exception of five reports (four anchored solely in personal experiences—see Chapter 4), the 3rd graders focused their reports exclusively on animals. For example, while six attributed the thematic origin of their reports to trade books, this attribution occurred after their implicit decision to join their peers in pursuing the topic of animals. Phil, who attributed his chicken report to a trade book, first decided to write about animals and then searched the classroom library for an animal book that held appeal. With respect to the experience-only writers—who, in general, attributed the thematic origins of their reports to their personal recreational experience—the triggering event was the call for "experts" to write nonfiction and subsequent class discussion (see Chapter 4). Thus, their thematic impulses were anchored in social interactions.

Organizing the Nonfiction Report

At the onset of this study, we anticipated that the 3rd graders would write reports that contained a report title and a paragraph or two. Seven did so, writing nine reports that included only a report title. Interestingly, all four writers who penned reports, based solely on their personal experiences included only a title with no division of content (see Chapter 4). Fourteen children, however, exceeded our expectations, crafting 19 reports that were organized into headings ($n = 6$) or chapters (replete with numbers and chapter headings) ($n = 8$).

The extent of our instruction at the beginning of phase 3 with respect to top-level structure included semantic mapping and heading-generation activities (see the Phase 3 section in Chapter 1). During the second session, the students were asked about the kinds of information a writer might include in a report on sharks. As the 3rd graders rattled off shark details, their responses were categorized on a semantic map. Students then generated headings for each clump of details; brief discussion about why authors organize their information under headings ensued. Table groups then were asked to generate headings for Cole's *Hungry, Hungry Sharks* (1986b), which is organized as continuous text with no organizational framework, and to share results. No instruction was presented on the construct of chapter, on the difference between headings and chapters, or on ways of organizing chapters. Yet seven writers whose top-level organizations were coded as multiple alignment included chapter numbers and headings across 10 reports. For example, the top-level organization of Sarah's report (Figure 2.2) was coded as multiple alignment because she consulted four books on dinosaurs and used headings from three of these books to create her "chapters." (*Note*: None of her intertexts organized content by chapters; each used headings only.) For example, Sarah revised the heading "Which Dinosaur Had the Most Teeth?" in Seymour Simon's (1990) *New Questions and Answers About Dinosaurs* to "Dinosaurs Teeth! Chapter 4," adding the chapter designation and number. She also revised Carroll's (1986) heading "Which dinosaurs ran the fastest?" in *How Big Is a Brachiasaurus?* to read: "Fast Dinosaurs! Chapter 3" in her report.

Four writers relied not only on two or more books for ideas about chapter headings but also on their own knowledge of the topic. For example, Colin's report (see Chapter 3) on penguins was anchored in two penguin books and in a penguin worksheet completed in 2nd grade. Only two of Colin's five "chapter" headings were paraphrased from the books he had read. For example, he created his own chapter title, "The History of Penguins" (not found in any of his sources), appropriated probably from his exposure to books in general or media.

Note that the word *chapter* is in quotes because, for Sarah and most of their peers, a "chapter" equated to a paragraph (see Figure 2.2). As already discussed, no instruction was provided on the construct of a chapter. And, interestingly, none of the trade books used by the children contained official chapters. Hence, their appropriation of the "chapter" can most likely be traced to Jessica's fossil/dinosaur report, which contained "chapters" and was showcased during our first lesson, or to their textbooks and nonfiction trade books. Caitlyn (Chapter 3) was the only 3rd grader who seemed to understand that a chapter is a major division of content that is often subdivided with headings.

As noted above, another impressive dimension of these multiple-alignment report writers was their use of multiple sources. Other than general discussion on the second day about the 3rd graders' contributions to the "What Makes a Good Report" chart, little attention was given to the research process that writers undertake until the final week of the study. Yet a number of the children strung their "chapters" together by consulting two or more resources. Undoubtedly, some of this multiple-book consultation was spurred by peer interaction; for example, Connor and Sarah, who sat at the same table, consulted the same four dinosaur books for their reports.

Dinosaurs

Chapter One Small dinosaurs!
Some small dinsaurs were
smaller than a human. The
Kompsognaythus was small as
a chicken. The smallest dinosaur
found yet is a parrot lizard
It was as small as a baby
bird.

Meat Eaters. Chapter 2
A Dimtrodon was a meateater
The Dimtrodon could adjust
his body tempcture. The
Nanotrannus was a meat
eater and a relitive of the
t-rex

FAST Dinosaurs! Chapter 3
The Stenonikunsawrus could
have run 50 miles per hour.
Ornithuhmymidz could run very
fast too. The cheetah could
run 70 miles per hour.

Figure 2.2. Sarah's (grade 3) report was coded as multiple alignment at top-level organization.

On the other hand, six writers whose top-level organization was coded self-alignment struck out on their own when organizing the content of their reports. For example, two 3rd graders who used a primary source that contained no organizational features created their own headings. Andrea read Seymour Simon's (1995) photo essay *Sharks*, which contains no chapters or headings (only continuous text), and used the information to create five "chapters," all of which began: "What I Know About [name of shark]." While Andrea couldn't verbalize her intertextual connection, it is likely that her familiarity with the KWL strategy that was implemented periodically in the classroom came into play here. Her friend Danielle, who consulted one primary source to write her fish report, ignored her author's headings, choosing to appropriate Andrea's idea, "Everything I Know About livbearsers [liverbearers]."

While three writers whose top-level organizational schemes were categorized as selected alignment surveyed their intertext's headings and selected headings that interested them for their reports, only one youngster appropriated verbatim the organization framework of his intertext. Patrick's four "chapters" aligned perfectly with the first four headings in *Birds* (Gill, 1990): "Our Interest in Birds," "Habitat," "Behavior," and "Flight."

At the paragraph level, the 3rd graders employed two alignment strategies extensively: selected alignment and self-alignment. For example, nine writers consulted particular paragraphs in their intertexts, and, rather than appropriating the exact sequence, they crafted their paragraphs by selecting some, but not, all of the sentences/ideas. We have already noted Phil's chicken example. While Sarah accessed multiple sources to shape the top-level organization of her report, she wasn't able to sustain this strategy at the paragraph level (Figure 2.2). For example, she used only one source, Carroll's (1986) *How Big is a Brachiosaurus?*, to draft her first paragraph ("Small dinosaurs!"). She paraphrased (in part or in whole) Carroll's first, third, seventh, and eighth sentences. On the other hand, eight writers who accessed no print material created paragraphs based on prior knowledge. These writers included those who based their reports solely on personal experiences (see Chapter 4) and those who wrote reports from memory (see Chapter 1). Their paragraphs were coded as self-alignment. With respect to the 11 paragraphs that aligned perfectly with the paragraphs in the intertexts, one writer accounted for 9 of these paragraphs. Examples of Kyle's perfectly aligned paragraphs are included in Chapter 5. And finally, our two most advanced writers penned 8 of the 9 paragraphs that were coded multiple alignment. Caitlyn and Colin, whose reports are presented in Chapter 3, merged information from more than one source to create their paragraphs.

In sum, our 3rd graders adopted a range of top-level organizational frameworks from reports with only titles to reports containing titles and headings to a report that contained a title, a table of contents, an introduction, chapter numbers and headings, and chapters divided into "Parts" (see Caitlyn's report in Chapter 3). Some writers actively appropriated the frameworks of their intertexts; others operated independently of text resources, preferring to call up organizational frameworks encountered in past texts. Less diversity of alignment was noted with respect to paragraph organization. Some closely aligned their paragraphs with those of their intertexts; others shuttled between paragraphs in two or more intertexts to create their own flow of sentences. Still others self-aligned their paragraphs, relying on past experiences and/or knowledge.

Voice and the Nonfiction Report

Bakhtin's (1981) claim that "the word in language is half someone else's" (p. 293) is borne out in the 3rd graders' nonfiction writing. Using a modification of Kamberelis and Scott's (1992) topology of voice, we interviewed the children about the point of view, or voice, they adopted when writing their nonfiction reports. For each sentence in each report, writers were asked, "Where did you learn this information?" Responses were coded as follows: direct quote, partial direct quote, textual paraphrase, personal-knowledge paraphrase, personal-experience paraphrase and stylization. As Table 2.2 reveals, the children readily acknowledged the voices they appropriated. Although the expectation was that the direct quote would constitute the most popular form of appropriation, it ranked behind the personal-knowledge paraphrase (28%)—the code applied to content paraphrased from memory (as opposed to content paraphrased from a published text, which was coded as a textual paraphrase). As noted earlier, however, 71% of these personal-knowledge paraphrases were attributed to four children who wrote their nonfiction reports exclusively from memory.

The personal-knowledge paraphrase, however, wasn't restricted to the memory-only writers. Seven other 3rd graders sprinkled 10 reports with information recalled from trade books, the media, and people. For example, Kyle, one of four writers to include information learned from the media, attributed the sentence "Hammerheads serch in groups like fish do" to the TV show *Kratts' Creatures*. Fourteen percent of the children's sentences were attributed to specific individuals. For example, in the opening "chapter" of his polar bear report, Jason included two sentences about their habitat that he said he learned from his 2nd-grade teacher. Eighteen sentences were coded as paraphrase—unknown when the writers reported that they "just knew" the information and were unable to cite a source. For example, Sarah began her introduction: "Anmals can be diffirent. Their all different kinds like the kitten, Bear, Dog, Bird." General knowledge of this kind, learned long ago, didn't lend itself to clear attribution.

The second prominent voice pattern was the unmarked direct quote. Recall that the issue of voice surfaced during the first week of instruction (see the Phase 3 section in Chapter 1). Asked whether they thought Joanna Cole copied sentences from another book when she wrote *Hungry, Hungry Sharks* (1986b), Colin noted: "No. You have to say it in your own words or it's like stealing." Brief discussion about the importance of paraphrasing ensued, but no instruction was offered on how and when to paraphrase. To their credit, a number of 3rd graders heeded this dictum. While 18% of the total number of sentences (*n* = 627) were coded as direct quotes, 13% were coded as textual paraphrases. As noted earlier, only three writers relied heavily on direct quotes, accounting for 67% of the total. Of the 14 children who relied on textual sources to write at least one report, 5 used no direct quotes. And 3 writers enclosed a verbatim sentence in quotation marks.

A finding of interest was the partial direct quote, which accounted for 12% of the total. All 14 writers who consulted print material while writing their reports included at least one partial direct quote, paraphrasing part of a sentence and copying a phrase or more from the original. Partial direct quotes ranged in frequency from 1 to 14, with 5 as the average. Interestingly, many perceived these partial direct quotes as genuine paraphrases, stating proudly that they "said it in their own words." A case in point is Connor's dinosaur report, which included 11 unmarked direct quotes, one marked direct quote that contained four sentences, 14 partial direct quotes, two paraphrases of captions, and one stylization. An example of one of his partial direct quotes follows:

ORIGINAL TEXT	CONNOR'S DIRECT QUOTE (CORRECTLY MARKED) AND PARTIAL DIRECT QUOTE
COMPSOGNATHUS (COMP-so-NAY-thus) One of the smallest dinosaurs was the Compsognathus. Its name means *fancy jawed*. Compsognathus was about the size of a pigeon. This dinosaur was like a bird in other ways as well. Parts of its body were covered with feathers. The feathers helped Compsognathus keep its body temperature the same all the time. (Simon, 1991a, p. 20)	The Smallest Dinosaurs "One of the smallest dinosaurs was the Compsognathus. Its name means fancy jawed. Compsognathus was about the size of a pigeon. This dinosaur was like a bird in other ways as well. Parts of its body were covered with feathers." The feathers helped them keep warm.

In asking why he put quotation marks around the first four sentences but not around the subject and simple predicate of the last sentence, Connor replied, "Yeah, that's because I copied the words [pointing to the correctly punctuated quote]. But I didn't copy the words here [pointing to the last sentence, which was coded as partial direct quote]." For Connor and his peers, the "Don't copy" dictum applied only to *entire* sentences. It was OK to copy some of a sentence as long as you changed the rest of it. Connor accepted clarification about his verbatim copying, as well as about the accuracy of his statement.

The fact that Connor and eight of his peers simultaneously entertained both partial direct quotes and paraphrases suggests that partial direct quotes may serve as a transition step to paraphrasing. Their use of partial direct quotes and direct quotes signals the need for extended discussion and demonstration of appropriation strategies.

Another interesting voice category was the personal-experience paraphrase. This paraphrase linked specifically to learning that had occurred as a result of firsthand experiences, with five writers accounting for the bulk (72%). Four of these youngsters wrote exclusively about their participation in recreational sports (see Chapter 4). At the time their pieces were written, all were taking lessons. When asked about their source of knowledge for individual sentences, these children cited these experiences. For example, when asked how she knew the information in her sentence "But if you [actor] mess up just keep going because the adicis will not know that you did a mitake," Vanessa replied, "It happened to me and I just kept going." Further probing, not surprisingly, revealed that her acting coach had shared this maxim many times. This category of personal experience acknowledges that nearly all of what the children considered to be their personally derived knowledge ("I know it because I do it.") had its origins in the mentors who taught these children. In addition to these experience-only writers, four other 3rd graders wove their personal-experience paraphrases into their text-based reports.

The voice pattern of stylization, which ranked third in popularity, appeared frequently in the reports of the above-mentioned experience-only writers. Without instruction in ways of engaging readers, these four 3rd graders summoned the strategies that advertisers, authors, and speakers use to attract and hold audiences: statements of dramatic effect, questions, personal opinions, and illustrations. For example, Kristin, in talking about Olympic gymnasts, offered the opinion: "But some times they make a mistake. And they don't get to much credit!" Of the 32 personal opinions logged, 69% were written by Jessica, whose memory-only report on fossils contained 19 opinions such as: "Fossils are really interesting to learn about. I love fossils." Five children who relied on textual resources also included at least one stylized statement in their reports. Phil, for example, opened his piece on chickens with the question: "Do you no that it takes 9 days for a chicken to form?"

In sum, voice was alive and well in the reports of these 3rd graders, who readily acknowledged the sources of their information. Encouraging was the finding that many had the confidence to integrate previously learned information and personal experiences and not allow their intertexts to monopolize their report writing. While verbatim copying was an issue (see Chapter 6), the viability of their textual paraphrases suggests a readiness for instructional intervention.

FINAL THOUGHTS

The 3rd graders in this study demonstrated a range of intertextual knowledge about the genre of report writing. This knowledge enabled them to pursue report writing of their own accord with confidence and enthusiasm; none of the children expressed a reluctance or inability to write nonfiction. Examination of the multifaceted nature of their intertextual understandings can best be accomplished by shifting the lens from our cross-sectional findings to case studies of individual writers. Building on the research of Many and colleagues (1996), our analysis of the three patterns of intertextuality suggests that the 3rd graders adopted four differing stances to the task of report writing. In order to describe these stances, we developed four categories of writers: strategic, experience-only, text-bound, and memory-only. Case studies that illuminate the first three categories are presented in Chapters 3 through 5. (*Note:* To the degree possible, the memory-only writers have been discussed in this chapter. The inaccessibility of sources used to write their reports from memory hindered full-fledged analysis.) A brief description of each category of writer follows:

- *Strategic.* Two writers, Caitlyn and Colin, profiled in Chapter 3, appeared to understand that nonfiction writing requires a deep knowledge of a subject—knowledge that is accumulated over time and in a variety of ways—and chose their topics accordingly. They consulted multiple sources but did not allow these sources to dictate their reports. Rather they engaged in much strategic decision making. They crafted their own organizational scheme and brought their own point of view to their work. They understood that information extracted from text sources should be paraphrased, not copied verbatim. They integrated information from multiple sources when constructing paragraphs. In essence, they understood the transformative nature of nonfiction report writing (Many et al., 1996).
- *Experience-only.* Unlike the strategic writers who accessed multiple sources including personal experiences, these writers tapped only their experiences. At the time of their report writing, most were involved in recreational lessons (e.g., karate, acting, gymnastics) and considered themselves "experts" on their topics. Their reports, presented in Chapter 4, exhibited a simple organizational framework: a title followed by a page-length paragraph that detailed what they had learned from instructors and peers. One striking feature of these experience-only writers was their sense of audience. Each writer included a number of stylizations (dramatic statements and opinions) to engage readers.
- *Text-bound.* This category includes a continuum of writers. At one end is Sarah, whose report was discussed earlier in this chapter (see Figure 2.2). At first glance, Sarah seems worthy of classification as a strategic writer.

Like Caitlyn and Colin, Sarah consulted multiple sources and reworked headings from various sections in three of these books to create her "chapters." While none of these authors labeled their headings as chapters, she exhibited some independent decision making with respect to her sequence of chapters, not allowing any one book to dictate her organizational framework. However, unlike Caitlyn and Colin, she didn't stand back from these texts and summon her prior knowledge (the class had studied dinosaurs a few weeks earlier) or text knowledge. Moreover, to craft each "chapter," Sarah used one primary source per "chapter," selectively aligning the flow of her sentences with those of her intertext. No integration of information across the books was evident. With respect to voice, Sarah primarily used partial direct quotes—paraphrasing part of a sentence while copying verbatim a phrase or two—although she did include a few paraphrases. With context-based instruction, Sarah is primed to adopt a more strategic stance toward nonfiction report writing.

More representative of text-bound writers are Patrick and Kyle, whose reports are presented in Chapter 5. While both tended to view texts as the sole source of authority, they approached certain aspects of report writing differently. For example, while Patrick relied on one trade book and initially aligned nearly every aspect of his report with this intertext, Kyle consulted multiple books and wrote pages of continuous text with little regard for coherence. Both copied verbatim major stretches of text; both eventually modified this affinity for verbatim copying after repeated demonstrations, illuminating how complex the construct of plagiarism is. Essentially, these writers allowed their sources to drive their reports.

We turn now to the reports and interviews of Caitlyn and Colin to illuminate the advanced understandings of the strategic writer. Drawing on the intertextual data gathered during the study, each child's knowledge about the thematic, orientational, and organizational dimensions of report writing is explored.

Strategic Nonfiction Writers: Caitlyn and Colin

IN THIS CHAPTER, we profile two writers, Caitlyn and Colin, who wrote reports that illuminated an expansive array of intertextual understandings. They understood the importance of planning while writing and of using multiple sources to carve out their point of view. Neither allowed the textual sources to drive their reports. Rather, they actively constructed meaning with the clear intent of making their reports their own. In essence, they adopted a *knowledge-transforming* rather than a *knowledge-telling* stance (Bereiter & Scardamalia, 1987).

As Table 1.1 reveals, both Caitlyn and Colin were academically strong students, functioning above grade level in literacy development. Caitlyn attended the gifted and talented program twice a week.

CAITLYN: INTERTEXTUAL PATTERNS

In early September, the 3rd graders penned their literacy histories. Caitlyn's autobiography revealed her passion for writing "long stories," especially about ponies. In discussing her autobiography, Caitlyn noted that she had been riding horses since she was 5 years old and that she had competed in local horse shows. With respect to her interest in writing, Caitlyn commented, "I'm like Harriet [in Fitzhugh's (1964) *Harriet the Spy*] because I write so much. I love to write."

Inspection of Caitlyn's writing notebook (see Table 1.2) attested to the marriage of her two passions, horses and writing. Her first entry, "Pony Ranch," was a two-page story containing two chapters. Caitlyn readily acknowledged the intertextual influence of *Misty of Chincoteague* (Henry, 1947), explaining that Pony Ranch was in the original story but that she "burned it down so Erin [Caitlyn's protagonist] could build it again." In addition, Caitlyn noted that her ending—"She put a saddle and bridle on him and rode him into the mist"—paralleled the original. This story was followed by a personal narrative about a pony she used to ride and then by three more pony stories and a Halloween story.

Woven throughout these stories was Caitlyn's considerable knowledge about horses. Excerpts from various stories included content such as:

- "I changed into my paddock boots and we led Genie outside to tack up."
- "He is black. He is 122 hands high."
- "I go get a pitch fork and wheel barrow to muck out. . . . After feeding, watering and mucking out, we practiced the jump course."

Therefore, we were not surprised that when the call to write nonfiction was sounded, Caitlyn responded. The day after Jessica and Kyle presented their reports to the class (see Phase 3 section in Chapter 1), Caitlyn began her report called, "Horses Around the World." The first three pages as well as page 5 of her seven-page report are reproduced in Figure 3.1.

We turn now to the three patterns of intertextuality—thematic, organizational and orientational—that underscore Caitlyn's report.

Thematic Intertextuality: "So Where Did You Get the Idea for Your Topic?"

When Caitlyn was asked about the thematic origin of her piece, she replied, "I got the idea from Jessica and Kyle because they were doing nonfiction things." When asked why she chose horses, she grinned, "Because I'm an equestrian."

As interviews continued over time, it became evident that, in addition to her extensive experience, Caitlyn had read many horse books, both fiction and nonfiction. "I have read the three whole series of *Saddle Club*, *Young Riders*, and *Pony Tails* and there's about 60 [books] in each series and I've read them all!"

She stated that she had "about 10" nonfiction books that she "reads all the time, especially the one on how to take care of a pony."

During interviews, Caitlyn also commented on the horse movies she had watched—*Black Beauty*, *The Black Stallion*, and *National Velvet*—and on her weekly viewing of "the Pony Channel on the Disney Channel." Having "lived" her topic in the presence of multiple experts, Caitlyn approached her report writing with confidence and knowledge.

Organizational Intertextuality: "Where Did You Get the Idea to Organize Your Report This Way?"

As discussed in Chapter 2, children possess varying levels of intertextual knowledge about organizational structure. Some children appropriate verbatim the organizational scheme of their primary text sources. Others are more selective about which headings, for example, they appropriate. Still others consult multiple sources in order to create their own framework.

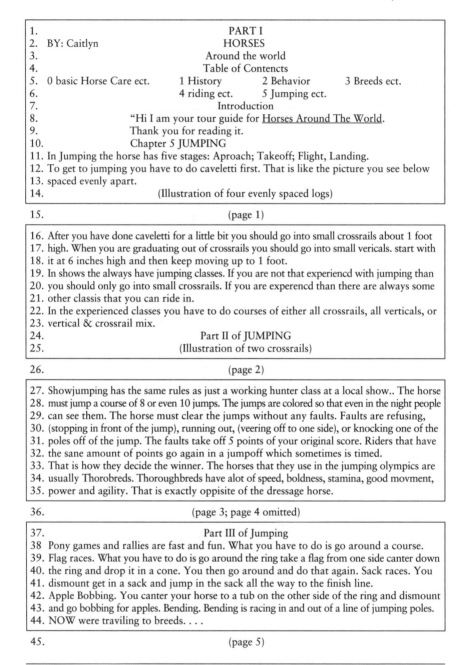

Figure 3.1. Four pages of Caitlyn's (grade 3) seven-page nonfiction report, "Horses Around the World."

In this section, we explore the degree to which Caitlyn's primary source, *Horses* (Budd, 1995), influenced the organization of her report at two levels: top-level text organization and paragraph organization. Recall that Caitlyn and her peers participated in a lesson that addressed how authors often use headings to organize their ideas. During this session, which occurred one day *after* Caitlyn began her report, the 3rd graders were handed sections of *Hungry, Hungry Sharks* (Cole, 1986b) and asked to generate headings and share them. No attention, however, was given to what a chapter is, to how some books are divided into chapters or headings, or to the difference between chapter headings and section headings.

Top-level text organization. In order to examine the top-level organizational links that Caitlyn forged, we begin with an overview of how Jackie Budd's (1995) book *Horses* scaffolded Caitlyn's report (reproduced in part in Figure 3.1). The cover of Budd's book shows the following title and subtitle:

HORSES

HISTORY   BEHAVIOR   BREEDS   RIDING   JUMPING

Budd's table of contents, however, does not align with the topics constituting her subtitle; rather, it includes four sections on other topics, which are not identified as chapters and are not numbered (see Figure 3.2). Inspection of lines 1–10 in Figure 3.1 reveals Caitlyn's active decision making with regard to Budd's organizational design. It is as if Caitlyn were debating: "Now, which of Budd's features do I want to use? Which do I want to revise? What features do I want to add?" Her deliberations resulted in the following appropriations.

Byline. For the first time in her writer's notebook, Caitlyn included a byline (Figure 3.1, line 2). When asked why, she replied, "Because it's a report and everyone is going to read it." When asked why she didn't write her name on the stories and personal narratives in her notebook, she commented, "Well, stories are only out of my mind. This is facts." The mystique of the "report" is pronounced for many young writers; from Caitlyn's perspective, the "real" knowledge of the nonfiction report carried greater import than the imaginative spin of storytelling.

Table of contents. Rather than appropriate Budd's table of contents (Figure 3.2), Caitlyn decided to transform the subtitle of Budd's book (HISTORY, BEHAVIOR, BREEDS, RIDING, JUMPING) into her table of contents (Figure 3.1, lines 4–6). When asked why she wrote "Table of Contents," rather than Budd's term, "Contents" (Figure 3.2), Caitlyn remarked, "Well, I read a lot of books

Caitlyn's "HORSES Around the World"

Table of Contents
0 basic Horse Care ect.   1 History   2 Behavior   3 Breeds ect.
4 riding ect.   5 Jumping ect.

Budd's HORSES: *History   Behavior   Breeds   Riding   Jumping*

CONTENTS

ALL ABOUT HORSES	4	IN THE PAST	39
The horse family	6	Myth and magic	40
Horse sense	8	Horses in war	42
Body talk	10	Going places	44
The paces	12	Pulling power	46
GOING RIDING	17	HORSES TODAY	48
Riding gear	18	Working horse	50
Bridles and bits	20	The entertainers	52
Saddles and stirrups	22	Young riders	54
Lifestyles	24	International sport	56
Grooming	32		
Food and feeding	35		

(Budd, 1995)

Figure 3.2. To design her table of contents, Caitlyn appropriated the subtitle of Budd's *Horses*.

that say 'Table of Contents.' I sort of do what other authors do." When I (Carol) asked why she chose to use the author's subtitle to structure her table of contents, instead of the entries in Budd's "Contents" (Figure 3.2), Caitlyn replied, "Because it had a lot of things. It would take forever to write everything. I have to pick out the main things." When asked why she added the chapter, "0 basic Horse Care ect." (see Figure 3.1, line 5) to her table of contents, Caitlyn explained, "Because you have to have this [chapter]. If you don't take care of a pony, it can get sick. Whoever reads my report will know all about everything for taking care of a horse." Caitlyn was the only 3rd grader to include a table of contents.

Introduction. Originally, Caitlyn followed her table of contents with the heading "Chapter" but decided to erase it in order to include an "Introduction" (Figure 3.1, line 7), the only 3rd grader to do so. Because Budd did not include an introduction in *Horses*, I (Carol) asked Caitlyn about the origin of this idea. She explained, "I have this book on snakes and it has one [an introduction]. It kind of tells what you're going to be talking about in your report, but not too much." This was the first of Caitlyn's many intertextual excursions to other sources. She understood that authors use this organizational feature to acclimate readers to their texts.

Chapter 5. Intrigued by her decision to start her report with Chapter 5 (Figure 3.1, line 10), I inquired as follows:

CAROL: Why are you starting with Chapter 5 instead of Chapter 1?
CAITLYN: I'm going to do it backwards so I'm going to do jumping and riding stuff first.
CAROL: Why is that?
CAITLYN: Because I did the exciting things first so that they'd [readers] keep on reading. They'd get really interested in it [the report] for Jumping and Riding first, and then Breeds.
CAROL: And why is the history chapter last?
CAITLYN: Because if kids read it first, they'll say, "Oh, history" [*groaning*]. But if it's jumping first, they'll say, "Oh, cool, jumping." And then it gets less [interesting] and less and less and less interesting until they're like, "Oh, history. Now I'm interested in horses so I think I'll go read it [history chapter]."

A keen sense of audience awareness informed Caitlyn's organizational scheme. She evaluated and then revised Budd's subtitle sequence, using her own experiences to engage reader interest. Although Caitlyn has yet to learn that audience interest is just one facet to which authors attend when they sequence chapters and that reader interest often hinges on the quality of the author's writing, not the topic per se, there is no question about the vitality of her thought processes.

Parts I, II, and III of Chapter 5. Although many 3rd graders divided their content into chapters, Caitlyn was the only child to understand tacitly that a chapter constitutes a major division of knowledge. Unlike peers who constructed "chapters" that were paragraphs of only three or four sentences, Caitlyn divided the content of Chapter 5 into Part I (Figure 3.1, line 1), Part II (Figure 3.1, line 24), and Part III (Figure 3.1, line 37). Note that she also incorporated four subheads into Part III to set apart each pony game: "Flag race" (line 39), "Sack race" (line 40), "Apple-Bobbing" (line 42), and "Bending" (line 43).

> CAROL: Where did you get the idea to divide Chapter 5 into parts?
> CAITLYN: Well, I've just learned how to jump, so I was talking about my own experiences and what my instructor told me.
> CAROL: Explain how you organized these parts.
> CAITLYN: Well, Part I is just about beginning jumping, about getting into jumping. The next part [Part II] is for teenagers because it's about show jumping and some breeds that I think are really good for show jumping.
> CAROL: And what about Part III?
> CAITLYN: It's just for kids, the fun part of jumping, the races and stuff. It tells you what it all is. If anyone is going to enter something, they need to know what it's about.
> CAROL: Why is Part I listed above the title of your report [see Figure 3.1, line 1]?
> CAITLYN: Because I didn't have room to write it down here [pointing to her title, Chapter 5].
> CAROL: When did you decide to divide Chapter 5 into parts?
> CAITLYN: When I got to the end of beginning jumping, I didn't want keep going with show jumping because it's not the same, so I made Part II.
> CAROL: Now, Jackie Budd doesn't break any of her sections into parts. Where did you get the idea to include parts?
> CAITLYN: I don't really know. Sometimes I see parts in my chapter books.

It was clear that Caitlyn had concluded that Budd's treatment of jumping was inadequate: "It [Budd's book] skips so much about jumping that I am putting in everything so everyone knows more about it."

The juxtaposition of Caitlyn's and Budd's texts suggests that Caitlyn appeared to take issue not only with Budd's light treatment of jumping but also with Budd's organizational decision to spread her jumping content across the book. To rectify this situation, Caitlyn searched Budd's book for any content related to jumping, reorganized it, and added new information in order to create her three-part chapter (see Figure 3.3).

Thus, Caitlyn's strategic decision making shaped the top-level organization of her report. Unlike some of her peers, who allowed original sources to dictate their organizational frameworks, Caitlyn assessed the organizational scheme of her primary source and revised it to suit her purposes.

Budd's Content on Jumping	Caitlyn's Content on Jumping
Pages 12–13. Four illustrations of a jump sweep across the pages. The caption reads: A true jump has five stages: (1) Approach—The horse steadies and dips its head. . . . (2) Take-off—it brings its quarters underneath and lifts its shoulders. . . . (3) Flight—the horse rounds its back and stretches out to clear the fence. (4) Landing—the forelegs . . .	*Part I.* Caitlyn's lead sentence (line 11) paraphrases Budd's caption. The remainder of Part I (lines 12–23), with its discussion of caveletti, crossrail, and vertical jumps, is anchored exclusively in Caitlyn's experiences. None of this content is in Budd's book.
Page 57. Show jumping has the same basic rules for a novice class at a local show and an international championship. The horse and rider must jump a course of colored fences without picking up any faults from knocking one over or refusing. Riders with equal faults go again in a "jump off," which may be timed to decide the winner.	*Part II.* Caitlyn uses Budd's three-sentence paragraph on show jumping to generate a more detailed description of jumping, integrating much personal knowledge and experience (lines 27–35). Caitlyn's attention to vocabulary is notable.
Page 55. In a subsection called, "Ready, get set, go!," Budd writes: Pony club games are like some of the races at a school sports day. The only difference is that the contestants are on horseback. Games include flag races, sack races, apple-bobbing, and bending (racing in and out of a line of poles). (Budd, 1995)	*Part III.* Ignoring Budd's first two sentences, Caitlyn expands Budd's final sentence into a section that describes each game (lines 38–44). Intertextual links are tied to multiple sources.

Figure 3.3. Caitlyn's reorganization and revision of Budd's content on jumping.

Paragraph structure. The same level of intellectual energy that Caitlyn brought to bear on her top-level text structure manifested itself in the organizational flow of sentences in her individual paragraphs. Recall that in Chapter 2 we discussed the strategies the 3rd graders devised while consulting textual sources to construct their paragraphs. The most popular paragraph strategy was selected alignment; many writers crafted paragraphs by selecting some, but not all, sentences from their original sources. The second prominent strategy was self-alignment (creating a paragraph independent of identified sources), followed by multiple alignment (creating a paragraph that merged information from more than one source). Another strategy called perfect alignment was employed by only three 3rd graders; these children essentially wrote paragraphs in which the sequence of their sentences aligned perfectly with that of their original source.

None of Caitlyn's paragraphs was coded as perfect alignment or selected alignment. At no point did Caitlyn allow Jackie Budd, the author of her primary source, to dictate the flow of the sentences in her paragraphs. Rather, Caitlyn remained in charge of her text, sometimes relying solely on her personal knowledge to construct her paragraphs (self-alignment) and sometimes integrating information from one or more sources. Examples of self-aligned paragraphs and multiple-aligned paragraphs follow.

Self-alignment. As mentioned above, Caitlyn commented that Budd gave minimal attention to the art of jumping in her book. To rectify this situation, Caitlyn inserted jumping information in Part I of Chapter 5, information that Budd did not include in her book. The lead sentence in Part I (Figure 3.1, line 11) was a paraphrase of Budd's captioned illustration that briefly described the five stages of a true jump. The remaining text in Part I (Figure 3.1, lines 12–23) on caveletti, cross rails, and small verticals was anchored in Caitlyn's equestrian training. In reference to her illustrated explanation of caveletti jumps, Caitlyn commented, "That's what I had to do first."

When asked about where she had learned about small cross-rail jumps, she noted, "I know that because my instructor told me." Caitlyn organized these paragraphs without the scaffold of a published text—hence the coding of self-alignment. Caitlyn crafted a text structure that paralleled the sequence of her own early jumping experience. Although she had had no prior instruction in the sequence text structure or in the use of signal words such as *first* and *after*, she allowed the nature of her experience to dictate this text structure. Similarly, in the subsequent paragraph on experienced and inexperienced jumpers in shows (Figure 3.1, lines 19–23), Caitlyn organized her information in the text structure of comparison/contrast. Once again, she appeared to choose the text structure warranted by the content. Undoubtedly, Caitlyn's appropriation of these text structures was fed by her informal exposure to sequence and compare/contrast paragraphs in her science and social studies textbooks, in nonfiction read-alouds, and in her recreational reading.

While there is no doubt that Caitlyn could have anchored her horse report solely in her experiences, she, in the spirit of a true nonfiction writer, cast her net wide. We turn now to Caitlyn's paragraphs that were informed by multiple sources.

Multiple alignment. Part III of Caitlyn's report (Figure 3.1, lines 37–44) illuminates an expanse of intertextual connections. Prompting this section of her report was Budd's subsection, presented here in its entirety and accompanied by an illustration of a pony race:

Ready, get set, go!

Pony club races are like some of the races at the school sports day. The only difference is that the contestants are on horseback. Games include flag races, sack races, apple bobbing, and bending (racing in and out of a line of poles). (Budd, 1995, p. 55)

Caitlyn, convinced that readers "might be wondering about all these games," decided to expand Budd's final sentence into a full section of her report. I asked Caitlyn about the sources of her information:

CAROL: Your book [Budd's *Horses*] doesn't explain flag races. How do know about flag races?
CAITLYN: This is flag racing [*pointing to the illustration in* Horses]. You have to come from this side of the ring. And see this cone [*pointing*]. You take the flags out, go around, and put the flags in this cone at this end.
CAROL: How do you know this?
CAITLYN: I've seen it done at shows. And I watched it on the Pony Channel.
CAROL: What is the Pony Channel?
CAITLYN: It's on the Disney Channel—shows all about horses.
CAROL: And did you get your information about sack races from the Pony Channel?
CAITLYN: No, I have a book that said they [the characters in her book] had seen a movie of that and so that's where I got it.
CAROL: What book was that?
CAITLYN: It's a fiction book, but the horse care parts are real. I think it's called *Blue Ribbon*. I read it at home.
CAROL: I'd love to see it. Can you bring it in?

Sure enough, there in Caitlyn's chapter book, *Maxine's Blue Ribbon*, were descriptions of the sack and apple-bobbing race. As you read the following excerpts from *Maxine's Blue Ribbon* and Caitlyn's report, note Caitlyn's ability to transform the language of fiction into the language of nonfiction.

MAXINE'S BLUE RIBBON	CAITLYN'S REPORT
"Wow, a sack race!" Pam said as the next event flashed on the TV screen. A bunch of kids were jumping toward a finish line, their legs stuffed into big cloth bags. And as they jumped, the kids had to lead their horses behind them! (Saunders, 1994, p. 18).	Sack races. You dismount get in a sack and jump in the sack all the way to the finish line. (Figure 3.1, lines 40–41)

Thus, to construct this part on pony games, Caitlyn interwove information from multiple sources: *Horses, Maxine's Blue Ribbon*, the Disney Channel, and her own experiences. She demonstrated this same level of intertextual fluidity in other paragraphs throughout her report.

Orientational Intertextuality: Appropriating the Voices of Others

Orientational intertextuality addresses the degree to which a writer adopts the point of view, or voice, of one or more other sources (e.g., books, people, films, songs, and so on). As discussed in Chapter 2, the 3rd graders were asked about the voice origin of each sentence in their reports ("Where did you learn this information?"). Seven intertextual patterns were noted: direct quote, partial direct quote, textual paraphrase, personal-experience paraphrase, personal-knowledge paraphrase, picture observation, and stylization.

With the exception of the direct quote and picture observation, Caitlyn adopted all of these voices while crafting her report. Not surprisingly, her most prominent pattern was the personal-experience paraphrase. Thirty-eight percent of her sentences connected to her experiences as an equestrian. For example, in Figure 3.4, we note Caitlyn's advanced ability to assess the density of Budd's second sentence and then to unpack its complexity by presenting readers with four coherent, logically sequenced sentences. These four sentences (numbered three through six in the figure) were coded as personal-experience paraphrases. For example, when asked how she knew about the five-point deduction for faults, she replied, "Because I've been in a couple of experienced shows. So whenever my horse did something wrong, they took off five points."

The personal-experience paraphrase, of course, acknowledges that what children learn through firsthand experience is scaffolded by the interactions

Budd's *Horses*	Caitlyn's Report
Show jumping has the same basic rules for a novice class at a local show and an international championship.	1. Show jumping has the same rules as just a working hunter class at a local show.
The horse and rider must jump a course of colored fences without picking up any faults from knocking one over or refusing.	2. The horse must jump a course of 8 or even 10 jumps.
	3. The jumps are colored so that even in the night people can see them.
	4. The horse must clear the jumps without any faults.
	5. Faults are refusing, (stopping in front of the jump), running out, (veering off to one side), or knocking one of the poles off of the jump.
	6. The faults take off 5 points of your original score.
Riders with equal faults go again in a "jump off," which may be timed to decide the winner. (Budd, 1995, p. 57)	7. Riders that have the same amount of points go again in a jumpoff which sometimes is timed.
	8. That's how they decide the winner.

Figure 3.4. Caitlyn's expansion of and alignment with Budd's text. The sentence numbers were added by the investigators for coding purposes.

of more knowledgeable others (Vygotsky, 1978). When asked about the source of her personal knowledge, Caitlyn was forthright in attributing much of it to her riding instructor, family members (also riders), and experts at horse shows.

Also noted in Figure 3.4 are the voice patterns of the partial direct quote and the textual paraphrase. Sentences 1 and 2 were coded as partial direct quotes. Like many of her peers, Caitlyn understood that it is not appropriate to copy verbatim a whole sentence. However, lifting a clause or phrase didn't appear to violate the copying sanction. When asked about the clause in the first sentence, "Show jumping has the same rules," Caitlyn remarked, "But I didn't copy all of it, so it's in my own words." While Caitlyn's report contained six partial direct quotes, a total of nine sentences were coded as textual paraphrases. We have already noted her textual paraphrase of the fictional description of sack races in *Maxine's Blue Ribbon* (Saunders, 1994); other examples include the following:

HORSES	CAITLYN'S REPORT
Riding ponies are suitable for young riders (Budd, 1995, p. 58).	They [referring to her list of ponies in the previous sentence] are great pony's for begining riders.
Jumping a natural fence at a working hunter show class (p. 54 [caption]).	You have to jump coops and fences and natural jumps.

And finally, notable across Caitlyn's report was the orientational pattern called stylization (see Chapter 2). Caitlyn internalized strategies that others use to draw in readers/listeners and infused her report with nine stylizations—statements of dramatic effect, personal opinions, questions, diagrams. For example, to introduce her report (Figure 3.1, lines 8–9), she wrote: "Hi! I am your tour guide for *Horses Around The World*." When asked about the origin of this idea, she replied, "When I was at the racetrack for my first time, there was a tour guide, and he said, 'Hi! I'm your tour guide for the Philadelphia racetrack.'"

Caitlyn recognized the appeal of the guide's introduction and decided to appropriate it for her report. This sentence was coded as stylization—dramatic effect. In another effort to engage her readers, Caitlyn prefaced her Chapter Two, "Breeds," with the statement: "Now we're traviling to breeds" (Figure 3.1, line 44). Caitlyn also incorporated two diagrams of jumping arrangements (caveletti and crossbars) to enhance her report (Figure 3.1, lines 14 and 25). When I noted that Jackie Budd didn't include diagrams in her book and asked about their origin, she commented, "I wanted to show a description so the readers can see what they're being talked to about because it's hard to tell it in words."

Caitlyn ended her report with "A Pony Game," attributing this intertextual connection to Patrick (a peer), "who did a word maze in his math journal and so I got the idea to make a learning game and who wins it will get a ride on my horse."

In conclusion, from her byline to her pony game, Caitlyn laid claim to her report. She understood that effective exposition takes strategic endeavor—searching for appropriate sources, judging the content of these sources in light of accumulated personal knowledge, shaping the direction of a report based on a merger of personal and text knowledge, and keeping reader interest at the forefront.

COLIN: INTERTEXTUAL PATTERNS

Thematic Intertextuality: "So Where Did You
Get the Idea for Your Topic?"

According to Colin's autobiography, he entered 3rd grade with a rather accomplished writing record, noting that he had written "10 stories, three poems, and one song." Interestingly, Colin made no reference to the nonfiction reports he had written in 2nd grade—reports he had saved and proudly shared during interviews. His affinity for story writing was evident in his writer's notebook (see Table 1.2). With the exception of two personal narratives in September, all entries were stories, primarily sports stories such as "Mo Vaughn on Halloween Night," "Rookie Season," and "The Magic Ice Rink." Given Colin's passion for sports, we were surprised when he chose to write about penguins (Figure 3.5).

CAROL: Where did you get the idea to write about penguins?
COLIN: Because I studied penguins last year in 2nd grade.
CAROL: Do you remember in class when Kyle shared his report about dinosaurs and I asked if there were other experts in the room? Do you remember what you said?
COLIN: That I'm an expert on baseball and hockey and all sports.
CAROL: Right, so I'm curious as to why you picked penguins, and not sports.
COLIN: 'Cause everyone was doing animals. Patrick's [who sat at his table] doing reptiles, Caitlyn's doing horses, so I picked penguins because I'm really interested in them and I know a lot about them.

Based on the sports knowledge in his stories, there was no doubt that Colin could have written a report on baseball or hockey. However, he opted to join the club of animal report writers. He chose penguins because of the unspoken norm established by the 3rd graders that there were only two acceptable categories of reports: animals or hobbies (e.g., karate, gymnastics). In accordance with this norm, no other topics were pursued (see Chapter 1).

Influential also in his topic choice was Colin's understanding that in order to write a successful report, he needed to select a topic about which he knew something. When probed about the source of his knowledge about penguins, Colin explained that his 2nd-grade teacher had read books about penguins, had shown films, and had taken the class to the New England Aquarium to observe penguins. He also explained that he had written a report on penguins in 2nd grade that he had brought to school, of his own volition, along with his 2nd-grade penguin handouts that included factual information and

1.	By Colin
2.	Penguins
3.	Chapter 1: The History of Penguins. A long time ago humans thought that penguins were just
4.	birds that could fly and lived everywhere. But now scientists have proved wrong. Because
5.	now we know that penguins are birds that can't fly and can onley live from the equator down
6.	south.
7.	Chapter 2: Penguins Big and Small. Penguins come from the size the small Blue fairy
8.	penguin to the huge Emporer penguin. The Blue Fiary penguin is about1 foot in size. Which
9.	lives in Astraula. The Gallopagose penguin is 2 feet tall in size and lives in the Gallopagose
10.	islands. The king penguin is about 3 feet 8 inches. Who lives in Antarctica and is the second

11.	(page 1)

12.	biggest penguin in size. The emperor penguin is the biggest penguin in size He is exactly 4
13.	feet tall.
14.	Chapter 3: Enemies
15.	Penguins can be eaton very easly, here are some of there enemies. The most dangeorus
16.	enemie of the penguin is, the Killer Whale. The Killer whale usauly feads on emperor
17.	penguins and seals. Another enemie of the penguin is the shark in the summer. Along with
18.	the lepord seal.
19.	Chapter 4: Penguins and Birds
20.	Penguins are very diffrent from birds, because bird lean forward more than Penguins. Also
21.	penguins can toboggan and birds can't because thier feet would get in the thier way.
22.	Penguins also can live in colder climates than birds and birds usauly fly south in the winter

23.	(page 2)

24.	but penguins can't do it because they can't fly!
25.	Chapter 5 Growing up
26.	In this chapter I'm going to tell you how a King penguin is hatched and how it grows up!
27.	first what happens the mother lays her egg and keeps it on her feet. Soon the penguin is
28.	ready to break out. It starts to chip away the edges. after it is out of the egg the penguin finds
29.	that the weather is cold and it doesn't have it's fluffy feathers yet! The baby sits on his
30.	mothers or fathers feet to keep worm. The penguin is now two months old and has grown it's
31.	downy feathers. He and other baby penguins huddle together to keep warm and safe. the

32.	(page 3)

33.	penguin is eight months old now and his parents are out fishing. When they come home they
34.	have food for him. The penguin is now losing it's fluffy feathers. Soon he will be able to
35.	swim. he is 13 months old now and his yellow feathers are turning orange and has a steak of
36.	pink on his beak.
37.	The End
38.	(Illustration of a penguin)

39.	(page 4)

Figure 3.5. Colin's (grade 3) four-page nonfiction report, "Penguins."

penguin poetry. As interviews continued over time, Colin also explained that he owned penguin books, one of which he brought to school to use for his report. Like Caitlyn, Colin entered into the act of report writing with a bank of knowledge. However, unlike Caitlyn, Colin's knowledge, for the most part, was outside the domain of his personal experience. While he had observed penguins at the New England Aquarium, he did not possess the cumulative firsthand experience that Caitlyn possessed. But, then, neither do many accomplished nonfiction writers. As Joanna Cole (1996), author of the *Magic School Bus* books, confesses:

> You probably know Arnold, the kid who likes to stay home who doesn't want to get too messy, too cold, too involved in anything. The kid who would rather watch a filmstrip than be an astronaut. Arnold is like me, too. I spend most of my time reading and writing. I sometimes thank my lucky stars that I am not at this moment on an expedition to the North Pole. (p. 31)

This lack of firsthand experience, however, did not prevent Colin or Joanna Cole from doing what nonfiction writers do: consulting multiple resources, absorbing and integrating information in order to hone a point of view. Thus, while the merger of personal experience and text/media knowledge is an optimal condition for nonfiction writing, it is not the only condition.

Organizational Intertextuality: "Where Did You Get the Idea to Organize Your Report This Way?"

Top-level text organization. Like Caitlyn, Colin accessed multiple resources while writing his report but allowed none to monopolize the organizational flow of his report. Colin's experience with nonfiction literature manifested itself in his decision to divide his report into chapters and to assign chapter headings to each. None of the trade books or teacher handouts that he consulted organized information into chapters; both of his primary sources used only headings. In addition, Colin's 2nd-grade report on penguins contained only two headings: "Emperor Habitat" and "Emperor Interesting facts." When asked where he got the idea to divide his information into chapters, he acknowledged the influence of a peer: "I just picked it up somewhere. Oh, now I know. When Jessica did her report on fossils [on the overhead], she put in Chapter 1." Jessica's report as well as his textbooks were two of probably many sources that contributed to his awareness about chapters.

What set Colin and Caitlyn apart from their peers was their ability to transcend the print materials in order to bring to bear their own sensibility. As reported earlier, Caitlyn rejected Budd's minimal treatment of horse jumping and decided to craft a full chapter on jumping, which she presented in three "parts" across three pages. Colin evidenced this same degree of independence by beginning his report with two self-generated chapters: "The History of the Penguins" (Figure 3.3, lines 3–6) and "Penguins Big and Small" (Figure 3.5, lines 7–13). None of his sources, including his 2nd-grade report, contained these headings or included content on history or on the comparative sizes of penguins.

> CAROL: Where did you get the idea to write a history chapter?
> COLIN: Well, I learned about it [the history] in the movies we saw in 2nd grade, about how people used to think penguins could fly, but they can't.
> CAROL: Why did you start your report with the history chapter instead of, for example, starting with the chapter "Penguins Big and Small?"
> COLIN: So people could know about the penguin and where it lives and just the true facts about it. If people thought that penguins lived all around the Earth, you could set them straight and tell them they only live from the equator down.
> CAROL: So you wanted readers to know the correct facts first. Tell me where you got the idea for Chapter 2. None of your books had a section that told about the sizes of different penguins.
> COLIN: Well, I learned about so many penguins in 2nd grade and I just remembered how big they were.
> CAROL: Did Ms. S show a chart that showed the sizes of various penguins?
> COLIN: No, but she had a blow-up balloon of the Emperor penguin who is four feet tall, so I got the idea to do from the smallest one to the biggest, which is the Emperor.

Thus, without consultation of print materials, Colin relied on his recall of information learned in 2nd grade and on his tacit understanding about exposition to structure his first two chapters. He then moved across multiple sources to construct his three remaining chapters, orchestrating a fairly logical flow. Colin acknowledged that he appropriated the title of his third chapter, "Enemies" (3.5, line 14), from *The Penguin* (Weaver, 1983), which contained a section called "Enemies of the Penguin." When asked why, unlike in his first two chapters, he had physically moved his paragraph under his Chapter 3 heading, Colin explained that this was the way it was in *The Penguin* and he copied the idea.

To create his heading, "Chapter 4: Penguins and Birds" (Figure 3.5, line 19), Colin, to our amazement, brought to school a penguin worksheet that he had completed in 2nd grade. He rejected the worksheet's title, "Moving on Land, Snow and Ice," deciding to paraphrase the worksheet directions: "Compare a penguin with a bird you see often, such as a sparrow" (Bernard, 1994, p. 39).

Colin then traveled to yet another source, *Penguin* (Ling, 1993), to compose his final chapter on the life cycle of the penguin, "Growing Up" (Figure 3.5, lines 25–36). Ling's book, written for emergent readers, is organized into eight two-page sections, each with its own heading (e.g., "Hatching in the cold," "Keeping warm"). Each section contains a total of five or six sentences with colorful penguin photographs. To design his chapter title, "Growing Up," Colin chose to paraphrase the series title, "See How They Grow," which appears above *Penguin* on the title page of the book. He then ignored Ling's headings, but used the content in each section to draft his final paragraph (see Figure 3.6). Colin's text has been parsed to show the alignment.

Paragraph organization. At the paragraph level, we continue to witness Colin's cognitive versatility. An engaging example of Colin's ability to integrate information from multiple sources into one paragraph is found in "Chapter 4: Penguins and Birds" (Figure 3.5, lines 19–24). As already noted, Colin appropriated the idea for this chapter from his 2nd-grade worksheet (Bernard, 1994). He surveyed this worksheet, which asked the reader to examine a penguin and a sparrow and to answer questions such as the following:

- What might happen if the penguin leaned forward like the sparrow?
- Sparrows can't toboggan like the penguins below. What might get in their way if they tried? (p. 39).

He used these questions (and his answers) to draft his first two sentences (Figure 3.5, lines 20–21). He then moved from this worksheet to his 2nd-grade report about Antarctica in order to write the first part of his third sentence, and then finished the sentence with information he had learned from his 2nd-grade teacher.

This pattern of merging personal knowledge and text knowledge occurred in all but Colin's first and final chapters. In his final chapter, he selectively aligned his text with that of *Penguin* (Ling, 1993). As Figure 3.6 shows, Colin attended closely to the author's flow of sentences, choosing only those sentences that he deemed central to his message.

Orientational Intertextuality: Appropriating the Voices of Others

Figure 3.6 also showcases Colin's advanced understanding about voice in nonfiction text. In comparing Colin's text with the original, note not only his skill at paraphrasing but also his genre-appropriate language. Colin transformed the atypical expository language of this book into the standard

Ling's *Penguin*	Colin's Report
	1. In this chapter I'm going to tell you how a king penguin is hatched and how it grows up!
My mother has laid her egg. She keeps it warm on her feet.	2. first what happens the mother lays her egg and keeps it on her feet.
I am growing inside the egg. I am the King penguin.	
I am ready to break out of my egg.	3. Soon the penguin is ready to break out.
I chip away the tough shell. It takes ages!	4. It starts to chip away the edges.
At last, I am free!	
I am one day old. It is very chilly out, even though the sun is shining. My fluffy feathers have not grown in yet. Brr! (Ling, 1993, pp. 6–8)	5. after it is out of the egg the penguin finds that the weather is cold and it doesn't have it's fluffy feathers yet!

Figure 3.6. Colin selectively aligned his text with Ling's. The sentence numbers were added by the investigators for coding purposes.

language of exposition: He substituted the third-person pronoun *it* or the word *penguin* for the book's first-person pronoun *I* and maintained the verb tense (present, not past) characteristic of exposition. While such sensitivity to the linguistic patterns of the nonfiction genre has been demonstrated by researchers (Duke & Kays, 1998; Kamberelis & Bovino, 1999; Pappas, 1991, 1993), Colin's ability to operate on his intertext at this level is notable.

While Caitlyn's most prominent voice pattern was the personal-experience paraphrase, Colin's was the textual paraphrase. Unable to call on extended direct experience with penguins, Colin did what most nonfiction writers do—paraphrased information from various sources. Seventy-five percent of his sentences were coded as textual paraphrases; another 18% were personal-knowledge paraphrases attributed to his 2nd-grade teacher. His knowledge about paraphrasing surfaced during the first week of instruction in connection with a class discussion about the criteria of a good report (see Phase 3 section in Chapter 1). In talking about whether the 3rd graders thought that Joanna Cole copied sentences from another book when she wrote *Hungry, Hungry Sharks*, Colin replied, "No. You have to say it in your own words or it's like stealing." Later, when probing the source of this knowledge, Colin explained that his 2nd-grade teacher had told the class that when writing their penguin reports, "We could say something like it [the book], but we had to say it in a different way." Colin abided by this instruction, incorporating no direct quotes and only two partial direct quotes into his report.

Finally, Colin's report contained two stylizations. The first is at the beginning of "Chapter 5" (Figure 3.5, line 26): "In this chapter I'm going to tell you how a King penguin is hatched and how it grows up!" With this statement, Colin introduced readers to the thesis of his chapter and attempted to interject enthusiasm with his use of the exclamation point. He also included an illustration of a penguin at the end of his report (Figure 3.5). In asking Colin what he did to keep readers interested, he replied, "I just did different topics so like it wasn't about one topic because after you kept reading and reading [about one topic], you'd get bored so I did different things like enemies and growing up and told all the interesting facts." Colin reminds us that ultimately it is the author's ability to weave intriguing details into the nonfiction story that holds the reader.

STRATEGIC WRITERS: PROFILE SUMMARY

Multiple Sources, Extended Knowledge, Self-Directed Writing

Children, like adults, dip into a vast and varied well of texts—oral or written—when creating nonfiction pieces. Caitlyn and Colin accessed multiple sources while writing their reports. Each had experienced his or her topic firsthand, learned from experts or more knowledgeable others, read a number of trade books, and watched media programs.

They appeared to choose their topics with the understanding that nonfiction writing requires a rich knowledge of and fascination with a subject, accumulated over time and in a variety of ways. Nonfiction writing was not what it was for some of their peers: Read a line in a text and then write it in your own words or just copy. Rather, it was a process of strategic decision making. They used their knowledge to chart the direction of their reports; they consulted text sources but did not allow these sources to dictate their focus.

Appropriation of Multiple Voices and Perspective-Taking

The most lively manifestation of voice occurred in the stylized statements that Caitlyn and Colin wove into their reports. Without any instruction, they called on one or more of the strategies that advertisers, authors, and speakers use to engage audiences: statements of dramatic effect, questions, personal opinions, and illustrations. Caitlyn in particular demonstrated sensitivity to the issue of audience, integrating nine stylized statements into her report. Because a number of 3rd graders also infused stylized statements into their reports, especially the experience-only writers (see Chapter 4), this dimension of voice may be a powerful starting point for discussion about ways in which writers leave their imprint on reports.

Bakhtin's (1981) claim that texts echo other texts is borne out not only in Caitlyn's and Colin's stylizations but also in the substance of their reports. Both readily acknowledged the voices that they appropriated. At times, they cited people who had conveyed the information; at other times, they cited the texts that they had consulted. When these texts were examined, it was evident that both children were fairly adept at paraphrasing others' words. They understood that, in Colin's words, "You have to say it in your own words or it's like stealing." Neither Caitlyn nor Colin included unmarked direct quotes; however, both included a small percentage of partial direct quotes, sentences that are part paraphrase and part direct quote. Their use of these partial direct quotes signals the need for more extended discussion and demonstration. It is important for young writers to know that borrowing text as minimal as a phrase still necessitates quotation marks. Moreover, it is helpful for them to understand that while the paraphrase is the standard form of appropriation, there are times when writers use direct quotes to lend authority to their piece or to enhance it with eloquent or riveting language.

Striking about their reports, as compared to those of their peers, was the degree of perspective-taking that Caitlyn and Colin adopted. Each had a nascent understanding of the kind of perspective-taking that nonfiction writers adopt as they research a topic in order to find their point of view. Both strove to delineate for readers what they believed to be important about their topic. With ongoing discussion about how acclaimed nonfiction writers stalk the terrain of their topics to hone their point of view, we make conscious what strategic writers understand tacitly (see Chapter 6).

Titles, Bylines, Multiple Chapters: Organizing the Nonfiction Report

Caitlyn and Colin possessed a working knowledge about the organizational dimensions of the nonfiction report. Although none of the textual sources they read were divided into chapters, both organized their content into numbered chapters, assigning a heading to each chapter. While discussions about how authors organize information under headings took place during our instructional sessions, no attention was given to what a chapter is, to how books are divided into chapters, or to the difference between chapter headings and section headings. Yet Caitlyn and Colin brought this knowledge, gleaned from exposure to nonfiction trade books, textbooks, and peers' reports, to their report writing. While a number of 3rd graders strung their chapters together by consulting one or more books and by selectively aligning their chapter titles with those of the original sources, Caitlyn and Colin distanced themselves from original sources in order to generate their own chapter headings ("parts" in Caitlyn's case). Both relied on their accumulated knowledge about their topics, in conjunction with textual sources, to chart the top-level structure of their reports. For example, while none of the books Colin used to write his report on penguins contained a section on the history of penguins or on the comparative sizes of penguins, he opened his report with these two self-generated chapters. It is this level of independent analysis and decision making that we want to bring to children's attention, along with the idea that authors give much thought to the sequence of their headings or chapters before, during, and after they write.

While both incorporated chapters, Caitlyn was the only 3rd grader to understand tacitly that a chapter is a major division of content. Her first chapter on jumping was four and a half pages in length, subdivided into three parts. Colin, on the other hand, like many of his peers, viewed a chapter as a paragraph of content, averaging about three or four sentences in length. Although young writers have yet to internalize the intricacies of text organization, their global understandings provide us with important teaching opportunities. We can begin by acknowledging these understandings and, through the use of quality trade books and research reports, work to refine this knowledge.

The strategic thought that characterized Caitlyn's and Colin's ability to orchestrate the top-level structures of their reports also characterized their ability to craft individual paragraphs. Rather than aligning the sentence flow of their paragraphs with the flow of original sources as many 3rd graders did, Colin and Caitlyn merged information from more than one source to generate their paragraphs. Caitlyn, for example, when constructing her paragraph on breeds, opened with a sentence derived from her own experience, followed this with three paraphrases of information she had learned on the Pony Channel, and ended with partial direct quotes from *Horses* (Budd, 1995). By repeatedly modeling how information from two or more sources can be integrated to create effective paragraphs, we can help children adopt the stance of a true nonfiction writer.

To conclude, this chapter has illuminated the multifaceted intertextual knowledge that Caitlyn and Colin brought to the genre of report writing, much of it appropriated from nonfiction literature and life experiences. As strategic writers, they knew that nonfiction writers use the following strategies:

- Consulting multiple sources (book, people, and media) to extend their knowledge base
- Charting the direction of their text, informed by multiple resources but not governed by them

- Dividing information into chapters
- Crafting paragraphs that integrate information learned from multiple sources
- Including their own experiences when appropriate
- Paraphrasing the ideas of others
- Stylizing statements to engage readers

Indeed, this expanse of understanding is impressive. However, this is not suggest that Caitlyn and Colin have mastered the complexity of report writing. For example, while both children extracted information from multiple sources, neither took notes while reading. While they both engaged in mental planning, they did so during the act of composing, not beforehand—no organizing webs or simple outlines were used. Both children wrote only first drafts of their reports; neither child revisited their reports to add, delete, or rearrange information.

The extent to which young children can grasp these and other understandings through instruction is unknown. Further research needs to be undertaken, especially in light of the Many and colleagues' (1996) finding that "the research subtasks—planning, searching, finding, recording, reviewing, and presenting" (p. 31) are so complex that even 6th graders have difficulty executing and integrating these tasks.

Given this caveat, Caitlyn and Colin remind us, though, not to underestimate the cognitive powers of children. Through interactions with peers, teachers, and others, they actively make sense of the world around them and then use this knowledge to participate in an array of social and literacy contexts. Through continual analysis of their social-constructive activity, we can ascertain the extent of their understandings and provide context-based instruction to fill in the gaps and to advance their knowledge. In essence, when we know what children can do through their own independent problem solving and what they can do with guidance from more knowledgeable others, we set the stage for optimal learning (Vygotsky, 1978).

Experience-Only Nonfiction Writers: Vanessa and Kristin

To launch the first lesson of our instructional phase (see the Phase 3 section in Chapter 1), I (Carol) placed Kyle's report, titled "fossils and Dinosaurs," on the overhead and asked him to read it. I asked the class where they thought he got the idea to write this report, recording their ideas on the board:

SARAH: From a book about fossils?
KRISTIN: From a magazine like *Time For Kids* because they had something about digging for dinosaurs.
DANIELLE: From our science book, which has stuff about fossils too.
CAROL: Kyle, will you circle the source or sources that gave you the idea? [*He circles the science book.*]
KYLE: We were learning about fossils in science. And I know a lot about fossils because I dug up dinosaur bones at Roger Williams Park and I saw lots of fossils in the museum [at the park]. . . . [*Excitement builds as students ask questions about the dinosaur dig.*]
CAROL: How fortunate we are to have two beginning experts on fossils [Jessica had also shared her fossil report]. And my guess is that there are other experts in this room who know a lot about particular nonfiction topics. For example, who in this room is an expert on horses?
CLASS: Caitlyn!
CAROL: Right. Who else is a beginning expert on a nonfiction topic?
PATRICK: I'm an expert on reptiles like snakes, Hilo monsters, and lizards. And John and me are experts on hockey and football. [*Begins a rush of other sports' experts.*]
PHIL: Vanessa is an actress; she takes acting lessons.
VANESSA: Phil is a blue belt in karate.

Taking our lead from writing experts such as Donald Graves and Lucy Calkins, we sent the message that successful nonfiction writing can be anchored in life experiences:

My dream is that all our classrooms will be filled with fanatics: with bird-watchers, detectives, rock hounds, star-gazers, with bands of enthusiasts that form around submarine models, sprouted acorns, and a barnacle-covered rock. . . . When children's interests and observations are invited into the classroom, the writing workshop will contain informational writing and children will move easily between nonfiction and all other genres. (Calkins, 1994, p. 434)

Five of our 18 3rd graders heeded our call for "budding experts"; four were categorized as experience-only writers because they relied exclusively on their personal experiences when drafting their reports. (Caitlyn, the fifth writer, whose report was presented in Chapter 3, was categorized as a strategic writer because she didn't restrict her report writing to personal experience.) In this chapter, we examine the reports of two experience-only writers: Kristin and Vanessa. (Danielle's topical fish report and Phil's karate report are referenced periodically.) As Table 1.1 reveals, Kristin's literacy level was rated advanced, while Vanessa was performing on grade level. Because these young writers did not consult any print material while crafting their pieces, they provide a window on intertextual patterns that are steeped in social interaction. We begin with thematic intertextuality—the genesis of their ideas for report writing.

"SO WHERE DID YOU GET THE IDEA FOR YOUR TOPIC?"

Vanessa: Thematic Intertextuality

During the second week of phase 3, Vanessa began her piece on acting (Figure 4.1). Up to this point, her writer's notebook had evidenced a strong af-

---

1. Acting

2. Hi! My name is Vanessa. Come Here. I'll show you around. If you want to do acting you

3. have to sighn up when you do you'll get a skirpt. And he/she will give you a part! You'll

4. have to partice and parctice! Then you have dress resreae [rehearsal]! The derector has to see

5. how fast you can dress. Because you have to chage real fast so you can have a new costume

6. on when you go on the stage. And you have a cuple of minits. And then on the day of the

7. play you go on the stage when its your turn and say your line. But if you mess up Just keep

8. going because the adicic [audience] will not know that you did a mistak.

9. The End

Figure 4.1. Vanessa's (grade 3) nonfiction report, anchored exclusively in personal experience.

finity for story writing (see Table 1.2). While Vanessa penned a few personal narratives during September, she was one of the first to shift to fiction, amassing a total of 16 stories by December, varying in length from one to six pages. Story titles such as "Anastasia takes over," "The girl who cird [cried] mice," and "The tale of nothing" revealed her appropriation of literature (Judy Blume's (1972) *Tales of a Fourth Grade Nothing* was a read-aloud); others such as "The Haunted Mainchon," "Tower of teror," and "The three whithis [witches]" were anchored in the Halloween writing spree that had taken hold of this classroom.

When the call for "experts" was made during the opening instructional session, Phil announced Vanessa an expert in acting. Vanessa reciprocated, noting Phil's blue belt in karate. Such public acknowledgment translated into reports by both.

> CAROL: Tell me about your acting lessons.
> VANESSA: I do acting—for 5 years. I know all about acting and what you're supposed to do and I decided that I just want to write about it.
> CAROL: My goodness, 5 years is a long time.
> VANESSA: Cause I've been in more than five plays. First it was "Little Drum." I was a little drum soldier. I dropped my little stick thing and I said "grrrrrrr" by accident and I picked it up and everybody laughed at me of course. And I was Bo-Peep, and then I was Jill in Jack and Jill, and that time I really had to change fast because in one part I was Jill and then I had to run upstairs, change into my summer shoes, and wait and go back on. And then I was princess, and I was a clown, and now I'm a person from outer space.

Vanessa continued to speak about acting with much authority, elaborating on the details noted in her report. When asked if she had consulted any books/materials while writing her piece, she noted that she'd never seen any books on acting.

Kristin: Thematic Intertextuality

Kristin, one of the strongest writers in the classroom, was one of the last children to compose a nonfiction report, "Gymnastics" (Figure 4.2). Her writing life prior to this nonfiction was anchored in personal narratives (see Table 1.2). In a classroom where children had total control over their choice of topics and genres, Kristin chose to write only personal narratives about home and school events during September, October, and November. So did the two other children, Kyle and Josie, at Kristin's table. Kyle was the first to digress by beginning a nonfiction report on fossils and dinosaurs. On

Gymnastic's by:
Hi! My name is _____.
I'm good at gymnastic's. Come on
I'll show you around the gym.
These are the un-even bars. You
can do things like, a pull-over,
and a pull-over-hip circle. This is the horse.
On the horse you can do things
like, jump, stands. This is the floor
you can do, handstands, cartwheels
hand stand forward rolls, and
forward rolls. You do things like this
in the Olmpics. You also do
things like, flips for the floor.
On the beam, in the Olmpics it's pretty
hard. The gymnasts learn to do
cartwheels on the beam! And
back flips and front flips and
stuff. All the time gymnasts are
getting gold metals. But sometim
es they make a mistake. And
they don't get to much credit!
But they try there Best. And even
though it's hard, they love it!

Figure 4.2. Kristin's (grade 3) nonfiction report, anchored in personal experience and the media.

the same day, Kristin began her first story of the year, called "Dazzling Diamonds," which was six pages in length, complete with nine chapters and chapter headings. As if to remain in solidarity with Kyle, who had decided to write about a curricular topic that had been studied in class, Kristin, too, chose to appropriate the content of a nonfiction magazine article the class had just read:

> CAROL: Where did you get the idea to do a story on diamonds?
> KRISTIN: Well, *Time for Kids*. It was an article called "Dazzling Diamonds." And I liked it so much I wanted to make up a story about it. And I wanted to put myself in it and I wanted to have a big brother, so I put Kyle in it.
> CAROL: Is there anything in your story that was mentioned in the article?
> KRISTIN: Well, it talks about the Blue Hope Diamond at the end of it.
> CAROL: And is the Blue Hope Diamond in your story?
> KRISTIN: Well, it's going to be at the end of it, but I haven't written about it yet.
> CAROL: I love this part of the story [*reading excerpt*]: "So Kristin ran back home and got their dad's tool's. Kristin took the hammer, wrench and screwdriver. Kristin tried the hammer, split in two. Tried the wrench, got twisted. Tried the screwdriver, blade chipped off. . . ." Where did you get the idea to write it this way?
> KRISTIN: I don't know. I just thought it up that way.
> CAROL: Are there any stories or poems you've read that used that kind of language?
> KRISTIN: No. I just thought of that.
> CAROL: Does the article in *Time for Kids* talk about how to chip diamonds from rocks?
> KRISTIN: Yeah. You chip it like this [*demonstrating*], like a thousand times to get it out.

Kyle drew on the content of fossils studied in class to write a piece about the same topic (co-thematic), in the same voice (co-orienting), and in the same genre (co-generic) as his social studies textbook (Lemke, 1992). Kristin also appropriated content (mining diamonds) she had read but chose to shift the genre and voice in her exploration of this topic. While this phenomenon was not within the purview of our study, we noted conversations with other 3rd graders who used nonfiction content to prompt fictional pieces. For example, Phil incorporated content learned in class about the food pyramid into two different stories and the content about the weather into another story. Other than preliminary research that documents this cross-genre activity (Cairney, 1990; Lancia, 1997), little is known about the intertextual links that young writers forge as they transfer nonfiction content to fiction. Given the recent interest in multigenre research projects (Allen & Swistak, 2004; Broaddus & Ivey, 2002; Grierson, Anson, & Baird, 2002; Romano, 1995, 2000), further research on co-thematic, genre-switching texts of young writers would be beneficial in order to document the expanse of children's intertextual understandings and to extend instructional theory and practice.

By the time Kristin began writing her nonfiction piece on gymnastics (Figure 4.2) in January, she was surrounded by nonfiction writers. When asked about the origin of her piece, Kristin replied, "Well, I do gymnastics." Kristin had been taking lessons for 3 years and was eager to explain and demonstrate moves such as a "pullover-hip circle." When asked about the source of her knowledge about the Olympics, she credited the media: "Because I've seen the Olympics on TV and I do jump stands and cartwheels and things like that at my gymnastics school where I do it, so I remembered it."

To conclude, two parallels can be drawn with respect to the thematic intertextuality of the four experience-only writers in the class. First, all wrote their nonfiction reports only after a call was sounded for budding "experts." Prior to this call, these writers may not have viewed their expertise as worthy of report writing. Thus, we may need to help children understand that "writers learn to breathe in the world wherever they are: in a bathtub, bed, church, Salvation Army" (Fletcher, 1996, p. 32)—or in a gym or on a stage. Second, the children who answered the call did so with a confidence rooted not only in personal experience but also in formal instruction. Three of the four experience-only writers (Vanessa, Kristin, and Phil) had been taking after-school lessons in their particular recreational activity for at least 2 years; Danielle had taken lessons in scuba diving and snorkeling during a number of trips with her parents.

"WHERE DID YOU GET THE IDEA TO ORGANIZE YOUR REPORT THIS WAY?"

During interviews, all 3rd graders were asked if they had consulted print materials while writing their drafts. Our experience-only writers confirmed our observations that no published materials were consulted during writing workshop. Thus, they organized their reports without the scaffold of text sources. In this section, we address the intertextual influences at both the top-level text organization and paragraph organization levels.

Top-Level Text Organization

Analysis of the four experience-only reports revealed marked similarity with respect to top-level organization. In contrast to the reports of the strategic writers such as Caitlyn and Colin (Chapter 3) that were coded multiple alignment (e.g., chapter headings or section headings created by consulting two to four resources), the reports of these writers were coded title-only. The only organizational feature in each report was its title (e.g., "Acting"). Like authors of photo essays (e.g., Simon in *Sharks* [1995] and *Earthquakes* [1991b]) or easy-to-read nonfiction (e.g., Cole in *Hungry, Hungry Sharks* [1986b]) who employ this basic top-level structure, our experience-only writers included a title followed by one page of continuous text with no division of content.

The organizational similarity across reports was a curious phenomenon in light of their exposure to Jessica's fossil report, which contained a title and content divided into "chapters" with chapter numbers and headings, and to direct instruction in headings (see Phase 3 section in Chapter 1). In retrospect, it would have been interesting to ask the experience-only writers to compare the top-level organization of their reports to Caitlyn's report (Figure 3.1).

Paragraph Organization

While many of their peers created paragraphs by consulting at least one published text and then aligning the sentences in their paragraphs to varying degrees with these sources, the experience-only writers had no such tangible scaffold. To construct their paragraphs, they established the purpose of their pieces (e.g., explain how to act) and then adopted text structures that "flowed naturally from the content" (Bamford & Kristo, 1998, p. 29). The result was use of the text structures that researchers have identified as prominent in exposition:

- *Description.* A text structure that includes information about the characteristics of a topic (person, event, idea) and employs signal words (also called connectives), such as *for example, in fact, characteristics are,* and *most important.*
- *Sequence.* A text structure in which events, ideas, or steps are logically and sequentially ordered and which uses signal words such as *first, then, finally, before,* and *after.*
- *Compare/contrast.* A text structure that details how two or more things are alike and/or unlike and uses signal words such as *alike, similar, different, in contrast, on the other hand,* and *however.*

- *Cause and effect.* A text structure that explains how events (effects) occur because of other events (causes) and uses signal words such as *because, therefore, if . . . then, thus,* and *as a result.*
- *Problem/solution.* A text structure that describes a problem and offers possible solutions and employs signal words such as *problem, question, solution, solved, answer,* and *if . . . then.* (Meyer, 1975; Meyer, Brant, & Bluth, 1980; on description, see also Vacca & Vacca, 1999)

Of course, most text structures are rarely found in pure form; authors often embed one or more structures in their pieces.

In all likelihood, our experience-only writers constructed passages that adhered to one or more of these text structures by summoning knowledge abstracted from their previous exposure to expository texts. These intertextual sources ranged from their science and social studies textbooks to nonfiction trade books to television programs and documentaries. We turn now to the insights of the young authors themselves.

Vanessa: Organizational intertextuality. Vanessa approached her piece on acting (Figure 4.1) as follows:

CAROL: Did you have a plan about how to organize this report before you started writing?

VANESSA: Huh?

CAROL: Did you write down some ideas about how you might want to organize this report before you started writing it?

VANESSA: No, I'd just stop and think and I say, "Now what do you do next?" And I'd say, "Oh yeah" and write it down.

CAROL: So you told readers the steps that they would follow if they were going to act in a play?

VANESSA: Yeah, I told everything from the beginning to the end so they'd know what to do. Like the first thing you have to do is change into your costume. You have to go out there and do your part in front of the audience and then you have to come back in. If you have another part, and if you have to get changed real fast, you have to go.

Vanessa was forthright about not preplanning this report. She essentially planned as she went, driven by the question, "Now what do you do next?" This question prompted the construction of a sequence text structure, from signing up for acting class, to practicing a script, to participating in a dress rehearsal, to finally executing the actual performance. Vanessa included a few temporal connectives such as *when, then,* and *on the day of* to alert readers to her sequence text structure.

It became clear during interviews that Vanessa's knowledge about acting far exceeded the skeletal sequence charted in the report. After reading certain sentences, Vanessa, of her own volition, digressed from the text to elaborate on that particular step in the sequence. For example, with regard to her sentence about getting a script (Figure 4.1, line 3), she noted, "The first time you come [to acting class], there's all these pages spread out and you get one, two, three, four, five [pages], you know, the one you make into a script. So then we put it into this folder and staple it and then you get a script." With regard to lines 3–4 ("You'll have to practice and practice!"), Vanessa remarked, "The week before the play, when you go up on stage . . . when the chairs are all set up and everything and the lights are shining on you, but no people are there and you have to see what you can do. But if you don't want that line, you can cut it off."

Vanessa, like most nonfiction writers, subsumed other text structures into her primary text structure of sequence. For example, she ended her piece with a problem/solution pattern: "But if you mess up, just keep going because the audience will not know that you did a mistake." This rather abrupt ending may be attributed to the fact that it was written the day before winter break. However, during the interview, Vanessa rounded out the sequence: "So then on the day of the play, you go out and say your lines, and, at the last part, they call your name and you have to go out there and stand in the position that you're supposed to stand. And then they don't throw roses at you, but you go down and take pictures and everything and there's a snack bar."

Kristin: Organizational intertextuality. After Kristin read her piece on gymnastics (Figure 4.2), I (Carol) commented, "I love how you organized this. Did you have a plan in your head before you started to write?" With the same look of confusion noted on Vanessa's face, Kristin asked, "Can you ask that question again?" Kristin, Vanessa, and a number of their peers gave anecdotal support to Bereiter and Scardamalia's (1987) finding that young writers do not separate planning from writing. Rather, they "plan only one point at a time" (p. 169), subscribing to a "think-write-think-write pattern" (p. 197).

> When in exploratory interviews, we told children that adults sometimes think for 15 minutes or more before starting to write, many children were incredulous. They could not imagine what there was to think about for that length of time. They were inclined, in fact, to think that such a slow start was a sign of incompetence and that expert writers, being smarter, should be quicker off the mark. (Bereiter & Scardamalia, 1987, p. 197)

With clarification, Kristin was able to explain how she organized her report:

CAROL: Well, this might have been your plan, [*reading from her piece*] "I'll show around the gym—the uneven bars." and then you tell about that.

KRISTIN: Yeah, 'cause as soon as you walk in the door you see the uneven bars first. Because this is the door [*taking out a piece of paper and drawing the floor plan*] and this is the uneven bars. And the horse is over here, and the floor is right in the middle. And the beams are over way, way right behind the horse.

CAROL: So, when I walk in, the first thing I see is the bar.

KRISTIN: Then the horse, then the floor. And I didn't put in the beam [*adding to floor plan*].

CAROL: So you organized this first half of your report by taking the reader on a tour of the gym. You tell the reader what he or she will see in the order of where things are placed in the room.

KRISTIN: Right. This comes first [*pointing to the bars on the diagram*], then this [*pointing to the horse on the diagram*].

Bereiter and Scardamalia (1987) put Vanessa's and Kristin's plan-as-you-write approach into perspective:

> The fact that children do little planning in advance of starting to write does not mean that they do not plan during other phases of composition. It is by now well known that expert writers often do much of their planning while they write rather than before they start writing. Nevertheless, planning in expert writers stands out as a distinct mental activity, concentrating largely though not exclusively in the early phases of producing a composition. (p. 194)

It is interesting to juxtapose Kristin's plan for organizing her report (a tour of the gym) with the report itself. Given her comments, the reader might expect a sequence report detailing the order in which the gym equipment is arranged, complete with temporal connectives such as *first, then,* and *last.* However, the sequence in Kristin's head doesn't materialize on paper. Rather, she seemed to employ a descriptive text structure, organizing her knowledge of the gym into a series of related couplets, which Newkirk (1987) describes as "two clause-units. These might include: identification + information, question + answer, statement + reason, or statement + example" (p. 126). Examples of Kristin's "identification + information" couplets include:

> These are the uneven bars. You can do things like, a pull-over and pull-over hip circle. This is the horse. On the horse you can do things like, jumpstand's. (Figure 4.2, lines 5–9)

In the second half of her report, Kristin shifted the text structure to comparison/contrast, both comparing her gymnastics preparation with that of the Olympics (Figure 4.2, lines 12–13) and contrasting it with Olympic contenders who must perform "cartwheels on the beam! And back flips and front flips" (lines 17–18) which she acknowledged were "pretty hard."

In sum, we noticed pronounced similarity among our experience-only writers with respect to organizational intertextuality. Without the scaffold of print material, each organized his or her report in the exact same fashion, namely, a title followed by a full page of continuous text. None divided the report into chapters or headed sections. To generate the content of the report, each ruminated about the nature of his or her firsthand experience and intuitively settled on a text structure (e.g., sequence, description, etc.) that aligned with his or her way of knowing.

APPROPRIATING THE VOICES OF OTHERS: ORIENTATIONAL INTERTEXTUALITY

Two types of voice appropriation predominated in the reports of our experience-only writers: stylizations, which are paraphrases that "contain both the semantic intention of the original source and the more personal intention of the child author" (Kamberelis & Scott, 1992, p. 371), and personal-experience paraphrases, which are restatements of information learned as a result of active participation in recreational lessons.

Stylizations

Statements of dramatic effect. One striking dimension of the reports of these experience-only writers was their affinity for statements of dramatic effect. Recall, for example, Caitlyn's opening in her horse report, "Hi! I am your guide for *Horses Around the World.* Thank you for reading it," an introduction appropriated from a tour guide she had encountered at a Philadelphia racetrack (see Figure 3.1). As the opening lines of three other experience-only writers show, Caitlyn was not the only writer to open her piece with an energetic salutation and a direct appeal to readers:

Hi! My name is Vanessa. Come Here. I'll show you around.

Hi! My name is Kristin. I'm good at gymnastics. Come on. I'll show you around the gym.

Hi my name is Phil. I take Karate and I'm a blue belt and this [is] all I had to go through to get it.

Notable with respect to these atypical expository leads was the fact that no other 3rd graders began their reports with such effusive informality. The lead, "Hi. My name is . . ." was not found in any other reports. Interestingly, when Vanessa and Phil (Kristin did not write a second report) wrote subsequent reports that were anchored in trade books (and not in their personal experiences), they did not break the rules of exposition as their opening lines reveal:

Although dolphins have fins and live in the sea, They are not fish. (Vanessa)

Do you no that it takes 9 days for a chicken to form . . . (Phil)

While the intertextual congruity noted among the "Hi! My name is . . ." leads would seem to suggest a high degree of appropriation among the writers themselves, such direct links can only be substantiated in some instances. For example, in inquiring about the parallel between Caitlyn's tour guide analogy and Vanessa's "Come here. I'll show you around," Vanessa noted that she was not even aware that Caitlyn was writing a report on horses (begun two days before Vanessa began her report). Vanessa and Caitlyn did not sit at the same table, did not usually play together, and did not, to our knowledge, confer during writing workshop. When asked why she included these lines, Vanessa replied, "'Cause it's what my teacher said to me when I was there on my first day [of acting class]. And she took me around to see the dressing room and the stage and things." However, Phil, who sat at Vanessa's table, had read her acting report during sharing time. While he didn't acknowledge appropriating Vanessa's lead, he may have.

In examining these leads, we noted three kinds of statements: a salutation (e.g., "Hi!"), a personal introduction (e.g., "My name is Kristin. I'm good at gymnastics."), and a direct appeal to the reader (e.g., "Come Here. I'll show you around."). These statements were coded as two types of stylizations: statements of dramatic effect (e.g., "Come Here. I'll show you around.") and statements of personal opinion (e.g., "I'm good at gymnastics.").

When I asked why she included her name and the statement "I'm good at gymnastics" (Figure 4.2), Kristin replied, "The readers have to know that I wrote this report because it's all true because I know everything about gymnastics." When I pointed out that she didn't introduce herself in any of the stories that she wrote, she noted, "But this is different. This is a report about something real, not just a made-up story." Kristin went on to explain that she had been taking gymnastic lessons for 2 years and that she planned to compete in the Olympics. While Vanessa didn't allude to her acting expertise in her text (Figure 4.1), she certainly did so during an interview: "I wanted to get everybody excited and tell them about me. And I know all about acting, what you're supposed to . . . I do acting for 5 years."

Thus, our experience-only writers attended to both writer credibility and audience awareness. While Langer (1986) found that only 21% of the 8-year-olds in her study expressed a concern for audience (as compared to 46% of the 11-year-olds) when they wrote reports (given the prompt), she noted that 67% replied affirmatively when asked if they would write their reports differently for different audiences. Langer's 3rd graders reported they would write longer and neater reports for older audiences. Interestingly, Langer (1986) found that none of the 8-year-olds began their reports with "Hello," although 36% did begin "their reports with topic starters such as 'I know a lot about horses.'" (p. 65).

Personal opinion. As Newkirk (1987) noted, young nonfiction writers often allow their own engagement with the topic to permeate their writing:

> i like birds, cats, dogs, cubs, and some bears. Some water animals are nice to me I like them and I think they are very, very, cute. Sharks are fish, if you didn't know that now you know that. The whale shark is very harmless to people. A shark does not have any bones. Baby sharks are called pups. (in Newkirk, 1987, p. 130)

This 2nd grader's propensity to merge statements of fact and feeling/ opinion—what Newkirk (1987) calls an attribute series—is common among 1st and 2nd graders. Newkirk, in his analysis of 1st, 2nd, and 3rd graders' expository writing, classified 22% of the 1st graders' pieces and 26% of 2nd graders' pieces as attribute series. Only 6% of the 3rd graders' pieces were classified as such. Newkirk (1987) viewed the attribute series as part of "the general developmental progression"(p. 126) through which children travel on their way to writing more conventional exposition, acknowledging, though, that "no claim is made that students must progress through" (p. 126) each specific category. Langer (1986) also found that 14% of the 8-year-olds in her study began their reports with an opinion or a commentary and 7% included opinions in ending paragraphs.

Statements of opinion punctuated the reports of our experience-only writers. For example, I (Carol) interrupted Kristin after she finished reading the lines (Figure 4.2, lines 20–22) "but sometimes they make a mistake. And they don't get to much credit!"

CAROL: Why do you say that?
KRISTIN: Because you know the girl who twisted her ankle really badly and she still did the beam and the horse. *She still did it!* And she didn't get the gold even with so much pain. She was just determined to do it. It was just like her goal, her destiny, or something like that. And it hurt so much, but she did it.

CAROL: I remember that. I couldn't believe Kerri went on the floor
    again. Is that how you feel about gymnastics?
KRISTIN: Yeah. Even though it's hard, I love it. Someday I hope I go
    to the Olympics.
CAROL: Did your gymnastics teacher talk about what happened to
    Kerri?
KRISTIN: No, I just watched the Olympics on TV and saw things
    like that.

While I didn't probe Kristin's use of words such as *determined, goal,
destiny*, it's not too much of stretch to attribute these appropriations to the
media, which she acknowledged as her primary intertextual source. Interviews in which the athletes talked about their determination and goals, along
with commentaries by the experts about athletes' destinies, are the staple of
Olympic media coverage. Subsequent talk with family members and friends
in all likelihood reinforced the primacy of these concepts. However, what
Kristin probably did not hear on television was any commentary that influenced the lines in her report "but sometimes they make a mistake. And they
don't get to much credit!" It appears that Kristin wanted to go on record
as questioning the standards of gymnastic competition. It is possible that
Kristin's opinion had its roots in the words of a family member or a peer
who expressed concern about the competitiveness of this sport; it is also
possible that it represented her "indelible mark" (Fletcher, 1993, p. 79) on
this situation.

A delightful example of a personal opinion that tied to direct experience (and ultimately to the words of a mentor) occurred during an interview
about Vanessa's ending (Figure 4.1, lines 7–8): ". . . you go on stage when
its your turn and you say your line. But if you mess up just keep going because the adicic [audience] will not know that you did a mistake."

VANESSA: If you mess up a line, you can't say, "Oh wait a minute."
CAROL: Why is that?
VANESSA: You have to keep going. They [the audience] won't even
    know, you know. Just keep on going.
CAROL: And who gave that advice to you?
VANESSA: My dance teacher. She tells us over and over and over.

Personal-Experience Paraphrase

As has been evident throughout this chapter, our experience-only writers
wrote and spoke with much authority about their varying realms of knowledge. They took pride in the fact that their knowledge was anchored in their
experiences, acknowledging that they wrote everything "from their heads"

without consulting a book or other resources. Simply put, they knew because they did. For that reason, nearly all their sentences, except those coded as stylizations, were coded as personal-experience paraphrases. However, when probed about the source of this firsthand knowledge, most readily attributed it to their instructors, parents, and/or peers. To illustrate, Vanessa, when asked where she had learned about the importance of practicing, replied:

> VANESSA: Well, you have to practice really, really hard because you can't mess up on the thing. Because I go to [name of acting school] and if you mess up on the day of the play, she [acting teacher] screams at you.
>
> CAROL: She does?
>
> VANESSA: I mean she *screams* at you.
>
> CAROL: It must be hard to memorize all those lines.
>
> VANESSA: Oh, yeah, yeah. And the day before it, she'll say, "I want this play to be perfect!, you know. And if you mess up, you'll be in big trouble." You'll just get screamed at. And that's when you have this fill out sheet and they'll write stuff.

EXPERIENCE-ONLY WRITERS: PROFILE SUMMARY

During our opening session (described at the beginning of this chapter), we showcased the reports of our first two nonfiction writers and sounded the call for other "experts." However, of the many who expressed expertise, only four followed through with reports that were anchored exclusively in their personal experiences without consultation of text resources. What appears to have distinguished these four writers is the formal instruction that characterized their experiences. All had taken or were taking classes over an extended period of time. When asked about the source of the knowledge in their reports, they frequently cited their firsthand experience. With further probing, they readily attributed this knowledge to their instructors, parents, and peers. Marked similarity was also noted with respect to the organizational structure of their reports. Each adopted the simple organizational scheme of a title followed by a paragraph of continuous text, one page in length. Their content was not divided into chapters or headings. They exhibited an affinity for stylized statements. For example, three of the four writers began his or her report with a version of "Hi. My name is . . ." and then proceeded to establish their credibility as experts. They also included personal opinions about their topic and statements of dramatic effect.

    If Caitlyn, the strategic writer profiled in Chapter 3, hadn't been in this classroom, we would have guessed that the kind of reports showcased in this chapter represent what 3rd graders are developmentally capable of doing when writing from firsthand experience. However, Caitlyn stretched the outer boundary of the zone of proximal development—"the distance between children's actual developmental levels as determined through independent problem solving and potential development as determined through problem solving under adult guidance or a collaboration with more capable peers" (Vygotsky, 1978, p. 86). Caitlyn's ability to center her horse report in her personal experiences as an equestrian paralleled that of her experience-only peers. However, Caitlyn's tacit understanding that nonfiction writing requires a deep knowledge of a subject led her to access multiple resources and then to merge both sources of data (personal and textual) into her report. Caitlyn let us know that this level of report writing is not outside of the reach of some 3rd graders.

Text-Bound Nonfiction Writers: Kyle and Patrick

IN 1996, MANY AND COLLEAGUES investigated the research and reporting processes of 11- and 12-year olds who were assigned the task of researching a self-selected topic on World War II and writing a report. Given 12 weeks to complete their reports, these Scottish youngsters had access to an impressive array of World War II materials (e.g., nonfiction books, newspapers, biographies, historical fiction, plays, films, slides, computer software, and artifacts, including ration books, identity cards, and gas masks). In addition, they interviewed family and friends about their war experiences and tape-recorded their accounts, adding them to the database. Mini-lessons on various strategies/skills were provided; for example, planning webs (graphic organizers) were introduced to help students organize their content. Many and colleagues (1996) found that these students adopted three different stances toward their research project. Some viewed research/report writing as a process of accumulating information, first locating a source, and then stringing together random bits of information, often copying text verbatim or photocopying and gluing information. Other students viewed their project as a process of transferring information, adopting a simple search and paraphrase stance. These students located a source relevant to their topic, closely paraphrased sentence by sentence (some copied verbatim), and then moved to the next source and repeated the cycle. Some used multiple sources, but in a fairly linear, nonintegrated fashion. Finally, some 6th graders viewed research/report writing as a process of transforming information, proceeding in purposeful, goal-driven ways. These "transformers" implemented a recursive strategy of reading multiple sources, brainstorming, rereading, searching, revising, and integrating information at each step. (Note that our strategic writers, Caitlyn and Colin, profiled in Chapter 3, exhibited some of these attributes.)

In this chapter, we address the reports of Kyle and Patrick. As Table 1.1 shows, Kyle was receiving academic support from the literacy specialist and Patrick was functioning on grade level. Both, in many respects, corroborate Many and colleagues' (1996) findings. Kyle essentially adopted the stance of "research as accumulating information" (p. 18) and Patrick, the stance of "research as transferring information" (p. 18). While Many and colleagues presented some distinctions between these two categories of writers, we think they would agree with our general conclusion that both groups were text-bound. As we will demonstrate, Kyle and Patrick viewed the text as the sole source of authority. That said, they were our nonfiction cheerleaders. Both exuded such enthusiasm when talking and writing about their topics that they brought others into the nonfiction fold.

KYLE: INTERTEXTUAL PATTERNS

You met Kyle in Chapter 1. He and Jessica were the first and only 3rd graders to choose to write nonfiction reports during the second phase of our study. Prior to drafting his first report on fossils/dinosaurs, Kyle had filled his writer's notebook (see Table 1.2) with personal narratives with the exception of two stories: "The Missing Meters" (intertextual link: a math program called "Square One" on *Children's Television Workshop*) and "Arthur Travels in Space" (intertextual link: Marc Brown's (1984) *Arthur Goes to Camp* and TV series; Kyle "wanted to write a movie he [Brown] didn't make yet").

On our second day of instruction, I (throughout the chapter, *I* refers to Carol) placed a picture of a Great White shark on the overhead projector and asked the 3rd graders to help me figure out what I might include in a shark report. Hands shot up. Kyle exclaimed, "You could write about their teeth!" This was one of many contributions Kyle offered during this semantic mapping activity. That same day, Kyle abandoned his dinosaur report and began his shark report. The first four pages of Kyle's six-page report are shown in Figure 5.1.

Thematic Intertextuality: "So Where Did You Get the Idea for Your Topic?"

Kyle readily acknowledged his thematic source during a conference the next day: "Because we were learning about sharks, I thought it would be a good idea to write about them." When asked if he knew a lot about sharks, Kyle replied, "Just a little. I had to get some information." It wasn't until four conferences later and five pages into his shark report that Kyle mentioned his personal experience with sharks:

> KYLE: I'm going to write about sharks in Florida [during February vacation]. If I'm gonna catch a shark while I'm going fishing and I'm going to write about it.
> CAROL: Do you think you will see any sharks?
> KYLE: Oh, yeah, if I go fishing. Well, my brother catched a shark. That's where I got the idea to write about sharks.
> CAROL: He caught one last year? What did he do with it?
> KYLE: He put it back. I wanted to keep it, but the guy said, "No."

1. Thinking about sharks can make you shiver with excitement. That's because sharks
2. are truly awesome creatures. When something is awesome, you feel respect, fear, and
3. wounder all at the same time. Most of us feel this way about sharks—a little scard,
4. but very curious. Sharks live in all the waters of the world. Certain kinds of sharks
5. stay in certain kinds of waters. Hammerheads, tiger and bull sharks usually like the
6. warm waters of tropical places. Only about 25 kinds of sharks have been known to
7. actually attack people. Most of the dangerous sharks are large, and usually eat big fish
8. and mammals. The sharks skin is made of cartilage. Sharks have been here when the
9. dinosaurs were alive. The awesome shark deserves to be respected, admired as well

(page 1)

10. as feared. We still have so much to learn about his fascinating fish. A shark called
11. Megalodon lived in the world's oceans until about 50,000 years ago. You can
12. imagine how big Megalodon was by comparing the size of its jaw. Because live
13. shaks are so hard to study, even scientists still have a lot to learn. They do know that
14. there are 350 kinds of sharks. Sharks such as the thresher, basking, mako, and blue
15. prefer water that is neither too warm nor too cold. Tiger Sharks live in warm waters
16. and they like to feed on Dollphins. Sharks can find a fish hiding in the sand. A
17. hammer head shark looks different but the head looks like a hammer. A great white

(page 2)

18. Chap 4 Shark can kill any kind a shark if it isn't spiky. A shark can be small and
19. some can be humungo. Sharks lived for millions of years. Sharks are so awesome
20. because there teeth are so cool. Once you get into a sharks teeth there isn't a way out.
21. Sharks are so fast because they are. The great white sharks teeth are very sharp and if
22. you get in the sharks mouth you would die in a minute. The hammerheads serch in
23. groups like fish do. The thresher shark hat the longest tail because its so long. Chap 5
24. Some sharks eat meat and others eat planckton like the wale sharks and the wale
25. shark has know teeth and it's bigger than a truck. The great white shark is the most
26. dangerous of all sharks. In size, it is as long as a bus. Great whites are found in
27. cool-to-warm waters.

28.   (page 3)

29. Chap 6 The great whites will eat almost any thing to smaller sharks, fish, Penguins,
30. or even people. Meat-eating sharks are known to have huge
31. and varied appetites. Chap 7 Some large cruise slowly near the surface. Chap 8 The
32. wale shark feeds during the day in deep, warm tropical oceans. Chap 9 Gill-slits are
33. like arches on a brige: As a shark swims, water passes through the gills slits and into
34. the gills. Chap 10 Not all sharks swim fast. Some, like the wobbing, rest on the
35. seafloor. The spotted wobbing moves from one rock pool to the next, searching for
36. crabs and other crustaceans. Chap 11 Long, sharp and poinnted teeth help a shark to
37. catch and hold onto slippery prey. Serrated teeth sliced through flesh. Flat crushing
38. teeth are found in sharks that eat crustaceans. Chap 12 A shark's ears are inside . . . .

(page 4)

Figure 5.1. Four pages of Kyle's (grade 3) six-page nonfiction report on sharks. Most of the intertextual links are tied to three trade books.

CAROL: Now I remember! You wrote a journal entry earlier in the year about this. Let's see if we can find it.

Kyle located his personal narrative and elaborated on the events of the day. It was interesting that Kyle didn't mention his brother's encounter with a baby hammerhead during our first conference (and unfortunate that I didn't recall this journal entry). This highlights the importance of probing for intertextual links across time so that the range of sources can be identified. It seems likely that both sources triggered the idea to write about sharks. Once his report was underway, hammerheads were mentioned on every page.

Organizational Intertextuality: "Where Did You Get the Idea to Organize Your Report This Way?"

We examined the influence of Kyle's primary sources on the organizational decisions that he made at two levels: top-level text organization (how his intertexts influenced the way he organized his information) and paragraph organization (how his intertexts influenced the flow of sentences in his paragraphs) (see Chapter 2). Two of his intertexts—Maestro's (1990) *A Sea Full of Sharks* and Simon's (1995) photo essay *Sharks*—contained no organizational features other than title. His third book, *Sharks* (Oakley, 1996), contained a table of contents, a heading per page, captioned illustrations, and an index, but no chapters.

Top-level text organization. Perusal of Kyle's first two pages (Figure 5.1, lines 1–9 and lines 10–17) reveals a sweep of continuous text with no title, no chapter designations, no headings—congruent, in large part, with that of his first primary source, *A Sea Full of Sharks* (Maestro, 1990). Maestro presents her content on each page in a block-paragraph format (3–6 sentences in length) and then fills the rest of the page with a large illustration. It's interesting to note that Kyle's decision to use continuous text occurred literally minutes after our lesson that highlighted the importance of using headings to organize content.

On page 3 of his report (Figure 5.1, lines 18–27), Kyle disrupted his use of continuous text by inserting "Chap 4" (line 18) and "Chap 5" (line 23). Because none of his intertexts included chapters and because our instruction didn't address the use of chapters, I initiated the following dialogue:

CAROL: Why did you decide to label this section [*pointing*] "Chap 4?"
KYLE: I want to start chapters now.
CAROL: Where did you get the idea to use chapters?

KYLE: Well, Kristin, she's writing this story about diamonds and I'm in it [*giggling*]. I'm her brother in the story.

CAROL: Yes, I've read Kristin's great story. She told me you were the "Kyle" in the story; I'm not surprised because you are such good friends. What does Kristin's story have to do with your use of chapters?

KYLE: Kristin had chapters in her story and I got the idea for my report.

Indeed, Kristin's six-page story, "Dazzling Diamonds," was divided into nine chapters with embedded chapter notations such as "Chap 2" and "Cha 3." Kyle adopted this same organizational scheme for his report. For example, on page 4 of his report, Kyle embedded "Chap 6" through "Chap 12" (Figure 5.1, lines 29, 31, 32, 34, 36, 38) within his text. By the end of page 6, 19 "chapters" had been logged. We suspect that Kyle, influenced by Kristin's nine-chapter story, hypothesized that the more chapters, the better the piece. Length is an important variable for many young writers (Many et al., 1996; Read, 2001). Intrigued by Kyle's construct of "chapter," I engaged Kyle in conversation:

CAROL: How do you decide when it's a new chapter?

KYLE: I just do short chapters, that's all.

CAROL: Let's reread chapters 7 and 8. [*Kyle reads.*] Why did you separate this information into two chapters?

KYLE: Oh, I don't know.

CAROL: Do you have a plan for when you make a chapter?

KYLE: No. I just do it like chapter by chapter.

CAROL: No plan?

KYLE: No plan [*giggling*]. I just like putting chapters down and writing a story.

CAROL: What is a chapter?

KYLE: I don't really know. Some sentences?

Kyle, like many of his peers, had yet to internalize the attributes of a chapter. Take, for example, "chapters" 14 and 15 on page 5 of his report:

chap 14 Sharks are realy big fish that lived about millions of years ago. Sharks lived in the sea with fish, eals, and DINOSAURS. *chap 15 Sharks are some cool creatures that are millions and millions years old.* All sharks live in all sorts of oceans.

Reference to the longevity of the sharks (italicized sentences above) was not only duplicated across these two "chapters" but had already been established in his report, as the following italicized sentences reveal:

- Page 1 (Figure 5.1, lines 8–9): The sharks skin is made of cartilage. *Sharks have been here when the dinosaurs were alive.* The awesome shark deserves to be respected admired as well as feared.
- Page 3 (Figure 5.1, lines 18–20): A shark can be small and some can be hummungo. *Sharks lived for millions of years.* Sharks are so awesome because there teeth are so cool.

Inquiries about a general planning strategy were broached during three different writing conferences. During the second conference:

CAROL: Tell me, Kyle, how you organized your report on sharks.
KYLE: Organize?
CAROL: Did you have a plan for what you were going to write at the beginning, middle, and end of this report?
KYLE: Not really, I just kept writing things down.

During the next conference, which focused on page 3 of his report (Figure 5.1), I asked about his plan again, to which he responded, "I just want to do it. I have no idea why I want to write about sharks. I think it's so cool."

At that point, I reminded him about our class discussion on how nonfiction authors often organize their information under headings. I asked if he recalled what we added to Joanna Cole's (1986b) *Hungry, Hungry Sharks* to help readers have a clearer idea about what was covered.

Kyle replied, "When doing the body parts? Like that?"

"Exactly," I affirmed and pulled out the overhead of the section from Cole's book that contained the heading that Kyle and his table peers had labeled. We then returned to page 3 of Kyle's report (Figure 5.1, lines 19–22) and reread his information on shark's teeth. I asked what heading he might have used for this section. Kyle noted aptly, "Sharks' Teeth." I asked which sentence he should move to another section because it didn't fit with this heading. He quickly identified the sentence, "Sharks are so fast because they are," explaining it wasn't about teeth.

While Kyle seemed to recognize the relationship between main ideas and details, he did not transfer this understanding to the last three pages of his report, which were written after the "sharks' teeth" conference. This disconnect between knowledge and application is not uncommon. For example, Many and colleagues (1996) noted that while some "accumulators" talked about the importance of planning, they didn't follow through. Wray and Lewis (1992) also found "a large gap between what children said about how to use information books and what they actually did when using them" during a reading project (p. 20).

While Kyle was unable to verbalize his approach to writing his report, analysis of his journey through his intertexts suggests his "plan" may have been: "Let me see what I can find in Maestro's book that I can put in my report. Now that I've gone through that book, I'll see what Oakley has to offer. I'm finished with Oakley, so I'll try Simon." As noted earlier with respect to the longevity of sharks and other examples, it didn't matter whether the same content was covered by these authors. If Kyle happened upon it, he repeated it. Kyle gives credence to Bereiter and Scardamalia's (1987) observation that some "young writers tend to start writing almost immediately and to write down additional items of content as they think of them. This 'what next' or 'knowledge-telling' strategy has little place in it for conscious goal setting or organizational planning" (pp. 195–196).

Paragraph organization. A quick scan of Kyle's shark report reveals six pages of continuous text with no indented paragraphs. The search for paragraphs (in accordance with Newkirk's [1987] definition of three related and logically connected statements) yielded nine paragraphs, eight that were coded perfect alignment and one that was coded selected alignment.

Recall that perfect alignment refers to the writer's decision to adopt the same sequence of sentences as the sequence of the intertext (regardless of whether the sentences are direct quotes, paraphrases, etc.). Such was the case with eight of Kyle's paragraphs. For example, because Kyle began his report (Figure 5.1, lines 1–4) by copying verbatim the opening paragraph of Betty Maestro's *A Sea Full of Sharks* (see below), it was coded perfect alignment.

> Thinking about sharks can make you shiver with excitement. That's because sharks are truly awesome creatures. When something is awesome, you feel respect, fear, and wonder all at the same time. Most of us feel this way about sharks—a little scared, but very curious. (Maestro, 1990, unpaged)

This was also true of Kyle's second paragraph (Figure 5.1, lines 4–6), copied directly from Maestro's eighth page. No other sections of Kyle's first page were classified as paragraphs (as defined by Newkirk [1987]). For example, the next two sentences, "Only about 25 kinds of sharks have been known to actually attack people. Most of the dangerous sharks are large, and usually eat big fish and mammals" (Figure 5.1, lines 6–8), also taken directly from Maestro's tenth page, didn't meet the three-sentence criterion of a paragraph. Neither did his two subsequent sentences (lines 8–9).

In addition to six other perfectly aligned paragraphs copied verbatim from Maestro (1990) or Oakley (1996), Kyle also included one paragraph that was coded selected alignment. This paragraph on sharks' teeth (see Figure 5.1, lines 36–38) was created by rearranging the captions found on page 10 of Oakley's book. As Figure 5.2 shows, Oakley's (1996) text includes a heading and one paragraph, followed by an illustration of a large shark's head. To the right of the shark's head are illustrations of four teeth; under

Oakley's *Sharks*	Kyle's Report

WHAT FINE TEETH YOU HAVE!

Sharks have several rows of teeth that come in different shapes and sizes, all designed to do different jobs. When a front tooth falls out, the tooth behind moves forward to take its place. Sharks lose at least one tooth a week!

(An illustration of a large shark's head follows. To the right of the head are four illustrations of sharks' teeth, captioned as shown below.)

Slicing Teeth
Serrated teeth slice through flesh.

Spiked Teeth
Spiked teeth grip and tear flesh.

Crushing Teeth
Flat crushing teeth are found in sharks that eat crustaceans.

Holding Teeth
Long, sharp, and pointed teeth help a shark catch and hold onto slippery prey.

(Oakley, 1996, p. 10)

Long, sharp, and poinnted teeth help a shark catch and hold onto slippery prey. Serrated teeth sliced through flesh. Flat crushing teeth are found in sharks that eat crustaceans. (lines 36–38)

Figure 5.2. A passage that was coded as selected alignment. Rather than appropriating the exact order of Oakley's captions, Kyle selected (reordered and omitted) certain captions.

each illustration is a descriptive caption. Kyle's paragraph was coded selected alignment because he decided to switch the order of Oakley's captions, using her final caption as his lead sentence. Kyle explained, "See first they [the sharks] use the holding teeth to hold the fish and then the ser, [*I pronounce "serrated"*], teeth to slice them up." In addition, he noted that he omitted Oakley's caption on the spiked teeth "because it's the same thing as the holding teeth." Thus, he reordered and revised Oakley's captions to have them match the actual eating sequence. I congratulated Kyle on his decision to assess Maestro's text and present his own sequence (with the caveat about copying and a discussion about spiked versus holding teeth). This was the only time that Kyle acted on an author's text.

In sum, Kyle began his report with no organizational framework (not even a title), perhaps influenced by his first intertext (Maestro, 1990), which was organized as continuous text with no organizational features. When he moved to a second primary text (Oakley, 1996) that contained headings, Kyle didn't appropriate this format. The only clear intertextual link was Kyle's appropriation of Kristin's "chapters" in her story; however, he did so without an understanding of what constituted a chapter. At the paragraph level, he revealed a penchant for perfectly aligning his text with that of his intertext. While major parts of Kyle's report were driven by various primary texts, there were sections where he inserted information based on his personal knowledge (learned from various sources) but was unable to organize this knowledge into cohesive paragraphs.

Orientational Intertextuality: Appropriating the Voices of Others

During our first conference, Kyle acknowledged his direct appropriation of Maestro's words:

CAROL: Where did you get your information for this report?
KYLE: I got all this information from this book [*showing Maestro's A Sea Full of Sharks*]. And some I knew. This is my library book. . . .
CAROL: So how did you use this book?
KYLE: Well, I just copied out some things.
CAROL: Let's see what you copied.
KYLE: I didn't copy off all of them, most of all of them.

As Kyle and I researched the origins of each sentence on the first page of his report (Figure 5.1), we discovered that all but two (lines 8–9: "The sharks skin is made of cartilage. Sharks have been here when the dinosaurs were alive.") were direct quotes from Maestro's book. We then moved to the sentence about the megalodon on page 2 (Figure 5.1, lines 10–12); Kyle was unable to locate the reference in Maestro's text. I asked if he had used a second book; Kyle replied, "Yeah, I had a small book, but I don't think I copied out of that one." Upon checking, we found that the megalodon sentences were direct quotes from Oakley (1996). When asked if he recalled the discussion we had had in class about copying from other authors, Kyle replied sheepishly, "Um, I forget."

I reviewed our class discussion on verbatim copying and reminded Kyle about the selective use of direct quotes and the importance of punctuating with quotation marks. To reinforce the concept of paraphrasing, I congratulated Kyle on his personal-knowledge paraphrase in Figure 5.1 (lines 8–9:

"Sharks have been here when the dinosaurs were alive."), information
recalled from the read-aloud of *Hungry, Hungry Sharks* (Cole, 1986b).
During the next writing workshop, Kyle went on a personal-knowledge
paraphrasing spree (see Figure 5.1, lines 17–22). When he arrived at our next
conference, he proudly announced, "I didn't copy. I did my own." As we
discussed the origin of each sentence, he was adept at recalling the corre-
sponding intertextual link, offering to bring in his *Really Wild Animal* videotape so I could verify his facts. These intertexts are provided in Figure 5.3.

Kyle's paraphrasing momentum, however, was interrupted by the hia-
tus of December break. When we met to review page 4 (Figure 5.1) of his
report in early January, it was evident that he had reverted back to copying.
Without even asking, Kyle offered a justification: "I didn't copy any of the
book part [*pointing to the block paragraph at the top of Oakley's (1996)
page 16*] because I know we can't do that. This is only the words for the
pictures."

Kyle's Report	Intertextual Sources of Paraphrases
Tiger sharks live in warm waters and they like to feed on Dollphins. (lines 15–16)	"I got that on *Kratts' Creatures* [TV program on National Geographic channel]."
A shark can be small and some can be hummungo. (lines 18–19)	"That's true. I just know it." (We had read about sizes in Cole's book earlier in the week.)
Once you get in a sharks teeth there isn't a way out. (line 20)	"I know sharks' teeth go like this [uses fingers to show how teeth cave in] and when they close there's no way out." ["How do you know this?"] "I just looked at the picture [pointing to page 6 of Oakley's *Sharks*]."
The hammerheads serch in groups like fish do. (lines 22–23)	"I knew that. Like schools . . . I got it from a movie . . . *Really Wild Animals: Deep Sea Dive*."
Some sharks eat meat and others eat plancktin like the wale shark and the wale shark has know teeth and it's bigger than a truck. (lines 24–25)	"Yup. *Deep Sea Dive*. They show all sorts of sharks."

Figure 5.3. Intertextual sources that Kyle tapped while writing pages 2–3
of his report.

Indeed, Kyle had strung together one caption after another, jumping from page 16 to 24 to 27 to 26 of Oakley's book. Kyle was gracious about receiving further clarification about copying and resumed his efforts at paraphrasing (both personal-knowledge and textual varieties) in order to finish page 5 of his report:

> chap 14 Sharks are realy big fish that lived about millions of years ago. Sharks lived in the sea with fish, eals and DINOSAURS. chap 15 Sharks are some cool creatures that are millions and millions years old. All sharks live in all sorts of oceans. The Atlantic ocean, The pacific ocean, The Arctic ocean, and The Indian ocean.

Given Kyle's extensive appropriation of published texts, it was not surprising to find that 63% of the sentences in his shark report were coded as direct quotes: 28% were copied verbatim from the main body of his intertexts and 35% were copied verbatim from Oakley's captions. Five sentences were coded as partial direct quotes, reflecting Kyle's awareness of audience. For example:

SHARKS	KYLE'S TEXT
You can imagine how big a megalodon was by comparing the size of its jaw to the people pictured below. [Accompanied by an illustration of the megalodon's jaw, opened wide, with a father and son standing in the jaw.] (Oakley, 1996, p. 6)	You can imagine how big a megalodon was by comparing the size of its jaw.

Because Kyle didn't include the accompanying picture, he omitted the prepositional phrase "to the people pictured below" (Oakley, 1996, p. 6). While readers are left wondering about the comparison, they are not as baffled as they would be if the entire sentence had been copied.

In addition to direct and partial direct quotes, 11 sentences (15%) were coded as personal-knowledge paraphrases (see examples in Figure 5.3). Four sentences were coded picture observation paraphrases; for example, examining a picture of a thresher shark in Oakley's (1996) book, Kyle wrote: "A thresher shark hat the longest tail because its so long" (Figure 5.1, line 23). Three sentences were coded as source-unknown paraphrases because Kyle couldn't recall where he learned the information; for example, "A great white Shark can kill any kind of shak if it isn't spikey" (Figure 5.1, lines 17–18). No reference to "spiky" sharks turned up during a recheck of his intertexts. None of his sentences was coded as textual paraphrases.

Kyle's report also contained three stylizations. For example, he included an opinion on page 3 of his report (Figure 5.1, lines 19–20: "Sharks are so awsome because there teeth are so cool.") as well as a statement of dramatic effect (lines 21–22: "The great white sharks teeth are very sharp and if you get in the sharks mouth you would die in a minute."). Discussion with respect to accuracy of this latter detail ensued. Kyle admitted that he "figured this was true because you could lose so much blood," but agreed that reports need verifiable facts.

In sum, Kyle zigzagged his way through his report, moving from verbatim copying to a stretch of personal-knowledge paraphrasing, back to verbatim copying and another stretch of paraphrasing, and ending with a page of direct quotes. Siegler (1995) reminds us that this is not unusual:

> The typical situation is one where individual children know and use a variety of ways of thinking, rather than just one, and where cognition involves constant competition among alternative ways of thinking, rather than sole reliance on a single way of thinking at any given age. Rather than stepping up from Strategy 1 to Strategy 2 to Strategy 3, children would be expected to use several strategies at any one time, with frequency of use of each strategy ebbing and flowing with increasing age and expertise. To capture this view in a visual metaphor, think of a series of overlapping waves . . . each wave corresponding to a different rule, strategy, theory or way of thinking. (pp. 409–410)

The "overlapping waves" of voice appropriation suggest that while young writers construct, test, and refine hypotheses about written language in increasingly sophisticated ways, many do not do so in an incremental fashion.

In sum, Kyle, as affable as they come, charged through his report with a sense of personal delight with his own efforts. With dogged determination, he accumulated information (Many et al., 1996) by journeying from one text to the next, copying large chunks of texts without attention to coherence or redundancy. Repeated conversations about verbatim copying and about the advantage of organizing content under headings and the like didn't seem to either deflate his confidence or modify his report writing in any notable way. With prompting, though, he was able to write stretches of paraphrased information learned from movies and TV shows in a stream-of-consciousness fashion. Initially, he imposed no organizational structure on his report; then he appropriated the idea of chapters from a friend's story, randomly inserting "chaps."

PATRICK: INTERTEXTUAL PATTERNS

With the exception of a few interspersed personal narratives, Patrick's notebook was filled with stories (see Table 1.2). Particularly prevalent in his writer's notebook was the Halloween story genre. Beginning in September and carrying through October, he authored the following multipaged stories, noting intertextual links during interviews: "The Timber Wolf Returns" (intertextual link: R. L. Stine's [1994] book, *The Return of the Mummy*), "The Dead Football Player" ("I kinda combined Halloween and Matt Christopher" [who writes sports fiction]); *Nate the Great* (Sharmat, 1977); "Daffy Duck on Halloween" ("I got the idea from Connor because he was writing about Halloween and Looney Tunes"); and "The Return of the Pumpkin People" ("I read a lot of *Goosebumps* like this!"). With Halloween behind him, Patrick spent most of November crafting "New England Patriots vs. Dallas Cowboys," a seven-page football story.

In early December, Patrick was working on another story, "Garfield and the Broken TV in Christmas," when we began our nonfiction instruction (see Phase 3 section in Chapter 1). During the lesson, Patrick responded to our call for budding experts, announcing, "I'm an expert on reptiles like snakes, Gila monsters, and lizards. And Colin and me are experts on hockey and football." This opened the door to a deluge of other sport aficionados claiming expertise in baseball, gymnastics, karate and so forth. We were certain that sports reports would dominate their nonfiction writing, but this was not the case. The fact that Patrick chose to write about reptiles, not football—a topic about which he possessed deeper knowledge—was influenced in large part by the social dynamic that rippled through this 3rd grade classroom.

Patrick began his nonfiction report the day of our introductory lesson. Five pages of his seven-page report, "Reptiles and Amphibians," are presented in Figure 5.4. We turn now to a discussion about the range of intertextual links that anchored this report.

Thematic Intertextuality: "So Where Did You Get the Idea for Your Topic?"

When asked where he got his topic idea, Patrick replied, "I'm reading a book on reptiles."

> CAROL: Tell me about your interest in reptiles.
> PATRICK: I was born to like animals, especially reptiles.
> CAROL: Born to love reptiles?
> PATRICK: When I was 2 years old, I started reading all these books about reptiles.
> CAROL: You mean someone read them to you?
> PATRICK: Yeah, because some words I didn't know. . . .
> CAROL: Do you have any reptile books at home?
> PATRICK: I have like a thousand. I've been doing research on reptiles since I was 4.

Chapter I

BY: Patrick

1. REPTILES
2. Reptiles are usually four-legged (except snakes and a few lizards); each foot with three to
3. five clawed toes; skin usually with horny scales, sometimes bony plates. Most lay eggs
4. with hard or leathery skin. Reptiles were in their heyday millions of year ago; now they
5. are only a remnant of a once-great group. Some are of direct value. We use the skin's of
6. Alligators, Lizards, and large snakes for leather.

(page 1)

---

7. Snakes
8. Green Snakes, slender and harmless, live in greenery where they are hard to see. The
9. smaller species (15 to 18 in) with smoother scales prefers open grassy places.
10. Rainbow Snake is a handsome species. Stripes vary from orange to red. The uderside
11. is red with a double row of black spots. This snake swampy regions often burrows and is
12. not commonly seen. The females lay 20 or more eggs, which hatch in about 60 days.

(page 2)

---

13. Lizards
14. The Chuckwalla is (16 in. long) is, next to the Gilamonster our largest lizard. It feeds
15. on flowers and fruit of catus and tender parts of desert plants, and usually eats well in
16. captivity.
17. Spiny and True Iguana., representing two groups of large American lizards, are not
18. found in the United States, but come to within 100 miles of our border. They are often
19. seen in zoos. About 10 or 11 speices of spiny of False Iguana (1 to 4 ft long) live on the
20. ground in lower California, Mexico and further south into Central America.

(page 3)

---

21. ALLIGATORS and CROCODILES
22. form a distinct group of reptiles of ancient lineage. Alligators and Crocodiles feed on fish,
23. turtles, birds, crayfish, crabs, and other water life. Crocodiles prefer salt marshes and even swim
24. out into the ocean. Alligators are not usually dangerous. They are not especially long-lived, an
25. 10-footer is 20 to 25 year old.
26. (Patrick drew and labeled a picture of a crocodile.)

(page 4)

---

27. Amphibians
28. are animals that live in water when there babies. And when there grown up they crawl on land
29. but some amphibians like the salamander some salarmande live in water there hole life. That
30. eather live to be about 10 or 25 years old.

(page 5)

---

31. Salamanders and Newts
32. Congo-Eel and Hellbender are large salamanders. The Congo-Eel grows to be 30 to 36 in. long.
33. The Hellbender grows to be about 16 to 20 in. long. The Hellbender is much more smaller then
34. the Congo-Eel. The female lays a mass of eggs under mud or rotted leaves.
35. Newts . . .

(page 6; the remainder of the report is shown in Figure 5.8)

Figure 5.4. First six pages of Patrick's (grade 3) seven-page report, "Reptiles and Amphibians." Almost all intertextual links are tied to the same trade book.

CAROL: Do you have a reptile of any kind at your house?
PATRICK: No, but I'm getting one, a True Iguana, and they grow to be 4 feet.
CAROL: Your parents are going to let you have this huge reptile?
PATRICK: Well, my dad will let me get a True Iguana, but my mom won't because it grows too big.

Patrick then retrieved his field guide, titled *Reptiles and Amphibians* (Zim & Smith, 1956), flipped to the page that featured these iguanas, commented that they live in trees, and delighted in the fact that they look like little dinosaurs. I quickly skimmed the entry and discovered that Patrick's facts about the size and habitat of these iguanas were correct. I asked when he had read about the True Iguana; he noted that he had done so that morning. He then excitedly showed me a picture of a Gila monster, stating that it was the "second fastest reptile"; the field guide, however, noted "slow and clumsy" (Zim & Smith, p. 69). Patrick then announced that the "fastest and smartest reptile in the whole entire world is the alligator." A quick glance at the field guide revealed no such information, so I asked where he had learned this. Patrick replied that he thought he learned it from a movie in 2nd grade. Noticing my quick skim, Patrick posited, "I know something that's not even in here [the field guide]. It's something that probably they [the authors of the field guide] don't even know. It's that the Chuckwalla can go at speeds of up to 50 miles." Given that the field guide stated that the lizard called the Chuckwalla is second in size only to the sluggish Gila monster (Zim & Smith, 1956), I began to surmise that, while his intrigue with reptiles was boundless, his knowledge was limited. Given this, I was not surprised by Patrick's decision to rely heavily on his intertext while writing his report. We turn now to Patrick's appropriation of Zim and Smith's (1956) organizational structure.

Organizational Intertextuality: "Where Did You Get the Idea to Organize Your Report This Way?"

Patrick was the only 3rd grader to create a title page for his report, "Reptiles and Amphibians," complete with a byline and a copy of the cover illustration of his intertext (Zim & Smith, 1956), which he had glued to this title page. In order to examine the degree to which this intertext influenced Patrick's top-level organization, we begin with a brief overview of the field guide's setup and then discuss his appropriation of its organizational scheme.

Top-level text organization. As Figure 5.5 shows, the opening page, titled "Using This Book," serves as a table of contents and glossary. It is divided into two sections, "Reptiles" and "Amphibians." Following a brief description of reptiles, four types of reptiles (turtles, lizards, snakes, alligators and

---

USING THIS BOOK

The first step in the use of this book is to learn the differences between reptiles and amphibians:

REPTILES (highlighted in blue)

Usually: four-legged (except snakes and a few lizards); each foot with three to five claws; skin usually with horny scales, sometime bony plates. Most lay eggs with hard or leathery skin.

1. TURTLES Leathery or bony shell. Four limbs, short tail. Head can be withdrawn wholly or partly into shell.

pages 18–43

2. LIZARDS In the United States, mostly small, four-legged, covered with equal-sized horny . . . scales. Most are egg-laying, fast-moving land reptiles.

pages 44–69

(Zim & Smith, 1956, p. 3)

Figure 5.5. Table of contents of Zim and Smith's field guide, *Reptiles and Amphibians.*

crocodiles) are listed and defined. The amphibian section of this table of contents is organized in the same fashion. Under the heading AMPHIB-IANS is its definition, followed by two categories—frogs and toads, and salamanders.

This table of contents is followed by 12 pages of introductory material (e.g., sections such as living/extinct forms of reptiles and amphibians, values, collecting advice). Then a 2-page spread with more detailed information on reptiles is presented, followed by a 2-page spread with information specific to turtles. The next 21 pages address various turtles (generally one page per turtle). This organizational pattern is repeated for the remaining reptiles and amphibians: a two-page spread of general information about the species (e.g., lizards) followed by single-page descriptions of specific types of lizards. Alligators and crocodiles round out the reptile section; amphibians (frogs/toads and salamanders) follow.

The single-page species' descriptions in *Reptiles and Amphibians* (Zim & Smith, 1956) constitute the bulk of the field guide. Figure 5.6 illustrates the typical page setup. The top half of the page contains an illustration of the animal in its environs; the bottom half includes one paragraph of text. Each entry begins with the name of the animal, in capitals and boldface, which serves as both a heading and the subject of the lead sentence. A map of the United States, with the regions to which the specific species is indigenous, sits in the bottom corner.

[A colorful illustration of a Chuckwalla perched on a rocky ledge and eating a cactus fruit occupies the top two-thirds of the page.]

CHUCKWALLA (16 in. long) is, next to the Gila-monster, our largest lizard. It feeds on flowers and fruit of cactus and tender parts of desert plants, and usually eats well in captivity. Chuckwallas sun themselves on rocks but, when disturbed, dart into crevices, where they inflate their bodies and are difficult to remove. Indians used to eat them. The young have bands across body and tail; the adults have tail bands only.

[A map of the United States with the Southwest corner highlighted to show the habitat range appears in the bottom right corner of the page.]

(Zim & Smith, 1956, p. 49)

Figure 5.6. Typical page from Zim and Smith's field guide, *Reptiles and Amphibians*. Each page contains a description of a particular species, along with an illustration and U.S. map .

   While Patrick's report did not include a table of contents, his first entry, "Reptiles," revealed significant appropriation of his intertext's organization. As noted above, Zim and Smith (1956) preceded their pages on specific reptiles with a two-page introduction to reptiles, which Patrick readily acknowledged: "The authors told about what reptiles were, then they gave kinds—turtles, lizards, snakes—but I'm doing snakes and lizards. The authors also wrote about amphibians, then crocodiles and alligators. I'm going to do crocs and alligators after I tell what amphibians are. It's not going to be in a different chapter. I'm going to erase Chapter 2 for snakes and it will be part of Chapter 1 on reptiles, then I'll write Chapter 2 about amphibians." (*Note*: While he incorrectly categorized crocodiles/alligators as amphibians in his explanation, he assigned them to the correct reptile section when he began writing that part of his report.) Notable is not only Patrick's acknowledgment and adoption of an introduction but also his decision to label his reptile entry as "Chapter 1." Figure 5.4 (line 1) shows Patrick's introduction on reptiles and, four pages later, his introduction on amphibians (Figure 5.4, lines 27–30). These two introductory entries were coded as perfect alignment because Patrick's top-level text organization matched Zim and Smith's (1956). Of his own accord, though, Patrick inserted "Chapter 1" at the top of his "Reptile" page (Figure 5.4, line 1); *Reptiles and Amphibians* (Zim & Smith, 1956) contains no chapters. When asked where he got the idea to use chapters, he replied, "Well, I've seen it in my other reptile books." (I asked Patrick to bring one of these books to school, but he did not follow through.)

When asked for clarification about his decision "to erase Chapter 2," Patrick explained, "All the reptiles should be in one chapter because they go together. Then all the amphibians together." This suggested an awareness that a chapter represents a major chunk of content, often subdivided into smaller chunks, although he did not actually label the introduction on amphibians as Chapter 2 when he reached that point in his report. Inspection of his subsequent report on birds, however, revealed the tenuous nature of his understanding. This report contained three "chapters," each containing two or three sentences. Perhaps what Patrick learned about the construction of chapters from his analysis of Zim and Sim's (1956) field guide was supplanted by his peers' notion that a few sentences on a topic constituted a chapter.

As already noted, Zim and Smith (1956) include a two-page spread of general information on snakes, using the first word of the lead sentence to count as a heading ("**SNAKES** are the best known reptiles. . . ." [Zim & Smith, 1956, pp. 70–71]). Patrick appropriated only the heading, Snakes (which he highlighted in yellow to approximate the boldface of the field guide—see Figure 5.4, line 7). Unlike Zim and Smith (1956), he included no general information about snakes prior to addressing his specific species (Green snakes and Rainbow snakes). During interviews, Patrick acknowledged the guide's two-page overview but explained that he just wrote the highlighted heading, Snakes, not the introductory information, because "It's too much and it would just tell a lot of the same stuff."

Of the 32 snakes profiled in *Reptiles and Amphibians* (Zim & Smith, 1956), Patrick chose to include two (Green and Rainbow). During an interview, Alice asked why had decided on these two species.

PATRICK: 'Cause they are, like, the most common.
ALICE: Okay. These two are the most common? How did you know that?
PATRICK: 'Cause I got a book at home, but it was my parents' book . . . and it said that the Rainbow snake and Green snakes were the most common.

Patrick repeated this organizational scheme (heading, followed by two specific types) throughout his report. For example, his Lizards page (Figure 5.4, line 13) featured the Chuckwalla and the Spiny and True Iguana. In asking why he made these choices, he repeated: "They are the most common. I know the most about them." His response varied with respect to this choice of salamanders/newts: "I want to do my favorite salamanders. I like how they got little bitty feet [*pointing to the Congo-eel*]. It's so cute."

A quick scan of the field guide revealed no reference to any of these species as being "most common"; in fact, with the exception of the Green snake, the maps suggested otherwise (e.g., the True and Spiny Iguana are not native to the United States). We suspect that Patrick made his selections based on personal interest.

Having established the significant influence that Zim and Smith's field guide had on Patrick's report, we turn now to the intertextual ties at the paragraph level.

Paragraph organization. In this section, we analyze the degree to which Patrick aligned the sentences in his paragraphs with those of his intertext, *Reptiles and Amphibians.* (*Reminder:* This analysis compares the flow of sentences at the paragraph level with that of the intertext, regardless of whether the sentences were direct quotes, partial direct quotes, or paraphrases.) Patrick's report included a total of 11 entries; 6 qualified as paragraphs (as defined in Chapter 2). Five were coded selected alignment (e.g., Rainbow snake, Spiny and True Iguana, Congo-eel, newts, and Robber frog) because he selected some, but not all, of the content from Zim and Smith's (1956) various paragraphs. One paragraph (i.e., amphibians) was coded self-aligned.

To illustrate selected alignment, examine the decisions that Patrick made with respect to the flow of content in Zim and Smith's (1956) entry on the Rainbow snake (Figure 5.7). Patrick recorded Zim and Smith's first four sentences and seventh sentence, omitting the less essential material (the comparison statement and the unknowns) when copying content for his Rainbow snake paragraph. However, this ability to sort major from minor content tended not to prevail in most of his appropriated passages. In discussing his penchant for selected alignment, Patrick cited reasons ranging from a concern about length to reader interest. For example, note that Patrick copied only the first two sentences (see Figure 5.4, lines 14–16) from Zim and Smith's Chuckwalla entry (Figure 5.6), explaining:

PATRICK: Well, see, there would be too much. There'd be too much 'cause it probably would go like all the way done to here [*pointing to bottom of his notebook page*]. And I won't have room for the Spiny and True Iguana. They're my favorite.

CAROL: Oh. Did you read the whole paragraph first and then decide you just wanted sentences 1 and 2?

PATRICK: I only copied the good stuff our class didn't know—well, some things they could know.

CAROL: You copied sentences that you think the readers don't know?

PATRICK: Yeah.

CAROL: So you decided that readers would know that the Indians used to eat the Chuckwallas?

PATRICK: Well, probably.

Zim and Smith's *Reptiles and Amphibians*	Patrick's Report
Rainbow Snake is a handsome species. Stripes vary from orange to red. The underside is red with a double row of black spots. This snake of swampy regions often burrows and is not commonly seen. It is smaller (40 in.) than the closely related Mud Snake (P. 75) and like it has a sharper "spine" at the end of its tail. Little is known of its life history and feeding habits. The female lays 20 or more eggs, which hatch in about 60 days. (Zim & Smith, 1956, p. 74)	Rainbow Snake is a handsome species. Stripes vary from orange to red. The underside is red with a double row of black spots. This snake swampy regions often burrows and is not commonly seen. The female lays 20 or more eggs, which hatch in about 60 days.

Figure 5.7. An example of how Patrick selectively aligned his report with his intertext.

Inspection of his next entry on iguanas (Figure 5.4, line 17) suggests that Patrick's original reasoning that "there would be too much" on the page if he copied every sentence per species, rather than reader knowledge, predominated. In this entry, Patrick copied the first three sentences and then omitted the remainder of the text that contained the key content.

During this interview on the iguanas, I decided to call into question Patrick's verbatim copying of *Reptiles and Amphibians*. (Bear with us while we simultaneously address both organizational intertextuality at the paragraph level and orientational intertextuality at sentence level as the two are interconnected.)

CAROL: Last week, we talked about what makes a good report [*pointing the poster*]. Do you remember what Colin said about not copying another author's words?
PATRICK: I don't know that.
CAROL: Well, Colin made the point that copying someone else's words is like stealing.
PATRICK: I don't know how to do the quotation marks.
CAROL: It's great that you know about quotation marks. Yes, that's what you'd use if you copied someone else's words. I can show you how to insert them.
PATRICK: I'm still adding on stuff, this stuff that's not in the book.

CAROL: That's a great idea to add things you know or that you've read in other books. You can write what you know in your own words. . . .

Patrick's reference to quotation marks and his plan to add "stuff that's not in the book" suggested that he knew that copying is not permissible. It was after this interview that Patrick adopted a new strategy for aligning the sentences in his paragraphs. He arrived at the next interview with his notebook open to his next entry, "ALLIGATORS AND CROCODILES" (see Figure 5.4, line 21), beaming with pride:

CAROL: What do we have here?
PATRICK: First I read it. I read what we did and then I thought about it and did it on my own words.
CAROL: You did?
PATRICK: But I don't know if they are the same sentences or not 'cause I closed the book after I read it.
CAROL: So you closed the book first. Were the ideas fresh in your memory?
PATRICK: Yeah.

In comparing Patrick's text with the original and noting once again his verbatim copying, I realized that Patrick's excitement centered on his decision to *rearrange* the authors' sentences. After copying the first sentence, he copied the ninth sentence, followed by the eleventh, fourth, and third. We talked about this decision to reorganize content as well as the flexibility that writers have when dealing with isolated facts about size, habitat, food, and so forth. That accomplished, I decided to address his verbatim sentence copying by recopying his alligator/crocodile entry as he watched, adding my byline, handing it to him, and asking him how he liked *my* report. Patrick smiled and said, "I know what you're doing." I asked what I would have to do to make it my report. Patrick answered, "Write your own one, not mine." So I wrote a few sentences that paraphrased the content to illustrate the point. I asked what he planned to write about next and he said amphibians. Confident about his rudimentary knowledge, I asked him to tell me what he knew about amphibians. As Patrick talked, I created a simple content map. I then explained he could read Zim and Smith's entry to check this information, add new content to his map, and write his entry using his content map. Patrick left promising to do the next report "in my own words."

Patrick did not disappoint. He arrived back the next day with his entry on "Amphibians" (Figure 5.4, lines 27–30), declaring "I knew all this from 2nd grade." In cross-checking Zim and Smith's two-page spread on amphibians, it was clear that Patrick neither aligned his sentences with this text nor copied any sentences in part or in whole. This was his first self-aligned, paraphrased paragraph. Because it was also clear that he hadn't read Zim and Smith's entry, choosing rather to write from the content map he had dictated, we talked about how writers must double-check their facts before publishing their books. Was he sure that some salamanders lived "in the water their whole lives"? Where did he learn that salamanders live "to be about 10–15 years old"? I watched his enthusiasm deflate; he had done what I had asked (in part) and now I was adding on the variable of accuracy with which he didn't have to contend when he copied from the text. I suggested that we both research these facts and then decide if we needed to revise. He asked if he could first write about his favorite salamander, the Congo-eel.

During the next conference, he placed his Congo-eel entry (Figure 5.4, lines 32–34) and the original text from the field guide side by side to "prove" that he wrote this piece in his own words. Both his first and last sentences were copied verbatim; however, his three middle sentences contained two partial direct quotes and one paraphrase. In addition, he had selectively aligned his text with Zim and Smith's (1956), rearranging their content (appropriating the first, second, sixth, and fourth sentences respectively). The fact that Patrick reverted back to reliance on his intertext in order to write this piece on the Congo-eel after crafting his piece on amphibians from memory highlighted the challenge of nonfiction writing. Without extended knowledge on the topic of Congo-eels, Patrick had little choice but to lean heavily on his intertext.

In sum, Patrick appropriated quite extensively from the top-level text organization of his intertext: title page, introductory sections, headings, and subheadings. He also incorporated "chapters," appropriating not from his intertext but from other reptile books he had read (and probably his textbooks and peer reports). At the paragraph level, Patrick selectively aligned the sentences of many of his entries with those of his intertext, stating that his selection was tied to audience awareness (but, in practice, his selection appeared to tie to personal interest). With coaching, he crafted a paragraph from personal knowledge that was coded self-alignment. From Patrick we learned that young writers can appropriate top-level organizational features of intertexts for their own reports quite successfully but that the business of organizing content at the paragraph level requires multifaceted, recursive demonstration. In the following section, we trace the evolution of Patrick's voice appropriations.

Orientational Intertextuality: Appropriating the Voices of Others

As already established, much of Patrick's report directly echoed his intertext, *Reptiles and Amphibians*. Of the seven orientational intertextual patterns— direct quote, partial direct quote, textual paraphrase, personal-knowledge paraphrase, personal-experience paraphrase, picture observation, and stylization—direct quotes predominated. Patrick copied verbatim every sentence from Zim and Smith (1956) for his first three pages (five entries). Of a total of 43 sentences in his seven-page report, 26 (61%) were direct quotes. As with Kyle, we pursued the issue of verbatim copying during conferences. Beginning with the iguana entry, Patrick was reminded about the inappropriateness of copying any author's work. As discussed in the previous section, Patrick interpreted these discussions to mean that if he rearranged the authors' sentences, he would no longer be an offender. With further clarification and the opportunity to demonstrate his knowledge via a content map, Patrick rallied to write his amphibian section without consultation of his intertext. He attributed his knowledge about amphibians to books and to watching a movie in 2nd grade. All these sentences were coded as personal-knowledge paraphrases.

This success was followed by the challenge of figuring out what do with his next entries on the Congo-eel and newts. Realizing that he didn't have the knowledge to write about these specific species and with an awareness that copying is "like stealing," Patrick demonstrated greater versatility with respect to voice appropriation in his newt entry (see Figure 5.8). During the interview about this entry, Patrick proudly declared that he didn't copy Zim and Smith (1956) and said everything "in my own words." As with every entry, he continued to appropriate verbatim the authors' lead sentence, explaining that he had to copy it "because it had the title, NEWTS, in it and I needed it." He followed with two partial direct quotes about the eastern and western newts, embedding two personal-knowledge paraphrases and a stylization. First, he calculated (erroneously) the newt's actual size ("that's 9 in. long"), a (redundant) fact not included by the authors. And to impress upon the reader just how large this newt was, Patrick inserted his only stylization (statement for dramatic effect) ("that's almost One foot."). Patrick ended this piece with the inference that the Western Newt is the largest newt in the United States. When asked how he knew this, Patrick replied, "It [the book] would have said it if there's a bigger one, and it didn't, so I know it is."

While issues of content redundancy and content verification loomed, this (and his previous) entry marked a significant step forward for Patrick. He moved out of his comfort zone with verbatim copying and tried his hand at partial direct quotes and paraphrasing using personal knowledge. Patrick also crafted one textual paraphrase in his Congo-eel entry (Figure 5.4, lines 33–34): "The Hellbender is much more smaller then the Congo-Eel." The original line read: "The Hellbender (16 to 20 in.) is shorter and broader, and lives farther north" (Zim & Smith, 1956, p. 139). While not as content-rich as the original, this textual paraphrase earned Patrick a word of praise.

In sum, Patrick included 26 (61%) direct quotes and six (14%) partial direct quotes (see examples in Figure 5.8). Like his peers (see Chapter 2), Patrick

Zim and Smith's *Reptiles and Amphibians*	Patrick's Report
NEWTS are attractive, interesting salamanders. Of the five species, the eastern (3 in. long) is perhaps the best known. . . . The Western Newt is about twice the size of the eastern species and differs in appearance too. (Zim & Smith, 1956, pp. 142–143)	NEWTS are attractive, interesting salamanders. *(Direct quote)* The eastern newt grows to be about 3 in. long. *(Partial direct quote)* The Western newt is about twice the size of the eastern newt. *(Partial direct quote)* that's 9 in. long. *(Personal-knowledge paraphrase)* that's almost One foot. *(Stylization)* The Western newt is the biggest newt in the United States. *(Personal-knowledge paraphrase)*

Figure 5.8. Patrick's transition to partial direct quotes and personal-knowledge paraphrases.

viewed these partial direct quotes as his own because he "changed around the words." Patrick also constructed seven (17%) personal-knowledge paraphrases, one textual paraphrase, one stylization, and two picture observations.

Toward the end of our study, Patrick presented us with his official "report." He had pulled the reptile/amphibian pages out of his notebook and stapled them together. Delighted with his "publication" (although it was not revised or edited), we expressed our gratitude. Patrick smiled, "If you think this one is good, wait till you see my report on birds. I've already started."

Patrick came to this task of report writing with a genuine fascination about his topic and with the knowledge that nonfiction authors organize their material using chapters and headings, select the material they want to cover, and create a visually attractive document. Along the way, he learned that unmarked verbatim copying was unacceptable, began to experiment with partial direct quotes and stylizations, and started to integrate personal-knowledge paraphrases.

TEXT-BOUND WRITERS: PROFILE SUMMARY

Kyle and Patrick were just 2 of the 11 3rd graders who wrote reports that were driven by the texts they consulted. Unlike the strategic writers profiled in Chapter 3, our text-bound writers didn't view research as a recursive process of reading across sources, reflecting, organizing, and synthesizing ideas for the purpose of establishing their perspective on their topic. Rather, most adopted a strategy of read one sentence in one book and copy it in part or in full. Some consulted multiple sources to write their reports but treated each source separately. For example, Kyle recorded information from one book, then moved onto the next, copying without regard for relevance, redundancy, or coherence. Lack of coherence was particularly apparent on the page in which he strung together caption after caption from various pages of his intertext. Others, like Patrick, latched onto one text resource and stayed close to this intertext both organizationally and orientationally. Some, like Patrick, engaged in mental planning during the act of composing; others, like Kyle, proceeded without a plan.

Undoubtedly, the most disconcerting attribute of our text-bound writers was their verbatim copying. Like most teachers, we warned against copying; like many kids, they went ahead and copied. The prevalence of this verbatim copying pushed us not only to reexamine our failure to provide effective instruction but also to probe the layers of misconception that young writers construct about plagiarism and to illuminate the disconnect between originality and plagiarism. We have devoted a section in Chapter 6 to this vexing problem.

It would be unfair to end this profile with the sense that Patrick and Kyle possessed little knowledge about reading and writing nonfiction. Both were the first at their tables to commit to nonfiction, generating an excitement about report writing that influenced their peers. Both chose to write about topics that fascinated them. While they had absorbed some general information from books, movies, and TV programs, they entered this report-writing process with the goal of learning more—not unlike acclaimed science writers (Cole, 1996; Gibbons, 2002) who, when asked how they chose their topics, often cite lack of knowledge as the impetus. Their fascination with their topics sustained their writing efforts over a couple of weeks. While neither was able to engage in the strategic decision making required for successful report writing, each demonstrated some fundamental understandings (e.g., Patrick—that reports have titles and an organizational structure; Kyle—that writers access multiple sources and include knowledge learned from nonprint sources).

Text-bound writers remind us that we need to start where they are and build on what they know. It is only through continual conversations with young writers about their reports that we can begin to sort out the intricacies of this complex endeavor and design instruction responsive to their needs.

Teaching Nonfiction Report Writing: Lessons Learned

IN THIS CHAPTER, we consider the pedagogical implications of our findings about children's nonfiction report writing, with a focus on lessons learned. We entered the instructional phase of our study with the goal of putting nonfiction center stage in order to ignite an interest in nonfiction literature and literacy. To guide their efforts, we targeted the "reports" of "Ms. Frizzle's kids" in Joanna Cole's *Magic School Bus* series as the intertextual prototype, with the hope that our 3rd graders would choose to write their own "little" reports. However, it quickly became evident that we had underestimated the children's affinity for and knowledge about this genre. As discussed in Chapter 1, once the call for nonfiction was made, our 3rd graders were out of the gate. They didn't wait for guidance from us. By the time we began instruction on the text structures (sequence, compare/contrast) in the *Magic School Bus* "reports" (which consist of very brief paragraphs, or bulleted summaries), many children were immersed in writing multipaged, multichapter reports, replete with chapter headings and stylized statements. The extent of our writers' intertextual understandings suggested that we had forgotten the cardinal developmental principle that knowledge begins globally and becomes increasingly differentiated and abstract over time (Gibson & Levin, 1975). This disconnect between what the 3rd graders were pursuing and what we were teaching characterized most of phase 3, which was probably inevitable given the freedom afforded by writing workshop. Accepting and exploiting this disconnect is just one of the pedagogical implications that we gleaned. We turn now to the other lessons learned in working side by side with our 3rd graders.

KINDLE A PASSION FOR NONFICTION LITERATURE, BUT DON'T WAIT FOR IMMERSION TO TRIGGER NONFICTION WRITING

The preliminary findings that elementary children struggle to read and write nonfiction (Alverman & Boothby, 1982; Britton et al., 1975; Chall & Jacobs, 1983) resulted in the call for nonfiction literature and literacy instruction (Daniels, 1990; Durkin, 1978–1979; Newkirk, 1987; Pappas, 1991). These experts argued that if we don't read nonfiction to children and don't show them how expository texts work, we can't expect them to succeed in school and in society in general. The ability to consume and generate multiple and varied forms of written discourse in socially and culturally appropriate ways is essential if they are to accomplish personal, professional, and civic goals (Christie, 1987; Kamberelis & Bovino, 1999; Kress, 1999; Stotsky, 1995).

If recent literature is an accurate barometer, teachers are infusing their classroom libraries and curricula with nonfiction literature (Broaddus & Ivey, 2002; Camp, 2000; Caswell & Duke, 1998; Doiron, 1994; Duke & Bennett-Armistead, 2003; Duthie, 1996; Fountas & Pinnell, 1996, 1999, 2001; Freeman & Person, 1998a, 1998b; Harvey, 1998; Oyler & Barry, 1996; Pinnell & Fountas, 2002; Ray, 2004; Stead, 2002; Sudol & King, 1996). Duke (2000) and Kamberelis (1999) remind us, though, that we have far to go in ensuring that all children interact in multiple ways with this literature. Duke (2000) observed 20 1st grade classrooms of high and low socioeconomic status (SES), logging the kinds of books that were available in each room as well as the range of print materials on walls and other surfaces. She found a pronounced scarcity of informational texts: 13% of the books and 4% of displayed print in the high-SES classroom were informational; only 7% of the books and 2% of displayed print were informational in the low-SES classrooms. Duke also found that children spent only 3.6 minutes per day engaged with nonfiction text, including cross-curricular endeavors. While we suspect that these percentages would increase with grade level, they suggest that nonfiction remains the literary stepchild.

This call for nonfiction is not meant to imply that attention to fiction should be diminished. The emergent literacy research is unequivocal about the centrality of story to children's language and literacy development (Chomsky, 1972; Clay, 1979; Durkin, 1966; Elley, 1989; Purcell-Gates, McIntyre, & Freppon, 1988; Snow, 1983; Sulzby, 1985). However, equal access to fiction and nonfiction is essential if we are to foster purposeful engagement with the expansive range of genres (Duke, 2000; Kamberelis & Bovino, 1999; Pappas, 1991). Two avenues of particular promise are informational storybooks—such as the *Magic School Bus* books, which merge fact and fiction—and text sets that pair fiction and nonfiction. Preliminary research shows that children absorbed significantly more scientific content from an informational storybook than from a nonfiction book on the same topic (Leal 1993; 1995). While we haven't been able to locate research specific to fiction/nonfiction texts sets, we suspect the use of such text sets (Camp, 2000; Livingston & Kurkjian, 2004) would have similar benefits. For example, Camp (2000) recommends linking the story *Stellaluna* (Cannon, 1993) with the informational book *Bats* (Bland, 1997); Livingston and Kurkjian (2004) recommend pairing Ruby Bridges's (1999) powerful autobiography, *Through My Eyes*, with Robert Coles's (1995) biography, *The Story of Ruby Bridges*.

Interestingly, guided reading collections have begun to include fiction and related nonfiction, printed opposite each other in the same book, accessed by flipping the book over (e.g., The Orbit Collection).

While research on the benefits of nonfiction to literacy development is still in its infancy, the promise is great (Dale & Farnan, 1998; Duke, 2000; Duke & Bennett-Armistead, 2003; Kamberelis & Bovino, 1999; Pappas, 1991). For example, surveys of children's reading interests have long reported on children's intrigue with nonfiction: (1) 1st and 2nd graders prefer books about animals and nature, followed by fantasy (Consuelo, 1967); (2) 2nd, 3rd, and 4th graders are more interested in reading books about real animals than stories about talking animals (Beta Upsilon Chapter, 1974; Kirsch, 1975); and (3) upper elementary boys show a strong preference for nonfiction (Lynch-Brown, 1977; Simpson, 1996; Smith & Wilhelm, 2002; Wolfson, Manning, & Manning, 1984), including books about "hobbies, sports, and activities they might engage in, and in informational resources" (Schwartz, 2003). In their review of studies on reading preferences, Monson and Sebesta (1991) concluded:

> A number of studies reported during the last two decades single out informational books as highly interesting to children in upper grades . . . and particularly to boys. Recent studies also show strong interest in biography for this group of students. It is difficult to view this finding, or any other related to reading choices, as unrelated to publishing trends. It is surely true that, in the last decade, students have had access to far more well-written informational books than at any time in the past. (p. 668)

This wealth of delectable informational books may be why 65% of the kindergartners in Pappas's study said that they preferred the informational texts to storybooks; in subsequent book sessions "almost all of the children" (Pappas, 1991, p. 461) maintained their preference for exposition. Findings such as these are important because of the strong correlation between voluntary reading and reading achievement (Anderson, Wilson, & Fielding, 1988; Morrow, 1983; Schiefele, Krapp, & Winteler, 1992). In a nutshell, children who read for pleasure outscore their peers.

In addition, immersion in nonfiction increases children's vocabulary and knowledge about the key features of exposition. When kindergartners were immersed in nonfiction for 4 months, they used significantly more past-tense verbs, generic noun constructions, information book beginnings, and comparative/contrastive constructions during retellings (Duke & Kays, 1998). Finally, immersion in informational text "is key because there appears to be a relationship between the kinds of text to which children are exposed and the kinds they chose to write and are able to write well" (Duke & Bennett-Armistead, 2003, p. 129).

Intrigued by this immersion/writing relationship, we experimented first with an invitation to write nonfiction and then with increasing doses of nonfiction literature over the first few months of the schoolyear (see Chapter 1). During the first week of school, we told our 3rd graders that they could choose their own genres and topics during writing workshop. Together, we brainstormed possible fiction and nonfiction topics, recording and posting ideas as well as a range of genres. None of the children responded to the invitation to write nonfiction during the first few weeks of school. During the first phase of our study, we read aloud one nonfiction book each week (along with three storybooks). We chose nonfiction literature that tied to the vernal pool science curriculum and that we hoped not only fostered intellectual engagement but also evoked aesthetic response (Rosenblatt, 1978; Spink, 1996; Tower, 2002)—books that would satisfy their endless fascination with animals (G. Anderson et al., 1985; Monson & Sebesta, 1991). None chose to write nonfiction. During the second phase, which included an increased diet of nonfiction literature (read-alouds three times a week), none chose to write nonfiction, with the exception of two who began reports in response to a dinosaur/fossil unit in their science textbooks.

In speculating on the reasons for this dearth of nonfiction, we raised questions about the literature we chose and about the construct of immersion but pointed to the social dynamic as pivotal (see Chapter 1). Granted the freedom to write in any genre, all of our 3rd graders chose to write personal narratives at the beginning of the year. Why? Because Alice, adhering to advice of Graves (1994), modeled personal narratives. At the end of September, Sarah wrote the first story, "The Good Haunted house," launching the Halloween story genre that triggered 28 other stories by the end of October. Story writing entered the classroom without any prompting from us, without any instruction. Why? A lifetime of story immersion at home and in school afforded the confidence needed to weave together basic story grammar elements. As each of these genres emerged, the 3rd graders jumped on the bandwagon in order to gain membership in the writing club (Dyson, 1993; Smith, 1988).

If someone, Alice or a child, had crafted and shared a report or biography or other nonfiction subgenre at the start of the schoolyear, would the 3rd graders have chosen to adopt nonfiction? Our findings suggest that many would have if the conditions of immersion, intention to write nonfiction, and responsive instruction were in place. To set the stage, we should have *shown* (not told) them what we meant by choice of genre.

SHOW (DON'T JUST TELL) YOUNG WRITERS WHAT IS MEANT BY CHOICE OF GENRE

In asking our 3rd graders to brainstorm the various types of writing (genres) that writers produce (with specific attention to nonfiction subgenres) and posting their responses, we thought we had set the stage for legitimate choice. In retrospect, we should have gone beyond merely "telling" the children that they could write in any genre. "Show, not tell," one of the commandments in the writer's Bible (Atwell, 1987; Calkins, 1991; Murray, 1989; Zinsser, 1985), needs to be applied not only to the context of genre-specific writing (e.g., "Show your character's state of mind, don't tell it") but also to the construct of choice itself. We needed to "show, not tell" our young writers what we meant when we said they could chose their own genre. (*Note*: This dictum obviously applies to the wide range of nonfiction subgenres [the letter, report, biography, etc.] as well as fiction and poetry.) We are convinced that if we had invited our 4th-grade guest speakers to present their Australian animal reports to our 3rd graders (see the Phase 3 section in Chapter 1) in early September and had followed their presentation with the call for other "experts," our students would have launched the nonfiction report–writing momentum much sooner in the schoolyear. Sowers (1985) attributed her 1st graders' earliest form of writing, the "all-about" book—a book in which they told everything they knew about a particular topic (e.g., dinosaurs)—to the direct exposure they had to the "all-about" books of 1st graders from previous years. Thus, the construct of choice must be coupled with demonstration: examples of nonfiction writing by published and peer authors and energized talk about where these authors got their ideas and knowledge to write nonfiction. Then the "social work" (Dyson, 1993, p. 59)—social interplay that simultaneously situates each young writer in nonfiction endeavor and in a web of peer relationships—will begin.

Such demonstration should also specify how their writer's notebook works in relation to the final product. Toward the end of phase 3, Patrick (see Chapter 5) pulled his report out of his notebook, created a cover page, stapled the pages together, and handed it to us for the classroom library, the only student to do so. Thanks to Patrick, we realized that we should have talked about the "product" from the get-go, which would have placed a premium on the writing processes of revision, editing, and publishing (processes that had been used by the 3rd graders on previous writing samples but not independently adopted for their reports) for a formal audience. This guideline applies to other genres. Perhaps none of the children chose to write letters of any kind because it didn't make much sense to draft a letter to a real person if the letter was going to stay in the notebook. Demonstration of how a writer could draft a letter in the notebook, and then revise and write/type the final copy on special letter paper, available at the writing center along with envelopes, would help children see the logic.

EXPECT A RANGE OF REPORT TYPES
DURING WRITING WORKSHOP

During phase 2 of our study, our two nonfiction trailblazers began writing reports by recalling knowledge accumulated from their curricular study and previous experiences, but they accessed no resources. The reports of these memory-only writers were discussed in Chapter 2. The day after we showcased these reports, three children chose to write reports: Danielle began a report on tropical fish based solely on her experiences (Chapter 4), Patrick began copying verbatim from a reptile book (Chapter 5), and Andrea began her report by interviewing a peer and recording what he knew about sharks. It was clear from the start that our youngsters, given no instruction during 3rd grade, approached report writing differently. Some relied totally on memory, others on their experiences or peers, and still others on the texts they consulted. During the next writing workshop, Caitlyn began her seven-page report on horses in which she successfully merged her extensive experience with horses with her consultation of both fiction and nonfiction trade books (see Chapter 3). This finding with respect to a range of task impressions (strategic, textbound, experience-only, and memory-only) corroborated the thrust of Many and colleagues' (1996) earlier research with sixth graders.

This taught us the importance of discussing stances early on with the goal of helping children move toward a more strategic stance. For example, for writers who crafted reports exclusively from their experiences, we would highlight the strength of integrating direct experience (checked for accuracy)—but also the limitations. We might use Kathryn Lasky's (1990) *Dinosaur Dig* to illustrate. This book traces the Lasky family's trip to the Montana Badlands to dig for fossils. Readers follow the family as they pack, travel west, descend treacherous buttes, and excavate fossils. We would ask why they thought Lasky didn't restrict her photo essay to just her family's experiences and why she integrated information about dinosaurs and fossils, including information learned from the onsite paleontologist. We would show that the effectiveness of *Dinosaur Dig* is tied to this integration of accurate science information and personal experience. We would then showcase Caitlyn's horse report (Chapter 3) and its history, and draw parallels between Lasky and Caitlyn: Both used their personal experiences and knowledge accumulated from multiple sources to create their pieces.

In addition, we would establish that not all writers write from direct experience. Many authors choose topics about which they know very little. As Joanna Cole (1996), author of the *Magic School Bus* series, explains: "When I write nonfiction, I often choose subjects I've always been curious about: evolution, how cuts and bruises heal, how a chick grows inside an egg" (p. 8). For example, we might brainstorm what Cole, who knew very little about baby chicks, had to do to write *A Chick Hatches* (1976) and then share her research process:

> In preparing to write a science book, I always read much more than one would think I needed to. I read as many books as I can find on the subject. I look in libraries and bookstores. I ask for help from librarians. I dig into the computer at the library. I try to find articles in scientific magazines, and I search for videos

on my subject. Sometimes, but not always, I read children's books to see how other authors have handled the subject. (Cole, 1996, p. 17)

We also would note that, unlike Kathryn Lasky (1993), who almost always has experienced her topic firsthand, Cole (1996) shies away from such experiences. At this point, we would ask Colin, author of a penguin report (see Chapter 3), to explain how he, like Joanna Cole, had to rely on a range of text sources for most of his report (noting that he did observe penguins at the aquarium when he was in 2nd grade).

In sum, we would build on their understandings and show how successful nonfiction writers, peer and published, adopt a strategic stance toward their work. In addition, we would "be aware of the explicit and implicit messages about the nature of research" (Many et al., 1996, p. 33) that we send. With our modeling of Ms. Frizzle kids' reports, for example, we sent the message that reports are very brief, often bulleted summaries. Fortunately, our 3rd graders were already pursuing their own ideas about reports when our introduction to *The Magic School Bus* reports began.

MAKE PUBLIC THE INTERTEXTUAL LINKS THAT PUBLISHED AND PEER WRITERS FORGE

The advent of literature-based programs in the 1980s spurred enormous interest in children's authors (Jenkins, 1999). While the bulk of author information in the form of autobiographies, biographies, videotapes, convention speeches, and journal articles ties to fiction writers, increasing attention is being given to nonfiction authors (Duthie, 1996; Jenkins, 1999; Keck, 1992; Robb, 2004). For example, autobiographical information about Joanna Cole can be located in her autobiography, *On the Bus with Joanna Cole* (1996); in the "Meet the Author" videotape available from Delta Education; and on her web site (http://www.evansday.com/cole.html). In addition, Cole is featured in *Meet the Authors and Illustrators* (Kovacs & Preller, 1991) as well as in the reference journals *Something About the Author* and *Children Literature Review*. As we will demonstrate in the sections that follow, these resources can be used to illuminate the research and writing processes of acclaimed nonfiction writers.

Show How Authors Cast Wide Their Nets for Ideas

Recall phase 3 of our study, which included continued immersion in nonfiction books and explicit instruction in the nonfiction report (Chapter 1). In the opening lesson, Kyle, our second nonfiction writer, placed his report, "fossils and Dinosaurs," on the overhead and read it to the class. The 3rd graders were asked to guess where he got his ideas. Their responses included "We're studying about fossils right now," "a book about fossils," "*Time for Kids* magazine because they had about digging for dinosaurs," "We watched a movie about dinosaurs," and "our science book." Kyle confirmed that he decided to write about fossils and dinosaurs "because we're learning about fossils," and added, "I dug up dinosaur bones at Roger William Park Zoo, and I saw *Jurassic Park*." This array of ideational sources—curriculum, print materials, media, human resources, and personal experience—continued to be reported during interviews with the 3rd graders (Chapter 2). Perhaps because of our thematic discussion, not one child who chose to write nonfiction lamented, "but I don't know what to write about." This suggests that such talk about the genesis of ideas is an important dimension in ensuring the pursuit of nonfiction writing. To reinforce and extend this base, the intertextual insights of published nonfiction authors should be included. For example, Joanna Cole (1996) explains where she got the idea to write her first book:

> Since my favorite subject in grade school had been science, and since I had been an avid watcher of insects as a child, I decided to write a children's book about insects. But all of the insects I thought of had already been done. My father told me about an article he had read in the newspaper about cockroaches, and how they were "living fossils," animals that hadn't changed much since prehistoric times. This interested me, so I wrote a book about cockroaches. (p. 4)

In sum, we do children a great service when we show them that all nonfiction writers, consciously or unconsciously, dip into the intertextual "Cauldron," as Tolkien (1965) called it, to find and develop their ideas. Essential also are the multiple public forums for sharing writing ideas—status of the class (Atwell, 1987), author's chair (Graves, 1994; Hansen, 1987), authors' circle (Harste, Short, & Burke, 1988), partner share, and so forth.

Explore How and Why Authors Organize Their Texts

As noted at beginning of this chapter, with the exception of introducing the organizational construct of heading, we essentially ignored this dimension of report writing. While our 3rd graders didn't take any formal steps to organize their information prior to drafting their reports, many appropriated the organizational schemes of their print resources (titles, chapter divisions and/or chapter headings, and/or headings) during the act of composing. In hindsight, we missed a golden opportunity at the beginning of our instruction to highlight the organizational features contained in our first nonfiction writer's report (see Chapter 1). Jessica presented her report on the overhead, reading the first three pages of her report, which included a title ("A report on Fossils") and numbered chapter headings (e.g., "Chapter 2

Are Fossils Old?"). While we discussed the thematic links that spurred Jessica's report, we did not probe her organizational links. At that point, we should have handed out copies of the Aliki books (e.g., *Digging Up Dinosaurs* [1988], *Fossils Tell of Long Ago* [1990], *My Visit to the Dinosaurs* [1985b], *Dinosaurs Are Different* [1985a]), which Jessica had read prior to beginning her report, and asked the children to examine Aliki's organizational framework. In concluding that Aliki used continuous text with no organizational features across all these books, we would probe Jessica as to the source of her decision to use chapters. As reported during her initial interview, Jessica attributed her appropriation to her science textbook and her father's "big" book on fossils. The stage would now be set for the following series of mini-lessons. We would ask the class to take out their science textbook, and examine its organizational scheme with the goal of helping children understand, for example, that a chapter is a major division of knowledge (not a single paragraph of content) that is often subdivided into sections, each section with its own heading. We then would examine Patricia Lauber's (1996a) *How the Dinosaurs Came To Be* and discuss parallels with the science textbook, noting that Lauber's book contains a table of contents, chapters that contain 6 to 10 pages, pages that contain an average of five or six paragraphs, illustrations on most pages but not all, headings that subdivide some chapters, and an index that also serves as a glossary. We then would compare Lauber's book to Simon's (1990) *New Questions and Answers About Dinosaurs*, noting that Simon organized each two-page spread as follows: a heading in question format, a one-page response consisting of two or three paragraphs, and a dinosaur illustration that filled one page and spilled over onto the text page. Discussion would center on why Simon didn't label these two-page spreads as chapters. To reinforce the construct of headings, Simon's other dinosaur books (e.g., *The Largest Dinosaurs* [1986], *The Smallest Dinosaurs* [1982]) as well as books such as *New Dinos* (Tanaka, 2002) could be analyzed. Returning to Aliki's books in conjunction with others, such as Pringle's (1995) *Dinosaurs! Strange and Wonderful*, and Markle's (2000) *Outside and Inside Dinosaurs*, we would analyze their book features (larger print, simpler sentences, one or two short paragraphs per page, illustrations on every page, no table of contents, no index, etc.) and infer why these authors chose not to use any organizational features. In addition, we would showcase some of Patricia Lauber's other books (e.g., *The News About Dinosaurs* [1989], *The True-or-False Book of Cats* [2001], *An Octopus Is Amazing* [1996b]) to illustrate the range of decisions that one author needed to make about text organization based on her target audience, the content to be included, and visual supports (illustrations, photographs, etc.). Rounding out this series of mini-lessons would be discussion of the difference between a report and a trade book with examples of former students' reports as well as trade books showcased.

Abandon the Notion of Voice as "Original" Authorship; Show How Polyphonic Voices Infiltrate Every Act of Writing

Voice reenvisioned. Donald Graves (1983), father of the writing process movement at the elementary level, has stressed the primacy of voice in writing: "Voice is the imprint of ourselves on our writing. It is that part of the self that pushes the writing ahead, the dynamo in the process. Take voice away and the writing collapses of its own weight" (p. 227). Over the last 20 years, writing-process experts (e.g., Calkins, 1994; Fletcher, 1993; Harvey, 1998) have echoed Graves's call for teachers to help children delve deep to find their unique voices:

> Everyone has an inner voice. . . . The writer may not know exactly what the inner voice represents (unconscious? superego? spirit?) but the writer does know one thing: the inner voice is spokesperson for the inner life. . . . The writer must learn to stalk the inner voice. (Fletcher, 1993, pp. 68–69)

However, as our findings and those of others (Cairney, 1990; Kamberelis & Scott, 1992; Donovan, 2001) have revealed, young writers first stalk the voices of those around them—authors, teachers, parents, peers, the media— and then use these voices to shape their message. As Bakhtin (1981) posited, "It becomes 'one's own' only when the speaker populates it with his own intention, his own accent, when he appropriates the word, adapting it for is own semantic and expressive intention" (p. 294). In essence, Bakhtin (1986) has forced a revision of the romantic view of writing as a process of "burrowing deep into subjectivity . . . to discover your authentic voice, and a voice that expresses who you are" (Lensmire, 1994, p. 11) to a view that recognizes writing as a process of spiraling outward to the voices that surround us in order to find our point of view (Lensmire, 1994). The instructional implications are huge. Rather than telling children to "burrow deep," we need to show them how all writers appropriate polyphonic voices in a variety of ways (Bakhtin, 1986).

The reports and transcript excerpts of our 3rd graders, particularly those of our strategic writers (see Chapter 3), are potent vehicles for demonstrating a range of voice appropriations specific to the nonfiction report. When Caitlyn and Colin were asked about the voice origin of each sentence in their reports ("Where did you learn this information?"), five of the seven primary intertextual patterns at the sentence level were noted: (1) personal-knowledge paraphrase (information recalled from the past, attributed to a person, a book, a television program, etc.); (2) personal-experience paraphrase (information usually learned through firsthand experience from a more knowledgeable other); (3) textual paraphrase (information paraphrased from print material); (4) partial direct quote (a sentence in which the writer paraphrased part

of the text and copied a phrase or more from the original); and (5) stylization (statements of dramatic effect or inquiry, personal opinion, and illustrations). Examples of each pattern would be presented for the purpose of
discussing the strengths and/or limitations of the various paraphrase patterns. For example, Caitlyn and Colin integrated information recalled from
sources such as TV shows and books. Tapping prior knowledge is an excellent starting point for revving up for report writing, as long as the writer
incorporates the additional step of verifying that the information recalled
is accurate.

Caitlyn and others also crafted stylizations in order to engage the interest of readers. Making public such stylizations in conjunction with those of
published nonfiction authors validates their understandings and expands their
repertoire. For example, both Caitlyn and Joanna Cole asked readers to
complete a comprehension check at the end of their works. Caitlyn, having
just included a list of the characteristics of different ponies, attempted to assess
her readers' recall with the inclusion of "A Pony Game" (see below); Cole
(1989), at the end of *The Magic School Bus Inside the Human Body*, checked
both recall and the distinction between fact and fantasy:

CAITLYN'S PONY GAME	JOANNA COLE'S TRUE-OR-FALSE TEST
What you have to do is look at the pony in the picture (with an arrow pointing to a picture of a pony) And try to name it.	1. A bus can enter someone's body and go on a tour. True or false? . . . 6. White blood cells actually chase and destroy disease germs. True or false? (Cole, 1989, p. 38)

One of the hallmark attributes of our strategic writers (see Chapter 3)
was their nascent understanding about the importance of paraphrasing ideas
found in texts. Both evidenced a burgeoning talent for constructing textual
paraphrases. Unlike some of their peers, neither Caitlyn nor Colin stole entire sentences from their intertexts, although both included a few partial direct quotes. With the exception of the experience-only writers, every 3rd
grader included at least one partial direct quote. Interestingly, many perceived
these partial direct quotes as genuine paraphrases, stating proudly that they
"said it in my own words." These partial direct quotes, which may signal a
developmental step toward internalizing the construct of a paraphrase, require instructional clarification (see next section).

While neither Caitlyn nor Colin included (unmarked) direct quotes, the
frequency with which a number of their peers copied verbatim spoke volumes to our lack of attention to these complex concepts. During the first week
of discussion about the criteria of a good report, the 3rd graders were quick

to equate direct quotes with "stealing." We dutifully reiterated the dictum: DON'T COPY. However, we didn't elaborate on why direct appropriation of others' words without attribution is unacceptable. Nor did we *show* them how to paraphrase, when to use a direct quote, and so forth. Our failing prompted us to take a hard look at the issue of verbatim copying.

Plagiarism and the nonfiction report. Undoubtedly the most glaring attribute of the text-bound writers profiled in Chapter 5 was their verbatim copying. Conversations with Kyle and Patrick (and their peers) suggested that they, like most youngsters, knew they were committing an offense (Lewis, Wray, & Rospigliosi, 1994) but neither genuinely understood this offense nor knew how to approach their task in any other way. As noted in Chapter 5, it was only through ongoing conversations about verbatim copying that we realized the layers of misunderstanding that entangled Kyle and Patrick. For example, recall that when challenged about his verbatim copying from *Reptiles and Amphibians*, Patrick decided that he would be in compliance as long as he rearranged the authors' sentences (which he copied verbatim). When this idea was rejected, he moved to partial direct quotes that he, like many of his peers, viewed as his own work. Similarly, when Kyle's copying was challenged, he decided to copy verbatim the captions of illustrations, explaining that captions were not the text per se. Thus, even with active coaching, neither fully grasped what it meant to not copy verbatim.

Misconceptions about the copying dictum extended to one of the 6th graders in Many and colleagues' (1996) study. Jean had copied a recipe from a book for her World War II report but told Many that she wasn't permitted to use the book any more, explaining: "Because I got in trouble—Mrs. Longman said I have to use my own stuff and can't get it from books" (p. 21). Consequently, Jean based her entire World War II report on oral accounts; she used no books. In talking to Jean's teacher, Many and colleagues (1996) learned that

> Jean had not been told specifically that she should not have copied the recipe (later in the day Mrs. Longman expressed surprise at Jean's interpretation, noting that a recipe would have been an acceptable thing to copy). However, the need to write information in the students' own words was stressed in sharing sessions throughout the term. Jean interpreted the statement that she had to write it in her own words to mean that she could not take material from books, and henceforth she avoided written texts. Instead, she looked for firsthand accounts and class discussions as sources for information. (pp. 21–22)

Thus, armed with our young writers' misconceptions about verbatim copying, we will be ready to provide instruction to help them understand that polyphonic voices echo in everyone's writing and that it is the writer's responsibility to acknowledge these voices and then to act upon them in some way—agree, extend, dispute, resist (Bakhtin, 1986). As Lunsford and Ede (1994) argue:

> Teachers of writing may best begin . . . by taking a rhetorically situated view of plagiarism, one that acknowledges that all writing is in an important sense collaborative and that "common knowledge" varies from community to community and is collaboratively shared. From this perspective, attribution of sources becomes not a means of avoiding the heinous sin of plagiarism, but of building credibility or writerly *ethos*, of indicating to readers that the writer is a full collaborative participant in the scholarly conversation surrounding whatever topic is at hand. (p. 437)

We will help students understand that when we say "write it on your own words," we are not asking them to invent "original" ideas. Rather we are asking them to use and acknowledge the ideas of many authors but to shape these ideas in a way that signals their point of view (Bakhtin, 1981). We'll explain how accomplished nonfiction writers work to find their angle. For example, Patricia Lauber (1992), award-winning nonfiction writer, speaks eloquently about perspective-taking with respect to her book, *Volcano: The Eruption and Healing of Mount St. Helens*, a book she did not plan to write until she happened upon a magazine photograph of a young plant sprouting through the thick volcanic crust of Mount St. Helens. In that instant, she found her point of view:

> I wanted to write a book that would examine the mechanics of a big eruption and put eruptions in perspective as a natural phenomenon that helps make the earth a planet of life, a book that would also be a celebration of life, of its resiliency, of its ability to survive and come back, of the earth's ability to heal itself. (p. 15)

Of course, decisions about voice appropriation begin during the research process. In the next section, we merge what we have learned from our 3rd graders and from the literature to address the issue of teaching voice.

Teaching voice. As noted in Chapter 2, none of our 3rd graders, including our strategic writers (Chapter 3), viewed research as a process separate from writing. None took notes in any form (e.g., list, outline, graphic organizer); none formally preplanned the organizational framework of their report. Rather, many adopted a plan-as-you-go strategy (Bereiter & Scardamalia, 1987); some proceeded with little or no attention to planning during the act of composing. Recall that at the end of our instructional sequence in phase 3, we read the aforementioned excerpt from Joanna Cole's (1996) autobiography about the numerous books she reads, videos she watches, and experts she interviews. We also should have emphasized the extent of reading she does to immerse herself in the topic to find her angle. In advising young writers about report writing, Cole (1996) explains:

> I wouldn't go [to] the encyclopedia as soon as I got home from school and start copying down information. I wouldn't make an outline. Some other writers might do these things successfully. But not me. First I would read. I would read in a very relaxing way. . . . I wouldn't want to pick out the first six facts that I found and write them down one after another without feeling a connection to my subject. I would want to see which information answered questions I've always had about leaves. Sometimes these might be questions I didn't know I had until I found the answers. (pp. 23–25)

Only when Cole (1996) has made a "connection" to her topic does she begin taking notes.

Cole's process of question generation can be replicated with a KWL chart or a variation called the Circle of Questions (Sampson, Sampson, & Linek, 1994/1995), which involves children in generating questions on a topic, writing them on tangents to a circle containing the name of the topic, and then organizing them into categories before reading any information on the topic. The children are then ready to appreciate the extent to which researchers go to find answers. Take, for example, Jean Fritz's (1969) *George Washington's Breakfast*. George W. Allen, named after George Washington, wondered what the first president ate for breakfast. After researching books on Washington, reading the diaries of Washington's friends, wandering through the Smithsonian, and visiting Mount Vernon to interview museum guides—all to no avail—George finally finds his answer in an old book of his grandfather's. Not surprisingly, George's research journey parallels that of his creator, Jean Fritz (1992):

> First I go to the library and read, read, read, read. Of course, I make notes as I go along. Then I travel to the places where my characters lived so I can get to know them on their own home ground. When I was writing my book, *The Great Little Madison*, I went to James Madison's home in Virginia. I took notes on everything I saw. I stood on the same steps where he once stood and looked out at his lovely plantation. I imagined him doing the same thing. (pp. 12–13)

Also not included in our instruction were the layers of scaffolded instruction needed to show the 3rd graders how to take notes. Next time around, we'll introduce note taking by implementing the gradual release of responsibility model (Pearson & Gallagher, 1983), which apportions the degree of responsibility that teachers and students assume when confronted with a new learning task. It assigns full responsibility to the teacher at the beginning of the instructional sequence who models and instructs students on the task. Learners then assume joint responsibility with the teacher, with a gradual release of responsibility to the students. The task is then turned over to the students, who independently practice and apply what they have learned. Fountas and Pinnell (1996) translate this model into levels of writing support such as shared writing, guided writing, and independent writing. Modeled writing would be added. To set a context, let's say that we begin a science unit on sharks with a KWL chart (for procedural information on this and other graphic organizers as well as comprehension strategies such as anticipations guides and reciprocal teaching, an excellent source is *Guiding Readers and Writers* by Fountas and Pinnell [2001]). In order to answer the questions listed on the KWL chart, we visit the New England Aquarium to observe and take notes on shark behavior and to interview an expert on sharks, we watch videos, and we read books (Graves, 1989, 1994). With their interest piqued, the 3rd graders decide to write a report that compares the five senses of sharks with those of humans (none of our resources pursued this particular angle). We decide to move through the first three phases of the gradual release of responsibility model (modeled writing, shared writing, and guided writing) by focusing only on the shark information. Hopefully students, at a later point, will be able to apply this knowledge to researching the five senses of humans during independent writing. Implementation of these phases might include the following lessons over several days.

Modeled writing. We set up two overhead machines side by side (Calkins, 2001), projecting the page on sharks' hearing from Simon's (1995) *Sharks* and a blank transparency on the other machine. As they watch and listen, we implement a think-aloud, explaining how we (1) read to sort relevant from irrelevant details, (2) take notes on only the important information, (3) paraphrase major ideas in the fewest words possible, guarding against using distinctive phrases or words unless enclosed in quotation marks, (4) explain why direct appropriation of others' words without attribution is unacceptable, (5) show how a marked direct quote can enhance our piece in rare instances, (6) record notes on a graphic organizer (e.g., spider map), (7) cite our source, and (8) reread notes to make sure they make sense (Elsbree & Mulderig, 1986). We then entertain questions.

Shared writing. To gauge their nascent understandings, clarify misconceptions, and extend their learning, we ask the students to help us take notes the following day. Because many 3rd graders accessed multiple resources but few integrated information across books at the paragraph level, we project the section on sharks' hearing from Markle's (1996) *Outside and Inside Sharks.* As we read, we note the overlap of information in both Simon's and Markle's books. We agree that there is no need to copy the same information, appreciating the verification of facts recorded yesterday. We concentrate on paraphrasing the new information found in Markle's book. At some point, someone notices contradictory information across the two books: (1) "They [sharks] can hear a wounded fish thrashing in the water from as much as 3,000 feet away" (Simon, 1995, unpaged); and (2) "Sharks can hear a wounded animal struggling for as far away as a football field" (Markle, 1996, p. 17). We brainstorm possible reasons for this discrepancy, emphasizing that writers have a responsibility to report accurate information. We read Markle's acknowledgment page in which she thanks seven scientists for their expertise; we note no such acknowledgment in Simon's book. We then segue to the value that Cole places on interviewing experts, not only to learn more about a particular topic but also to have her information verified by experts. "Part of my research is finding an expert on my subject. For instance, in 1980, when I was writing *A Snake's Body*, I needed to talk to a snake scientist. I had some specific questions to ask, and I wanted someone to read what I had written and tell me if I'd got it right" (p. 19). We ask the 3rd graders what we might do to resolve this discrepancy about sharks' hearing and invite them to take on the challenge of finding the answer(s) over the next few days.

The following day, we introduce an article on sharks from *Time for Kids*, asking the students to note any new information about a shark's hearing that can be added to our spider map. With information across three sources (Simon, Markle, and *Time for Kids*) integrated onto our spider map, we are ready to collaboratively draft our paragraph(s) on the shark's sense of hearing. We emphasize that when we write from our map that contains paraphrased phrases of information, we shouldn't have to worry about plagiarism. This drafting stage assumes that our 3rd graders have already had had instruction in main ideas and details—that they know how to write topic sentences and supportive details.

Guided writing. We hand out copies of Simon's and Markle's sections on sharks' teeth. We read the texts chorally; we pass out spider maps and ask the students to individually take notes. We tell them that they will write the next paragraph of our report tomorrow using only their spider maps. As children try their hand at paraphrasing information, we move through the room, complimenting successes, probing misconceptions if verbatim copying occurs, and using our findings to revisit the issue. We revisit verbatim copying by projecting excerpts of plagiarized nonfiction texts, using the children's own work (see Chapter 5), other students' work from previous years, or examples we have created ourselves, and then discussing them as follows:

- Reexplaining what verbatim copying is and that it applies to all aspects of text, including captions

- Showing that rearranging an author's sentences (copied verbatim) is inappropriate
- Introducing examples of partial direct quotes (see Chapter 2), explaining that while part of a sentence has been paraphrased, part has been copied directly and needs to be restated
- Demonstrating again what it means to paraphrase—to write something "in your own words"—and making it clear to the children that when they paraphrase, they are not coming up with their own ideas but rather restating others' ideas with attribution

It may also be instructive at some point, depending on the grade level, to introduce recent cases of plagiarism that have rocked the publishing world, showing, for example, age-appropriate excerpts of the passages that historian and Pulitzer Prize winner Doris Kearns Goodwin plagiarized while writing *The Fitzgeralds and the Kennedys* (Crader, 2002). The website *Plagiarism Hyperquest* (Christie, 1994) is a good source for further information on this and a wide variety of other plagiarism (and alleged plagiarism) scandals, including, for example, Dr. Martin Luther King Jr.'s doctoral dissertation; several books by the historian Stephen Ambrose; unfounded charges against J. K. Rowling, the author of the *Harry Potter* books; some of Senator Joseph Biden's speeches; the case of Jayson Blair, who plagiarized many of his *New York Times* articles in addition to fabricating many others (the latter also being a good kickoff point for another day's discussion, about the undesirability of "making up facts"); and the lawsuit against Disney Studios claiming that the animated fish in the movie *Finding Nemo* was plagiarized from an illustration of a character in a children's book (another useful kickoff point for a supplementary discussion, about how "pictures can be plagiarized, too"). In addition to discussing these examples, we can point out the serious consequences each offender has endured. More important, we can illuminate the missed opportunity these writers had to add their contribution to the work of their predecessors. When we plagiarize, we cheat ourselves of the intellectual challenge of weighing in (with grateful attribution) in order to advance an existing body of work.

Independent writing. With shark paragraphs drafted, we are ready to turn over the newly learned research/writing process to our 3rd graders. In small groups or with partners, they chose a particular sense of the human body and read materials that we have tagged with Post-its so that they can get right down to business. They read and complete their spider maps; they write their paragraphs. We confer with writers throughout, providing guidance, additional instruction, and so forth.

The last leg of this instructional journey—introducing the text structure of compare/contrast so that we can complete our initial mission (compare/

contrast human and shark senses)—returns us to the phase of modeled writing or shared writing in which we present the challenge of merging these two knowledge bases to the 3rd graders. We examine how other authors organize their compare/contrast text structures; we focus on signal words (*like, unlike, different, similar*) inherent in this structure. We take one sense (hearing) and complete a Venn diagram as we discuss similarities and differences. We then use this diagram to draft our text. Over the next few days, they then work in groups to create their Venn diagrams for other senses and write their paragraphs. We end the sequence by completing the writing process (with which they are well acquainted) with final revision, editing, and publication.

Ultimately, the fruits of our labor unfold during future writing workshops as students independently chose to write a nonfiction report anchored in the research and writing processes that we have modeled and reinforced. While we anticipate that many will adopt a strategic stance toward nonfiction writing, we will be ready to provide additional modeling and coaching. Because preliminary research indicates that some children plagiarize texts that are too difficult to comprehend (Lewis et al., 1994; Wray & Lewis, 1992), we will first monitor the readability levels of their sources, and then show them how to use the five-finger method to choose nonfiction books, preferably at their independent reading level (Veatch, 1968). This method directs the reader to select a full page of text (of approx. 100 words) from a trade book, to raise one finger each time an unfamiliar word is encountered, and to count the number of raised fingers at the end of the page. Zero to one fingers suggests that the book can be read independently, without teacher support; two to five fingers indicate that the book will be somewhat challenging; six fingers or more indicate that the book will frustrate the reader.

At some later point, we will revisit note taking, introducing alternative formats. For example, children delight in taking notes the Joanna Cole (1996) way:

> As I read, I absorb an enormous amount of information. I take some notes, but I'm not very traditional. I don't keep files of carefully coded index cards, for instance. But that isn't to say I'm not well organized. . . . Then as I read, I write down on sticky notes any special information I don't want to forget and attach the notes on the appropriate dummy pages. (p. 18)

Cole's note-taking strategy can be compared to that of Kathryn Lasky, who prefers outlining. Of a book she wrote on censorship, Lasky noted: "I kept breaking it down. . . . I outlined the first few chapters. Then I kept outlining smaller and smaller pieces" (quoted in Kovacs & Preller, 1993, p. 103). Lasky ended up with 11 outlines. While we haven't been able to locate any acclaimed authors who take notes in the form of graphic organizers (e.g., semantic maps, concept maps, KWL, I-charts, think sheets), we advocate instruction on such organizers (Merkley & Jefferies, 2001; Raphael & Englert, 1990).

Because we think it is important for young writers to understand that there is no one way of keeping track of the key information, we suggest that teachers introduce them to the array of note-taking/outlining strategies and give them practice in these variations with the goal of having each writer adopt the strategy that works best for him or her. Excellent resources to support such instruction can be found in Buss and Karnowski's (2002) *Reading and Writing Nonfiction Genres*, Fountas and Pinnell's (2001) *Guiding Readers and Writers: Grades 3–6*, Harvey's (1998) *Nonfiction Matters*, Kletzien and Dreher's (2004) *Informational Text in K-3 Classrooms*, Portalupi and Fletcher's (2001) *Nonfiction Craft Lessons*, and Robb's (2004) *Nonfiction Writing: From the Inside Out*.

Suspend Writing Workshop and Pursue a Collaborative Report Writing Project

How do we do all of the above? We recognize that time is a precious commodity in this age of state-mandated curricula. Therefore, it makes sense to suspend writing workshop for 2 or 3 weeks in order to pursue a collaborative report-writing project of the nature just described. Such projects have received strong endorsement from writing experts (Calkins, 1994; Duke & Bennett-Armistead, 2003; Harvey, 1998; Stead, 2002; Tompkins, 2004). Because thematic curricular units in science and social studies immerse children in a topic of study via trade books, guest speakers, films, computer programs, and field trips, they provide a natural scaffold for nonfiction writing (Calkins, 1994; Graves, 1994).

Another case in point is Sylvia Read (2001) and her 1st and 2nd graders whose school garden was inundated with praying mantises, providing the catalyst for their collaborative writing project. Together, they observed these creatures and searched the library for information. After reading each book, Sylvia asked the children what they had learned, recording notes on posters. As books were read throughout the week, old notes were revisited before new notes were added. Saturated with knowledge about praying mantises, the youngsters were asked to dictate their own book to Sylvia without reference to their notes. This book became their text for shared reading the following week; eventually it was bound and placed in the school library. These youngsters then researched and wrote their own nonfiction books with marked success (Read, 2001).

In sum, because report writing is a complex undertaking for writers of all ages (Many et al., 1996), we help children to begin to grasp this complexity when we involve them in a collaborative writing project that is anchored in these layers of support. Such a project enables us to walk young writers through the multifaceted and recursive steps of reading, planning, researching, note taking, integrating information, and writing reports. When possible, collaborative projects should include the research and writing processes of acclaimed authors. As we move through each phase of the report-writing process, we shuttle back and forth between what acclaimed authors do and decide what we will do. Of course, if children have been independently writing reports in writing workshop, we should have them share their ways of knowing. On completion of our project, we resume writing workshop, turning the children loose to try their hand at independent report writing.

FINAL THOUGHTS

John Dewey (1902/1956) ended his classic essay "The Child and the Curriculum" by answering the question, "How then, stands the case of Child vs. Curriculum?" (p. 30) as follows:

> The case is of Child. It is his present powers which are to assert themselves, his present capacities which are to be exercised; his present attitudes which are to be realized. But save as the teacher knows, knows wisely and thoroughly, . . . that thing we call the Curriculum, the teacher knows neither what the present power, capacity, or attitude is, nor yet how it is to be asserted, exercised, and realized. (p. 31)

When we designed our instruction, we thought we knew, to some degree, "the present powers, capacities . . . attitudes" of the young nonfiction writer, based on our own observations and the research literature (Chapman, 1995; Hicks, 1990; Langer, 1986; Newkirk, 1987; Pappas, 1991; Sowers, 1985; Zecker, 1996). While researchers have documented the increasingly sophisticated ways in which children abstract the features of non-narrative discourse, they have also acknowledged that their control of nonfiction isn't as stable as their control of fiction (Hicks, 1990; Kamberelis & Bovino, 1999). For example, Kamberelis and Bovino (1999) found that while the K–2 sample in their study had enough genre knowledge to produce stories and nonfiction science reports, their story writing far surpassed their nonfiction report writing. Moreover, many youngsters produced hybrid reports that combined features of both fiction and nonfiction. As students advance through the elementary grades, nonfiction writing continues to be a challenge, according to recent publications of the NAEP's *Nation's Writing Report Card* (Applebee et al., 1990; Greenwald, Persky, Campbell, & Mazzeo, 1999; Persky, Daane, & Jin, 2003). These findings, combined with our observation that children chose not to write nonfiction during writing workshop, prompted us to tread lightly, to think "small" when designing our instructional goal of having our 3rd graders write nonfiction reports on a par with those of the fictional kids in Ms. Frizzle's classroom. Fortunately, our 3rd graders began writing their nonfiction reports, shaped by a range of intertextual influences, before our instruction could define their efforts. These young writers validated Kamberelis and Bovino's (1999) finding with respect to the power of text to scaffold nonfiction writing. They validated Dyson's call for widening of Vygotsky's (1978) zone of proximal development to include not only the skilled teacher who scaffolds children's writing development but also the vibrant social network of peers who constitute the "collective" zone and who serve as writing colleagues and social mediators—listening, responding, expanding, challenging, accepting, rejecting, and so forth. And finally, our 3rd graders validated the place of instruction. For example, while they had absorbed and applied information about the textual attributes of the nonfiction report, many did not approximate the research and writing processes integral to this genre. Induction into these ways of knowing may best be accomplished through the insights of acclaimed and peer writers, explaining how they approach the art and craft of nonfiction.

Whether these validations, however, hold true for children from more diverse sociocultural backgrounds remains to be seen. Will children from low-income homes who have not taken horseback riding lessons, snorkeled in Aruba, dug fossils in Roger Williams Zoo Park—as the middle-class 3rd graders in our study had—forge a similar range of intertextual links while writing nonfiction? While the answer to this question or the even broader question about the acquisition and development of nonfiction literacy across the social and cultural spectrum has yet to be investigated (Duke, 2000; Kamberelis & Bovino, 1999), there are hopeful signs. Recent case studies of struggling young readers and writers have revealed the potency of nonfiction literature to usher children into literacy. Caswell and Duke (1998) traced the literacy journeys of two boys, one a special-needs working-class 1st grader and the other a poor 4th grader from Cape Verde. Both boys' interventions began with predictable books to strengthen concepts about print, word analysis skills, fluency, and comprehension. Their interest in nonfiction first became evident in their self-chosen writing topics: dinosaurs, football, and elephants. Their literacy tutors recognized the power of nonfiction to tap their background knowledge; to elicit more accurate, fluent reading; and to engender more purposeful reading and writing (Caswell & Duke, 1998). Animals and sports appear to be topics of universal appeal for children from all walks of life. Promising, too, are Kamberelis and Bovino's (1999) findings that culturally diverse youngsters—58% of whom were from working-class homes and 42% from middle-class homes—wrote significantly better animals reports under the scaffolded condition (asked to write the report by recalling information from books read/heard during an animal unit) than under the nonscaffolded condition (simply asked to write an animal report).

Coiled at the center of this question, though, is the pernicious indictment that poor children are devoid of "worthy" life experiences and consequently have no reservoir to tap when it's time to write. Researchers such as

Heath (1983), Dyson (1989, 1993, 1997, 2000), Kamberelis and Scott (1992), Morrow (1992), and Moll and Gonzalez (1994) have pointedly warned educators not to cast aspersions on the experiences of children from low-income families, as such assertions may launch the cycle of lowered academic expectations, insufficient instruction, and poor performance. For example, Gonzalez and colleagues (1993) have forcefully argued that if teachers are to serve children from diverse families, they must enter their lives as ethnographers to document their "funds of knowledge." They describe these funds of knowledge and their impact as follows:

> Funds of knowledge refers to those historically developed and accumulated strategies (e.g., skills, abilities, ideas, practices) or bodies of knowledge that are essential to a household's functioning and well-being. . . . A key finding from our research is that these funds of knowledge are abundant and diverse and may include information about, for example, farming and animal husbandry (associated with households' rural origins), construction and building (related to urban occupations), and many other matters, such as trade, business, and finance on both sides of the U. S. Mexican border. (Gonzalez et al., 1993, p. 6)

Poor children's experiences, then, are not the problem. Far more vexing to the literacy progress of poor children are the social and economic realities that teachers, passionate about their mission and armed with the best teaching practices, can't fix. In a sobering synthesis of the research on the achievement gap, Evans (2005) pinpoints pivotal factors, such as the 15,000-word differential between the vocabulary of low-income, culturally diverse children (5,000 words) and middle-class peers (20,000), and other differentials, such as the total number of books in the home, the amount of television watched, academic ground lost over the summer, the attrition rates in city school, and Kozol's (1991) "savage inequalities," to name a few. Evans (2005) sums up this bleak picture as follows: "As Howard Gardner has observed, we can accurately project a child's chances of completing college and her eventual income by knowing only ZIP code" (p. 584). Evans is forthright about the fact that while individual schools and individual teachers have been successful in narrowing the gap and will continue to be vehicles for social change, they cannot single-handedly transform the social and economic realities. Evans joins others in calling for high-quality preschools and after-school programs, education for parents, resolution of the fiscal inequalities that plague city schools, recruitment of the best teachers, and a proven track record of research on the best ways to teach poor children to read and write.

Clearly, the scope and complexity of the achievement gap is daunting. Each of us must decide on the level of social activism that we wish to bring to bear on parents, colleagues, administrators, the community, and legislators. With the advent of the critical literacy movement, teachers have been urged to "tie language to power, tie text interpretation to societal structures, tie reading and writing to perpetuating or resisting" (Edelsky, 1994, p. 254). This construct of literacy as social analysis and political action, first advocated by Paulo Freire (1970), was embraced by a number of literacy academics in the 1990s (Edelsky, 1994, 1996; Fairclough, 1992; Gee, 1990; Pappas & Pettegrew, 1998; Shannon, 1990, 1992, 1993; Shor, 1992; Shor & Pari, 1999). More recently, critical literacy has taken hold in a number of American and Australian classrooms (Bomer, 2004; Creighton, 1997; Duncan-Andrade, 2005; Fehring & Green, 2001; Foss, 2002; Heffernan & Lewison, 2003; Jennings & O'Keefe, 2002; Vasquez, 2003). These teachers strive to implement two fundamental principles of critical literacy. First they guide children—those who are privileged and those who are disenfranchised—to interrogate texts: "How is this text trying to position me?" "Whose voices are heard and whose are missing?" "How might this text be critiqued and redesigned?" (Luke & Freebody, 1997). Second, teachers engage students in praxis—considered reflection and prudent action to address a social injustice (Cadiero-Kaplan, 2002; Giroux, 1996; Heffernan & Lewison, 2003; Vasquez, 2003). While the intersection of critical literacy and informational literacy has only begun to be explored (Bomer, 2004; Heffernan, 2004; Kamberelis & Scott, 1992; Jennings & O'Keefe, 2002), it is ripe with potential.

A first step entails examining our existing curriculum for issues that lend themselves to social analysis. For example, recall that our 3rd graders studied Thanksgiving in the context of *Tapenum's Day* (Waters, 1996) and *People of the Breaking Day* (Sewall, 1990) as well as Martin Luther King Jr. and the civil rights movement. The social, cultural, and historical issues inherent in these books invite dialogue about social injustice, then and now. A natural extension is analyses of social concerns in the children's immediate world and opportunities to promote social action. One potent form of social action is writing. Enter the news article, the editorial, the persuasive letter, the biography. For the subgenre of choice, we would tap the children's prior knowledge, including intertextual connections; immerse them in exemplary models of this subgenre; build on what they know as we discuss/teach primary attributes and any intertextual information available; and then collaborate with the class to write this artifact for a genuine audience and purpose, making public all intertextual ties. In this way, we would position children not only to understand the power of language but also to use written language to take a stand.

References

Allen, G. (2000). *Intertextuality*. New York: Routledge.

Allen, C. A., & Swistak, L. (2004). Multigenre research: The power of choice and interpretation. *Language Arts, 81*(3), 223–232.

Alverman, D., & Boothby, P. (1982). Text differences: Children's perceptions at the transition stage in reading. *The Reading Teacher, 36,* 298–302.

Anderson, G., Higgins, D., & Wurster, S. (1985). Differences in the free-reading books selected by high, average, and low achievers. *The Reading Teacher, 39,* 326–330.

Anderson, R. C., Hiebert, E. H., Scott, J. A., & Wilkinson, I. A. (1985). *Becoming a nation of readers: The report of the Commission on Reading.* Washington, DC: National Academy of Education, The National Institute of Education, and Center for the Study of Reading.

Anderson, R. C., Wilson, P. T., & Fielding, L. G. (1988). Growth in reading and how children spend their time outside of school. *Reading Research Quarterly, 23*(3), 285–303.

Applebee, A., Langer, J., Mullis, I., & Jenkins, L. (1990). *The writing report card, 1984–1988: Findings from the nation's report card.* Princeton, NJ: Educational Testing Service.

Atwell, N. (1987). *In the middle: Writing, reading, and learning with adolescents.* Portsmouth, NH: Heinemann.

Avi (1991). Author's commentary. In G. Selnick & S. Gunton (Eds.), *Children's literature review* (pp. 1–15). Detroit: Gale Research.

Bakhtin, M. (1981). *The dialogic imagination: Four essays of M.M. Bakhtin* (C. Emerson & M. Holdquist, Trans.). Austin: University of Texas Press.

Bakhtin, M. (1984). *Problems of Dostoevsky's poetics* (C. Emerson, Trans.). Minneapolis: University of Minnesota Press.

Bakhtin, M. (1986). *Speech genres and other late essays.* Austin: University of Texas Press.

Bamford, R., & Kristo, J. (1998). *Making facts come alive: Choosing quality nonfiction literature K–8.* Norwood, MA: Christopher Gordon.

Barthes, R. (1977). *Image–music–text* (S. Heath, Trans.). New York: Hill & Wang.

Bearse, C. I. (1992). The fairy tale connection in children's stories: Cinderella meets Sleeping Beauty. *The Reading Teacher, 45,* 688–695.

Bereiter, C., & Scardamalia, M. (1987). *The psychology of written composition.* Hillsdale, NJ: Erlbaum.

Beta Upsilon Chapter, Pi Lamba Theta. (1974). Children's reading interest classified by age level. *The Reading Teacher, 27,* 694–700.

Bissex, G. (1980). *GNYS AT WRK: A child learns to write and read.* Cambridge, MA: Harvard University Press.

Blackburn, E. (1985). Stories never end. In J. Hansen, T. Newkirk, & D. Graves (Eds.), *Breaking ground: Teachers relate reading and writing in the elementary school* (pp. 73–82). Portsmouth, NH: Heinemann.

Bloome, D., & Egan-Robertson, A. (1993). The social construction of intertextuality in classroom reading and writing lessons. *Reading Research Quarterly, 28,* 304–333.

Bomer, R. (2004). Speaking out for social action. *Educational Leadership, 62*(2), 34–37.

Bradley, R. (1996). *Won way phonics.* Upton, MA: Bradley Institute for Reading and Language Arts.

Britton, J. (1993). *Language and learning* (2nd ed.). Portsmouth, NH: Boynton/Cook.

Britton, J., Burgess, T., Martin, T., McLeod, A., & Rosen, H. (1975). *The development of writing abilities.* London: Macmillan.

Broaddus, K., & Ivey, G. (2002). Surprising the writer: Discovering details through research and reading. *Language Arts, 80*(1), 23–30.

Burkhalter, N. (1995). A Vygotsky-based curriculum for teaching persuasive writing in the elementary grades. *Language Arts, 72,* 192–199.

Buss, K., & Karnowski, L. (2002). *Reading and writing nonfiction genres.* Newark, DE: International Reading Association.

Cadiero-Kaplan, K. (2002). Literacy ideologies: Engaging the language arts curriculum. *Language Arts, 79*(5), 372–381.

Cairney, T. (1990). Intertextuality: Infectious echoes from the past. *The Reading Teacher, 43,* 478–485.

Cairney, T. (1992). Fostering and building students' intertextual histories. *Language Arts, 69,* 502–507.

Calkins, L. (1983). *Lessons from a child.* Portsmouth, NH: Heinemann.

Calkins, L. (1991). *Living between the lines.* Portsmouth, NH: Heinemann.

Calkins, L. (1994). *The art of teaching writing* (2nd ed.). Portsmouth, NH: Heinemann.

Calkins, L. (2001). *The art of teaching reading.* New York: Longman.

Cambourne, B. (1988). *The whole story: Natural learning and acquisition of literacy in the classroom.* New York: Ashton Scholastic.

Camp, D. (2000). It takes two: Teaching with twin texts of fact and fiction. *The Reading Teacher, 53*(5), 400–408.

Casbergue, R. (1996, May). *The chrojen hors: Emergence of expository writing.* Paper presented at the Annual Meeting of the International Reading Association, Atlanta.

Caswell, L. J., & Duke, N. K. (1998). Nonnarrative as a catalyst for literacy development. *Language Arts, 75*(2), 108–117.

Chall, J. S., & Jacobs, V. A. (1983). Writing and reading in the elementary grades: Developmental trends among low SES children. *Language Arts, 60,* 617–626.

Chall, J. S., Jacobs, V. A., & Baldwin, L. E. (1990). *The reading crisis: Why poor children fall behind.* Cambridge, MA: Harvard University Press.

Chapman, M. (1994). The emergence of genres. *Written Communication*, 11(3), 348–380.

Chapman, M. (1995). The sociocognitive construction of written genres in first grade. *Research in the Teaching of English*, 29, 164–192.

Charney, R. (1991). *Teaching children to care: Management in the responsive classroom*. Greenfield, MA: Northeast Foundation for Children.

Chomsky, C. (1972). Stages in language development and reading exposure. *Harvard Educational Review*, 42, 1–33.

Christie, A. (2004). *Plagiarism hyperquest*. Retrieved October 16, 2005, from http://www.west.asu.edu/christie/emcc/plagiarism.html

Christie, F. (1987). Genres as choice. In I. Reid (Ed.), *The place of genre in learning: Current debates* (pp. 24–34). Geelong, Australia: Deakin University Press.

Christie, F. (1993). Curriculum genres: Planning for effective teaching. In B. Cope & M. Kalantz (Eds.), *The powers of literacy: A genre approach to teaching writing* (pp. 154–178). New York: Falmer.

Clay, M. (1979). *The early detection of reading difficulties*. Portsmouth, NH: Heinemann.

Cole, J. (1996). *On the bus with Joanna Cole: A creative autobiography*. Portsmouth, NH: Heinemann.

Consuelo, Sister M. (1967). What do first graders like to read? *Catholic School Journal*, 67, 42–43.

Cope, B., & Kalantzis, M. (Eds.). (1993). *The powers of literacy: A genre approach to teaching writing* (pp. 154–178). New York: Falmer.

Crader, B. (2002, January 28). A historian and her sources. *The Weekly Standard*. Retrieved October 4, 2004, from www.weeklystandard.com/Utilities/printer_preview.asp?idArticle=793&R=9D0F2C0D9

Creighton, D. (1997). Critical literacy in the elementary classroom. *Language Arts*, 74(6), 438–445.

Cullinan, B., & Galda, L. (1994). *Literature and the child*. New York: Harcourt Brace.

Dale, K., & Farnan, N. (1998). *Children's writing: Perspectives from research*. Newark, DE: International Reading Association.

Daniels, H. (1990). Young writers and readers reach out: Developing sense of audience. In T. Shanahan (Ed.), *Reading and writing together: New perspectives for the classroom* (pp. 99–125). Norwood, MA: Christopher Gordon.

Delpit, L. D. (1988). The silenced dialogue: Power and pedagogy in educating other people's children. *Harvard Educational Review*, 58, 280–298.

Dewey, J. (1956). *The child and the curriculum and the school and society*. Chicago: University of Chicago Press. (Original work published 1902)

Doiron, R. (1994). Using nonfiction in a read-aloud program: Letting the facts speak for themselves. *The Reading Teacher*, 47(8), 616–624.

Donovan, C. A. (2001). Children's development and control of written story and informational genres: Insight from one elementary school. *Research in the Teaching of English*, 35(3), 394–447.

Donovan, C. A., & Smolkin, L. B. (2002). Genre and other factors influencing teachers' book selection for science instruction. *Reading Research Quarterly*, 36(4), 417–441.

Duke, N. (2000). 3.6 minutes per day: The scarcity of informational texts in first grade. *Reading Research Quarterly, 35*(2), 202–225.

Duke, N. K., & Bennett-Armistead, V. S. (2003). *Reading & writing informational text in the primary grades.* New York: Scholastic.

Duke, N., & Kays, J. (1998). "Can I say 'once upon a time'?" Kindergarten children developing knowledge of information book language. *Early Childhood Research Quarterly, 13,* 295–318.

Duncan-Andrade, J. M. (2005). Developing social justice educators. *Educational Leadership, 62*(2), 70–73.

Durkin, D. (1966). *Children who read early.* New York: Teachers College Press.

Durkin, D. (1978–1979). What classroom observations reveal about reading comprehension. *Reading Research Quarterly, 15,* 481–533.

Duthie, C. (1996). *True stories: Nonfiction in the primary classroom.* Portland, ME: Stenhouse.

Dyson, A. (1989). *Multiple worlds of child writers: Friends learning to write.* New York: Teachers College Press.

Dyson, A. (1993). *Social worlds of children learning to write in an urban primary school.* New York: Teachers College Press.

Dyson, A. (1997). *Writing superheroes: Contemporary childhood, popular culture, and classroom literacy.* New York: Teachers College Press.

Dyson, A. (2000). Writing and the sea of voices: Oral language in, around, and about writing. In R. Indrisano & J. Squire (Eds.), *Perspectives on writing: Research, theory, and practice* (pp. 45–65). Newark, DE: International Reading Association.

Edelsky, C. (1994). Education for democracy. *Language Arts, 71*(4), 252–257.

Edelsky, C. (1996). *With literacy and justice for all.* Bristol, PA: Taylor & Francis.

Eggins, S., Wignell, P., & Martin, J. R. (1993). The discourse of history: Distancing the recoverable past. In M. Ghadessy (Ed.), *Register analysis: Theory and practice* (pp. 75–109). London: Pinter.

Elley, W. B. (1989). Vocabulary acquisition from listening to stories. *Reading Research Quarterly, 28*(2). 174–187.

Elsbree, L., & Mulderig, G. (1986). *The Heath handbook.* Lexington, MA: D.C. Heath.

Englert, C., & Hiebert, E. (1984). Children's developing awareness of text structure in expository materials. *Journal of Educational Psychology, 76,* 65–74.

Evans, J. (2005). Reframing the achievement gap. *Phi Delta Kappan, 86*(8), 582–589.

Fairclough, N. (1992). *Discourse and social change.* Cambridge, UK: Polity.

Fehring, H., & Green, P. (Eds.). (2001). *Critical literacy: A collection of articles from the Australian Literacy Educators' Association.* Newark, DE: International Reading Association.

Finn, C., & Ravitch, D. (1988). No trivial pursuit. *Phi Delta Kappan, 69*(8), 559–564.

Fletcher, R. (1993). *What a writer needs.* Portsmouth, NH: Heinemann.

Fletcher, R. (1996). *Breathing in, breathing out.* Portsmouth, NH: Heinemann.

Foss, A. (2002). Peeling back the onion: Teaching critical literacy with students of privilege. *Language Arts, 79*(5), 393–403.

Fountas, I. C., & Pinnell, G. S. (1996). *Guided reading: Good first teaching for all.* Portsmouth, NH: Heinemann.

Fountas, I. C., & Pinnell, G. S. (1999). *Matching books to readers: Using leveled books in guided reading, K–3.* Portsmouth, NH: Heinemann.

Fountas, I. C., & Pinnell, G. S. (2001). *Guiding readers and writers: Grades 3–6.* Portsmouth, NH: Heinemann.

Freedman, A. (1993). Show and tell? The role of explicit teaching in the learning of new genres. *Research in the Teaching of English, 27*(3), 222–251.

Freedman, R. (1992). Fact or fiction? In E. Freeman & D. Person (Eds.), *Using nonfiction trade books in the elementary classroom: From ants to zeppelins* (pp. 2–10). Urbana, IL: National Council of Teachers of English.

Freeman, E. B., & Person, D. G. (1998a). *Connecting informational children's books with content area literacy.* Boston: Allyn & Bacon.

Freeman, E. B., & Person, D. G. (1998b). *Using nonfiction trade books in the elementary classroom: From ants to zeppelins.* Urbana, IL: National Council of Teachers of English.

Freire, P. (1970). *Pedagogy of the oppressed.* New York: Continuum.

Freire, P. (1985). Reading the world and reading the word: An interview with Paulo Freire. *Language Arts, 62*(1), 15–21.

Gardner, H. (1999). *The disciplined mind: What all students should understand.* New York: Simon & Schuster.

Gee, J. P. (1989). Literacy, discourse, and linguistics: Introduction. *Journal of Education, 171*(1), 5–17.

Gee, J. P. (1990). *Social linguistics and literacies: Ideology in discourses.* New York: Falmer Press.

Genishi, C. (1992). Developing the foundation: Oral language and communicative competence. In C. Seefeldt (Ed.), *The early childhood curriculum: A review of current research* (pp. 85–117). New York: Teachers College Press.

Giacobbe, M. (1988). A writer reads, a reader writes. In T. Newkirk & N. Atwell (Eds.), *Ways of observing, learning and teaching* (pp. 168–177). Portsmouth, NH: Heinemann.

Gibbons, G. (2002). Gail Gibbons in her own words. Retrieved May 25, 2005, from www.gailgibbons.com

Gibson, E., & Levin, H. (1975). *Psychology of reading.* Cambridge, MA: MIT Press.

Giroux, H. (1996). *Living dangerously: Multiculturalism and the politics of difference.* New York: Peter Lang.

Glaser, B., & Strauss, A. (1967). *The discovery of grounded theory: Strategies for qualitative research.* Chicago: Aldine.

Gonzalez, N., Moll, L. C., Floyd-Tenery, M., Rivera, A., Rendon, P., Gonzalez, R., & Amanti, C. (1993). *Teacher research on funds of knowledge: Learning from households.* Santa Cruz: University of California, Center for Research on Education, Diversity & Excellence.

Graves, D. (1973). *Children's writing: Research directions and hypotheses based upon an examination of the writing process of seven year old children.* Unpublished doctoral dissertation, State University of New York at Buffalo.

Graves, D. (1983). *Writing: Teachers and children at work.* Portsmouth, NH: Heinemann.

Graves, D. (1989). *Investigate nonfiction.* Portsmouth, NH: Heinemann.

Graves, D. (1994). *A fresh look at writing.* Portsmouth, NH: Heinemann.

Greenwald, E. A., Persky, H. R., Campbell, J. R., & Mazzeo, J. (1999). *NAEP 1998 writing report card.* Washington, DC: National Center for Educational Statistics, U.S. Department of Education.

Grierson, S. T., Anson, A., & Baird, J. (2002). Exploring the past through multigenre writing. *Language Arts, 80*(1), 51–59.

Haneda, M., & Wells, G. (2000). Writing in knowledge-building communities. *Research in the Teaching of English, 34*(3), 430–457.

Hansen, J. (1987). *When writers read.* Portsmouth, NH: Heinemann.

Harris, P., Trezise, J., & Winser, W. N. (2002). "Is the story on my face?": Intertextual conflicts during teacher–class interactions around texts in early grade classrooms. *Research in the Teaching of English, 37*(1), 9–54.

Harste, J. C., Short, K. G., & Burke, C. (1988). *Creating classrooms for authors: The reading-writing connection.* Portsmouth, NH: Heinemann.

Harvey, S. (1998). *Nonfiction matters: Reading, writing, and research in grades 3–8.* Portland, ME: Stenhouse.

Heath, S. (1983). *Ways with words: Language, life and work in communities and classrooms.* New York: Cambridge University Press.

Heffernan, L. (2004). *Critical literacy and writer's workshop.* Newark, DE: International Reading Association.

Heffernan, L., & Lewison, M. (2003). Social narrative writing: (Re)Construction kid culture in the writer's workshop. *Language Arts, 80*(6), 435–443.

Hepler, S. (1998). Nonfiction books for children: New directions, new challenges. In R. Bamford & J. Kristo (Eds.), *Making facts come alive: Choosing quality nonfiction literature K–8* (pp. 3–18). Norwood, MA: Christopher-Gordon.

Hicks, D. (1990). Narrative skills and genre knowledge: Ways of telling in the primary school grades. *Applied Psycholinguistics, 11*(1), 83–104.

Hicks, D. (1997). Working through discourse genres in school. *Research in the Teaching of English, 31*(4), 459–485.

Holdaway, D. (1979). *The foundations of literacy.* Sydney, Australia: Ashton Scholastic.

Holdaway, D. (1986). The structure of natural learning as a basis for literacy instruction. In M. Sampson (Ed.), *The pursuit of literacy* (pp. 56–72). Dubuque, IA: Kendall/Hunt.

Huck, C., Hepler, S., & Hickman, J. (1987). *Children's literature in the elementary school.* New York: Holt, Rinehart & Winston.

Jenkins, C. B. (1999). *The allure of authors: Author studies in the elementary classroom.* Portsmouth, NH: Heinemann.

Jennings, L., & O'Keefe, T. (2002). Parents and children inquiring together: Written conversations about social injustice. *Language Arts, 79*(5), 404–414.

Kamberelis, G. (1999). Genre development and learning: Children writing stories, science reports, and poems. *Research in the Teaching of English, 33*(4), 403–460.

Kamberelis, G., & Bovino, T. (1999). Cultural artifacts as scaffolds for genre development. *Reading Research Quarterly, 34*(2), 138–170.

Kamberelis, G., & Scott, K. (1992). Other people's voices: The coarticulation of texts and subjectivities. *Linguistics and Education, 4,* 359–404.

Keck, J. (1992). Using a nonfiction author study in the classroom. In E. Freeman & D. Person, *Using nonfiction trade books in the elementary classroom: From ants to zeppelins* (pp.123–130). Urbana, IL: National Council of Teachers of English.

Kirsch, D. (1975). From athletes to zebras—Young children want to read about them. *Elementary English, 52,* 73–78.

Kletzien, S. B., & Dreher, M. J. (2004). *Informational text in K–3 classrooms.* Newark, DE: International Reading Association.

Kovacs, D., & Preller, J. (1991). *Meet the authors and illustrators.* New York: Scholastic.

Kovacs, D., & Preller, J. (1993). *Meet the authors and illustrators* (Vol. 2). New York: Scholastic.

Kozol, J. (1991). *Savage inequalities.* New York: Crown.

Kress, G. (1993). Genres as social process. In B. Cope & M. Kalantz (Eds.), *The powers of literacy: A genre approach to teaching writing* (pp. 154–178). New York: Falmer.

Kress, G. (1999). Genre and the changing contexts for English language arts. *Language Arts, 76* (6), 461–469.

Kristeva, J. (1986). *The Kristeva reader.* New York: Columbia University Press.

Kucera, C. (1995). Detours and destinations: One teacher's journey into an environmental writing workshop. *Language Arts, 72,* 179–187.

Lancia, P. (1997). Literary borrowing: The effects of literature on children's writing. *Reading Teacher, 50*(6), pp. 470–475.

Langer, J. A. (1986). *Children reading and writing: Structures and strategies.* Norwood, NJ: Ablex.

Langer, J. A. (1992). Reading, writing and genre development. In J. Irwin & M. Doyle (Eds.), *Reading/writing connection: Learning from research* (pp. 32–54). Newark, DE: International Reading Association.

Lasky, K. (1993). Shuttling through realities: The warp and the weft of fantasy and nonfiction writing. *The New Advocate, 6*(4), 235–242.

Lauber, P. (1992). The evolution of a science writer. In E. Freeman & D. Person (Eds.), *Using nonfiction trade books in the elementary classroom: From ants to zeppelins* (pp. 11–16). Urbana, IL: National Council of the Teachers of English.

Leal, D. (1993). Storybooks, information books and informational storybooks: An explication of the ambiguous grey genre. *The New Advocate, 6,* 61–70.

Leal, D. (1995). When it comes to informational storybooks, the end of the story has not yet been written: Response to Zarnowski's article. *The New Advocate, 8,* 197–201.

Lemke, J. (1992). Intertextuality and educational research. *Linguistics and Education, 4,* 257–268.

Lensmire, T. J. (1994). *When children write: Critical re-visions of the writing workshop.* New York: Teachers College Press.

Lewis, M., Wray, D., & Rospigliosi, P. (1994). ". . . And I want it in your own words." *The Reading Teacher, 47,* 528–536.

Livingston, N., & Kurkjian, C. (2004). Literature links: Expanding ways of knowing. *The Reading Teacher, 58*(1), 110–118.

Luke, A., & Freebody, P. (1997). Shaping the social practices of reading. In
S. Muspratt, A. Luke, & P. Freebody (Eds.), *Constructing critical literacies*
(pp. 185–225). Cresskill, NJ: Hampton.

Lunsford, A. A, & Ede, L. (1994). Collaborative authorship and the teaching of
writing. In M. Woodmansee & P. Jaszi (Eds.), *The construction of authorship:
Textual appropriation in law and literature* (pp. 417–438). Durham, NC: Duke
University Press.

Lynch-Brown, C. (1977). Procedures for determining children's books' choices:
Comparison and criticism. *Reading Horizons, 17,* 243–250.

Many, J. (1996). Patterns of selectivity in drawing on sources: Examining students'
use of intertextuality across literacy events. *Reading Research and Instruction,
36,* 51–63.

Many, J., Fyfe, R., Lewis, G., & Mitchell, E. (1996). Traversing the topical land-
scape: Exploring students' self-directed reading-writing-research processes.
Reading Research Quarterly, 31, 12–35.

Martin, B. (1972). *Sounds of language* (Teacher's Edition). New York: Holt, Rinehart
& Winston.

Martin, H. (1985). *Factual writing: Exploring and challenging social reality* (Teacher's
Edition). Geelong, Victoria, Australia: Deakin University Press.

Merkley, D. M., & Jefferies, D. (2001). Guidelines for implementing a graphic organizer. *The Reading Teacher, 54*(4), 350–357.

Meyer, B. J. F. (1975). *The organization of prose and its effects on memory.*
Amsterdam: North-Holland Publishing.

Meyer, B., Brandt, D., & Bluth, G. (1980). Use of top-level structure in text: Key
for reading comprehension of ninth-grade students. *Reading Research Quarterly, 16*(1), 72–103.

Moffett, J. (1968). *Teaching the universe of discourse.* Boston: Houghton Mifflin.

Moffett, J., & Wagner, B. J. (1976). *Student-centered language arts and reading,
K-13: A handbook for teachers.* Boston: Houghton Mifflin.

Moll, L. C., & Gonzalez, N. (1994). Lessons from research with language-minority
children. *Journal of Reading Behavior, 26*(4), 439–456.

Monson, D., & Sebesta, S. (1991). Reading preferences. In J. Flood, J. Jensen,
D. Lapp, & J. Squire (Eds.), *Handbook of research on teaching the English
language arts* (pp. 664–673). New York: Macmillan.

Morrow, L. M. (1983). Home and school correlates of early interest in literature.
Journal of Educational Research, 76, 221–230

Morrow, L. M. (1992). The impact of a literature-based program on literacy achievement, use of literature and attitudes of children from minority backgrounds.
Research Reading Quarterly, 27(3), 251–275.

Moss, B. (1995). Using children's nonfiction tradebooks as read-alouds. *Language
Arts, 72*(2), 122–126.

Murray, D. (1989). *Expecting the unexpected: Teaching myself—and others—to
read and write.* Portsmouth NH: Heinemann.

New London Group. (1996). A pedagogy of multiliteracies: Designing social futures.
Harvard Educational Review, 66(1), 60–92.

Newkirk, T. (1987). The non-narrative writing of young children. *Research in the Teaching of English, 21,* 121–145.

Oyler, C., & Barry, A. (1996). Intertextual connections in read-alouds of information books. *Language Arts, 73* (5), 324–329.

Pappas, C. (1991). Fostering full access to literacy by including information books. *Language Arts, 68,* 449–462.

Pappas, C. (1993). Is narrative "primary"? Some insights from kindergartners' pretend readings of stories and information books. *Journal of Reading Behavior, 25*(1), 97–129.

Pappas, C., & Pettegrew, B. (1998). The role of genre in psycholinguistic guessing game of reading. *Language Arts, 75*(1), 36–44.

Pearson, P. D., & Gallagher, M. C. (1983). The instruction of reading comprehension. *Contemporary Educational Psychology, 8,* 317–344.

Persky, H. R., Daane, M. C., & Jin, Y. (2003). *The nation's writing report card: Writing 2002.* Washington, DC: National Center for Educational Statistics, U.S. Department of Education.

Pinnell, G. S., & Fountas, I. C. (2002). *Leveled books for readers: Grades 3–6.* Portsmouth, NH: Heinemann.

Portalupi, J., & Fletcher, R. (2001). *Nonfiction craft lessons: Teaching information writing K–8.* Portland, ME: Stenhouse.

Publishers Weekly. (1998). (Review of *Harry Potter and the Socerer's Stone* on book jacket.)

Purcell-Gates, V., McIntyre, E., & Freppon, P. (1988). Learning written storybook language in school: A comparison of low-SES children in skilled and whole language classrooms. *American Educational Research Journal, 32,* 659–685.

Putnam, L. (1991). Dramatizing nonfiction with emerging readers. *Language Arts, 68,* 463–469.

Raphael, T. E., & Englert, C. S. (1990). Writing and reading: Partners in constructing meaning. *The Reading Teacher, 43*(6), 388–400.

Ray, K. W. (2004). Why Cauley writes well: A close look at what a difference good teaching can make. *Language Arts, 82*(2), 100–109.

Read, S. (2001). "Kid mice hunt for their selfs": First and second graders writing research. *Language Arts, 78*(4), 333–347.

Robb, L. (2004). *Nonfiction writing: From the inside out.* New York: Scholastic.

Romano, T. (1995). *Writing with passion: Life stories, multiple genres.* Portsmouth, NH: Boyton/Cook.

Romano, T. (2000). *Blending genre, altering writing style: Writing multigenre papers.* Portsmouth, NH: Boyton/Cook.

Roop, P. (1992). Nonfiction books in the primary classroom: Soaring with the swans. In E. B. Freeman & D. G. Person (Eds.), *Using nonfiction trade books in the elementary classroom: From ants to zeppelins* (pp. 106–112). Urbana, IL: National Council for Teachers of English.

Rosenblatt, L. (1978). *The reader, the text, the poem: The transactional theory of the literary work.* Carbondale, IL: Southern Illinois University Press.

Saltman, J. (2002). Harry Potter's family tree. *Journal of Youth Services in Libraries, 15*(3), 24–28.

Sampson, M. B., Sampson, M. R., & Linek, W. (1994/1995). Circle of questions. *The Reading Teacher, 48*, 364–365.

Schickedanz, J. (1990). *Adam's righting revolutions: One child's literacy development from infancy through grade one.* Portsmouth, NH: Heinemann.

Schiefele, U., Krapp, A., & Winteler, A. (1992). Interest as a predictor of academic achievement: A meta-analysis of research. In K. A. Renninger, S. Hidi, & A. Krapp (Eds.), *The role of interest in learning and development* (pp. 183–211). Hillsdale, NJ: Erlbaum.

Schwartz, W. (2003). Helping underachieveing boys read well and often. *ERIC Digest.* Retrieved May 22, 2005, from http://www.ericdigest.org/2003–2/boys.html.

Shannon, P. (1990). *The struggle to continue: Progressive reading instruction in the United States.* Portsmouth, NH: Heinemann.

Shannon, P. (Ed.). (1992). *Becoming political: Readings and writings in the politics of literacy education.* Portsmouth, NH: Heinemann.

Shannon, P. (1993). Developing democratic voices. *The Reading Teacher, 47*(2), 86–94.

Shor, I. (1992). *Empowering education.* Chicago: University of Chicago Press.

Shor, I., & Pari, C. (1999). *Education is politics: Critical teaching across differences.* Portsmouth, NH: Heinemann.

Short, K. (1992). Researching intertextuality within collaborative classroom learning environments. *Linguistics and Education, 4*, 313–334.

Siegler, R. (1995). Children's thinking: How does change occur? In W. Schneider & F. Weinert (Eds.), *Memory performance and competencies: Issues in growth and development* (pp. 405–430). Hilldale, NJ: Erlbaum.

Simmons, J. (1990). Portfolios as large-scale assessment. *Language Arts, 67*, 262–267.

Simmons, J. (1992). Portfolios for large-scale assessment. In D. Graves & B. Sunstein (Eds.), *Portfolio portraits* (pp. 96–113). Portsmouth, NH: Heinemann.

Simpson, A. (1996). Fictions and facts: An investigation of reading practices of girls and boys. *English Education, 2*(4), 268–279.

Sipe, L. (2001). A palimpsest of stories: Young children's construction of intertextual links among fairytale variants. *Reading Research and Instruction, 40*(4), 333–352.

Smith, F. (1988). *Joining the literacy club.* Portsmouth, NH: Heinemann.

Smith, M. W., & Wilhelm, J. D. (2002). *Reading don't fix no Chevys: Literacy in the lives of young men.* Portsmouth, NH: Heinemann.

Snow, C. (1983). Language and literacy: Relationships during the preschool years. *Harvard Educational Review, 4*, 165–189.

Sowers, S. (1985). The story and the all-about book. In J. Hansen, T. Newkirk, & D. Graves (Eds.), *Breaking ground: Teachers relate reading and writing in the elementary school* (pp. 73–82). Portsmouth, NH: Heinemann.

Spink, J. K. (1996). The aesthetics of informational reading. *The New Advocate, 9*(2), 135–149.

Stead, T. (2002). *Is that a fact? Teaching nonfiction writing K–3.* Portland, ME: Stenhouse.

Stotsky, S. (1995). The uses and limitations of personal or personalized writing in writing theory, research and instruction. *Reading Research Quarterly, 30*(4), 758–777.

Sudol, P., & King, C. (1996). A checklist for choosing nonfiction trade books. *The Reading Teacher, 49*(5), 422–424.

Sulzby, E. (1985). Children's emergent reading of favorite storybooks: A developmental study. *Reading Research Quarterly, 20*, 458–481.

Sulzby, E., & Teale, W. (1987). *Young children's storybook reading: Longitudinal study of parent–child interaction and children's independent functioning* (Final report to the Spencer Foundation). Ann Arbor: University of Michigan.

Tolkien, J. R. R. (1965). *Tree and leaf.* Boston: Houghton Mifflin.

Tomlinson, C. M., & Lynch-Brown, C. (1996). *Essentials of children's literature.* Boston, MA: Allyn & Bacon.

Tompkins, G. (2004). *Teaching writing: Balancing process and product.* Columbus, OH: Pearson Education.

Tower, C. (2002). "It's a snake, you guys!": The power of text characteristics on children's response to information books. *Research in the Teaching of English, 37*(1), 55–88.

U.S. Census Bureau. (2000). *United States Census, 2000.* Washington, DC: U.S. Department of Commerce.

Vacca, R. T., & Vacca, J. L. (1999). *Content area reading: Literacy and learning across the curriculum.* New York: Longman .

Vardell, S., & Copeland, K. (1992). Reading aloud and responding to nonfiction: Let's talk about it. In E. B. Freeman & D. G. Person (Eds.), *Using nonfiction trade books in the elementary classroom: From ants to zeppelins* (pp. 76–85). Urbana, IL: National Council of Teachers of English.

Vasquez, V. (2003). *Getting beyond "I like the book": Creating space for critical literacy in K–6 classrooms.* Newark, DE: International Reading Association.

Veatch, J. (1968). *How to teach reading with children's books.* New York: Citation Press.

Vygotsky, L. (1962). *Thought and language.* Cambridge, MA: MIT Press.

Vygotsky, L. (1978). *Mind in society.* Cambridge, MA: Harvard University Press.

Wolfson, B. J., Manning, G., & Manning, M. (1984). Revisiting what children say their reading interests are. *Reading World, 24*, 1–10.

Wollman-Bonilla, J. (2000). Teaching science writing to first graders: Genre learning and recontextualization. *Research in the Teaching of English, 35*(1), 35–65.

Wray, D., & Lewis, M. (1992). Primary children's use of information books. *Reading, 26*, 19–24.

Yeh, S. S. (1998). Empowering education: Teaching argumentative writing to cultural minority middle-school students. *Research in the Teaching of English, 33*(10), 49–83.

Yolen, J. (1991). The route to story. *The New Advocate, 4*, 143–149.

Zecker, L. (1996). Early development in written language: Children's emergent knowledge of genre-specific characteristics. *Reading and Writing: An Interdisciplinary Journal, 8*, 5–25.

Zinsser, W. (1985). *On writing well* (2nd ed.). New York: Harper & Row.

Children's Literature References

Aliki. (1985a). *Dinosaurs are different*. New York: HarperCollins.
Aliki. (1985b). *My visit to the dinosaurs*. New York: HarperCollins.
Aliki. (1988). *Digging up dinosaurs*. New York: HarperCollins.
Aliki. (1990). *Fossils tell of long ago*. New York: HarperCollins.
Bernard, A. (1994). *Penguins*. New York: Teaching Resources/Scholastic.
Bernhard, E., & Bernhard, D. (1993). *Dragonfly*. New York: Holiday House.
Billings, C. (1981). *Salamanders*. New York: Dodd Mead.
Bland, C. (1997). *Bats*. New York: Scholastic.
Blume, J. (1972). *Tales of a fourth grade nothing*. New York: Dutton.
Bridges, R. (1999). *Through my eyes*. New York: Scholastic.
Brown, M. (1984). *Arthur goes to camp*. Boston, MA: Little, Brown, and Company.
Budd, J. (1995). *Horses*. New York: Kingfisher.
Cannon, J. (1993). *Stellaluna*. New York: Harcourt Children's Books.
Carroll, S. (1986). *How big is a brachiosaurus?* New York: Platt & Munk.
Cole, J. (1976). *A chick hatches*. New York: Morrow.
Cole, J. (1983). *A bird's body*. New York: Morrow.
Cole, J. (1986a). *A dog's body*. New York: Morrow.
Cole, J. (1986b). *Hungry, hungry sharks*. New York: Random House.
Cole, J. (1986c). *Magic school bus at the waterworks*. New York: Scholastic.
Cole, J. (1987). *The magic school bus inside the earth*. New York: Scholastic.
Cole, J. (1989). *The magic school bus inside the human body*. New York: Scholastic.
Cole, J. (1990). *The magic school bus lost in the solar system*. New York: Scholastic.
Cole, J. (1992). *The magic school bus on the ocean floor*. New York: Scholastic.
Cole, J. (1994). *The magic school bus in the time of the dinosaurs*. New York: Scholastic.
Cole, J. (1995a). *The magic school bus inside a hurricane*. New York: Scholastic.
Cole, J. (1995b). *My new kitten*. New York: Morrow Junior Books.
Cole, J. (1996). *The magic school bus inside a beehive*. New York: Scholastic.
Coles, R. (1995). *The story of Ruby Bridges*. New York: Scholastic.
Dorris, M. (1992). *Morning girl*. New York: Hyperion.
Fitzhugh, L. (1964). *Harriet the spy*. New York: Harper & Row.
Freedman, R. (1991). *The Wright brothers: How they invented the airplane*. New York: Holiday House.
Fritz, J. (1969). *George Washington's breakfast*. New York: Putnam & Gosset.
Fritz, J (1992). *Surprising myself*. New York: Richard Owens.
George, W. (1989). *Box turtle at Long Pond*. New York: Trumpet Club.
Gibbons, G. (1993). *Frogs*. New York: Holiday House.
Gill, P. (1990). *Birds*. Mahwah, NJ: Troll Associates.

Hakim, R. (1991). *Martin Luther King, Jr. and the March Toward Freedom*. New York: Millbrook.

Henry, M. (1947). *Misty of Chincoteague*. New York: Macmillan.

King, M. L. (1997). *I have a dream*. New York: Scholastic.

Lamb, S. (1992). *My great aunt Arizona*. New York: HarperCollins.

Lasky, K. (1990). *Dinosaur dig*. New York: Morrow Junior Books.

Lauber, P. (1989). *The news about dinosaurs*. New York: Alladin.

Lauber, P. (1992). *Volcano: The eruption and healing of Mount St. Helens*. New York: Bradbury.

Lauber, P. (1996a). *How dinosaurs came to be*. New York: Simon & Schuster.

Lauber, P. (1996b). *An octopus is amazing*. New York: HarperCollins Children's Books.

Lauber, P. (2001). *The true-or-false book of cats*. New York: National Geographic Society.

Ling, M. (1993). *Penguin*. New York: DK Publishing.

MacLachlan, P. (1991). *Journey*. New York: Delacorte Press.

Maestro, B. (1990). *A sea full of sharks*. New York: Scholastic Inc.

Markle, S. (1996). *Outside and inside sharks*. New York: Atheneum.

Markle, S. (2000). *Outside and inside dinosaurs*. New York: Atheneum.

Martin, B. (1967). *Brown bear, brown bear, what do you see?* New York: Henry Holt.

Martin, B. (1991). *Polar bear, polar bear, what do you hear?* New York: Henry Holt.

Martin, B. (2003). *Panda bear, panda bear, what do you see?* New York: Henry Holt.

Numeroff, L. (1985). *If you give a mouse a cookie*. New York: HarperCollins.

Numeroff, L. (1991). *If you give a moose a muffin*. New York: HarperCollins.

Numeroff, L. (1998). *If you give a pig a pancake*. New York: HarperCollins.

Oakley, M. (1996). *Sharks*. New York: Ladybird.

Patent, D. H. (1993). *Killer whales*. New York: Holiday House.

Pringle, L. (1995). *Dinosaurs! Strange and wonderful*. Honesdale, PA: Boyds Mills Press.

Saunders, S. (1994). *Maxine's blue ribbon*. New York: HarperPaperbacks.

Sewall, M. (1990). *People of the breaking day*. New York: Atheneum.

Sharmat, M. (1977). *Nate the great*. New York: Yearling.

Simon, S. (1982). *The smallest dinosaurs*. New York: Crown.

Simon, S. (1986). *The largest dinosaurs*. New York: Macmillan.

Simon, S. (1990). *New questions and answers about dinosaurs*. New York: Trumpet Club.

Simon, S. (1991a). *Dinosaurs*. New York: Trumpet Club.

Simon, S. (1991b). *Earthquakes*. New York: Morrow.

Simon, S. (1995). *Sharks*. New York: Scholastic.

Srine, R. L. (1994). *Return of the mummy*. New York: Scholastic.

Tanaka, S. (2002). *New dinos*. New York: Atheneum Books for Young Readers.

Tsuchiya, Y. (1997). *Faithful elephants*. Boston: Houghton Mifflin.

Waters, K. (1996). *Tapenum's day*. New York: Scholastic.

Weaver, N. (1983). *The penguin*. Mahwah, NJ: Watermill.

Zim, H. S., & Smith, H. M. (1956). *Reptiles and amphibians*. New York: Golden Press.

Index

About the Authors

CAROL BRENNAN JENKINS has worked in the field of literacy for more than 30 years as a classroom teacher, literacy specialist, and teacher educator. She currently teaches courses in literacy at Boston University and coordinates the university's elementary education program. In addition to conducting literacy workshops for teachers, parents, and administrators, she works side-by-side with teachers in classrooms, tapping their expertise and supporting their efforts. She is a recipient of the International Reading Association and Massachusetts Reading Association's Celebrate Literacy award. Her publications include *The Allure of Authors: Author Studies in the Elementary Classroom* and *Inside the Writing Portfolio: What We Need to Know to Assess Children's Writing*, as well as numerous articles.

ALICE EARLE came late to a teaching career, graduating from Simmons College with a BA/MAT in early childhood and elementary education the year she turned 30. She has taught for 25 of the past 28 years since then, with time out for the birth of her quadruplet sons and the pursuit of a CAGS in education. She holds certifications in elementary education (K–6) and reading (K–12), and is currently pursuing her license as a principal. She is an active member of the Greater Boston Council of the Massachusetts Reading Association, has presented at numerous conferences, and has been a guest lecturer at the Boston University School of Education for several years. She also contributed a chapter to *Inside the Writing Portfolio*.